US 8th Air Force
in Europe

US 8th Air Force in Europe

The Eagle Spreads Its Wings:
'Blitz Week - Black Thursday, Blood and Oil'

Martin Bowman

Pen & Sword
AVIATION

First published in Great Britain in 2012 by
PEN & SWORD AVIATION
An imprint of
Pen & Sword Books Ltd
47 Church Street
Barnsley
South Yorkshire
S70 2AS

ISBN 978 1 84884 747 7

A CIP catalogue record for this book is available from the British Library

Pen & Sword Books Ltd incorporates the Imprints of Pen & Sword Aviation,
Pen & Sword Family History, Pen & Sword Maritime, Pen & Sword Military,
Pen & Sword Discovery, Wharncliffe Local History, Wharncliffe True Crime,
Wharncliffe Transport, Pen & Sword Select, Pen & Sword Military Classics,
Leo Cooper, The Praetorian Press, Remember When, Seaforth Publishing
and Frontline Publishing

For a complete list of Pen & Sword titles please contact
PEN & SWORD BOOKS LIMITED
47 Church Street, Barnsley, South Yorkshire, S70 2AS, England
E-mail: enquiries@pen-and-sword.co.uk
Website: www.pen-and-sword.co.uk

Contents

CHAPTER 1

The Raid That Failed

Double, double, toil and trouble;
Fire burn and cauldron bubble.'

Macbeth, *Act IV*

Captain Bill Cameron was slightly puzzled. And the twenty-three-year old pilot from California was not alone. After six months of combat operations in very cold and hostile winter skies over Europe, the combat crews at Shipdham were told that for the time being, at least, there would be no combat. And it was springtime. The 'Eightballers' did not understand then that this relatively pleasant interval was designed to prepare them for an exceptional mission, one that would put it on the line for all of them. There were new crews and new B-24Ds to replace those that had been lost and losses had been severe. Fate had spared Cameron. In the words of Ernie Pyle it could be said that, 'He is a fugitive from the law of average.' He was the only remaining pilot originally assigned to the 67th Squadron, which had lost five of its original nine crews including his own. After the loss of *Little Beaver* on 14 May 1943 Cameron was made an aircraft commander and with Lieutenant Bill Dabney, an American transfer from the RAF, a new crew was formed. They were given a new Liberator, which Cameron christened *Buzzin' Bear*. The name was partly inspired by the grizzly bear, which first adorned his home state's flag in 1846. Also, Cameron was a product of UC Berkeley, 'The Golden Bears'. 'Buzzing' or low flying was a popular trait among pilots. If he got through his next few missions Cameron knew that he would be able to return home; to Hanford, not far from the central Pacific coast that stretches from the Monterey Bay south through Big Sur to San Luis Obispo Bay. In his novels John Steinbeck immortalized Monterey's Cannery Row and the Salinas Valley. Henry Miller, another author who found a home on the Central Coast, called this place 'a paradise'. Cameron would one day make his home here in Carmel with wife, Alison, one of General 'Vinegar Joe' Stillwell's daughters after a combat career that stretched to twenty-nine months and thirty-eight missions and would be equalled by few in the 8th Air Force. Courage and compassion were characteristics that Cameron combined throughout his long combat performance.

The 'Flying Eightballs' were shifted, without explanation, to low-level formation practice over the green fields of East Anglia. It was the same story at Hethel and Hardwick. Between 11 and 25 June 1943 the 389th flew into their base at Hethel, just outside Norwich, to begin low level training alongside the 'Flying Eightballs' and the 'Travelling Circus'. Colonel Jack W. Wood, the thirty-six-year-old 389th CO, a veteran pilot from Fairbault, Minnesota, who had graduated from Flight School in 1928, was under pressure to get his group operational. A temporary ground echelon was seconded to Hethel pending the arrival of the regular ground personnel. After a five-day orientation course crews began flying low-level practice missions over East Anglia at less than 150 feet en route to their target range over the Wash. Rumour and speculation increased as ground crews sweated to remove the Norden bombsights and replace them with low-level sights. Heavier nose armament and additional fuel tanks in the bomb bays gave the men clues as to their new role. 'Since everything was Top Secret' wrote 'Tommie' Holmes, 'we were told only that we were going to Libya.' Only higher headquarters knew what was in the offing. Early in June General Brereton was informed that the three Groups would be joining his 98th 'Pyramiders' and 376th 'Liberandos' Bomb Groups for a second attack on the important strategic oilfields at Ploesti in Romania, which produced 60 per cent of all Germany's needs.[1] By increasing the Liberator's fuel capacity to 3,100 gallons they could just make it to the target from North Africa.

At Hardwick, Colonel Addison Baker led his Liberators flying wing tip to wing tip at 150 feet over the hangar line on the base, which served as a target. On some days the 44th and the 389th joined the 'Travelling Circus' in flights over the base in waves of three aircraft. Crews had been trained in the art of high-altitude precision bombing and were quite unused to low-level flying. On 25 June two 389th Liberators were involved in a mid-air collision. One made it back to Hethel but the other crash-landed and one man was killed. When they departed for North Africa at the end of June the 389th, the youngest and most inexperienced of the three Groups, had completed only two weeks' training in Norfolk.

By 25 June forty-one Liberators were available at Shipdham for the Ploesti mission, which was codenamed Operation *Statesman*. Five days later the three groups began their flight to North Africa via Portreath in Cornwall. Forty-two B-24s took off from Hardwick and thirty more left the runways at Hethel. However, a few 389th aircraft remained behind in Norfolk for training and air-sea-rescue duties. For the 93rd the long overseas flight meant a return to the African desert they had forsaken in February 1943. The 124 Liberators flew to Libya, where they came under the control of the 9th Air Force. After weeks of preparation the 'Eightballs' took off singly early one dark morning and flew, at very low altitude, to an airfield in the southern part of England. The next day, they crossed the Bay of Biscay, again low enough to escape German radar and passed through the Straits of Gibraltar to Oran in Algeria. *The Oklahoman*, which was flown by twenty-four-year-old Lieutenant John 'Jack' C. Martin Jr, was commandeered by Colonel Jack Wood when his aircraft lost an engine and went with the rest of the Group to Benina Main, one of Mussolini's former airfields, fifteen miles from the coastal city of Benghazi. This left Jack Martin's crew in Oran with an engine change to do. *The Oklahoman*, whose insignia was an Indian maid, sitting on top of a covered wagon, was named by Martin, who though he was born in Richmond, Virginia, was educated in Tishomingo, Oklahoma, graduating from high school there in 1937 and from the Murray State School of Agriculture in 1939. Before enlisting in the AAC he was a printer and photo-engraver on the *Madill Record*. He had met Vae Hogan at Lowry Field where she was a lieutenant in the Station hospital and they married on 25 May 1943 just before he left for overseas duty. Martin's kid brother was a private first class with the marine paratroopers in the south Pacific. By the time Martin and his crew arrived at Benina in Colonel Wood's aircraft the 389th would have flown four combat missions.

It was nearly dark when Bill Cameron and the crew climbed down from the *Buzzin' Bear* and waited to be directed to their billet. As they waited – and waited – Sergeant Gerald Sparks, the radio operator from Meridian, Mississippi, entertained them with his guitar. Eventually, someone came by in a truck and threw off a large canvas bundle, which they were informed was their 'billet'. Cameron knew then that they were not destined to feel at home in this strange new environment – and they never did. Hundreds of wrecked Axis aircraft still littered the area for hundreds of miles around and the words 'Believe, Obey, Fight' were inscribed on the walls of the hangars. 'Tommie' Holmes wrote: 'We had no idea what a contrast in climate we would encounter and how very hot and desolate this land would be. The temperature would rise to 130 degrees and we would be assaulted by lots of hot wind, dirt, grasshoppers and scorpions.' The 9th Air Force accused the 8th of being undisciplined and given to gross exaggeration of 'kills', while the 8th complained when it was discovered that the 98th were withholding the best rations. By using up the less desirable items and keeping back the best foodstuffs, only the choicest rations would remain for the 98th when the 'Eightballs' returned to England. Colonel Leon Johnson took the matter up with Colonel John 'Killer' Kane, the 'Pyramiders' CO, but things did not improve during the stay of the 'Eightballs' at Benina Main. One of the 389th personnel claimed that the only thing that resembled food was the bread baked every day.

We did get plenty of protein. The swarms of locusts made up for the lack of mutton, beef or pork. It took a few days to get acclimatized. You could tell a rookie in the mess. He can't eat after a few locusts land in his greasy mess kit; a veteran of a few missions will remove the locusts and continue eating; an old timer cannot eat without a few locusts in his mess gear.

There were two proven methods of cleaning your mess kit. Either scrub it with sand and make it glisten, or mix up a packet of powdered lemonade in your cup and let it stand overnight. It would glow in the morning. If the powdered lemonade dissolved the grime in your cup, imagine what it did to your stomach.

One afternoon, crews at Benina Main were hastily summoned to report to the briefing room. Bill Cameron learned that his crew would join his CO, Jim Posey, and another crew in a low-level sortie over Benghazi. Apparently, the natives were demonstrating in the town, putting pressure on the British for more local control. *Buzzin' Bear*, living up to its name and the other two aircraft, buzzed the city in a show of 'gunboat diplomacy'. After missions over such targets as Messina, Catania, Foggia and Naples, Bill Cameron completed his required twenty-five in a borrowed ship, the *Suzy-Q*, over Rome on 19 July. He recalls:

We then plunged into low-level formation practice once again but this time it was over the dry Libyan Desert. It occurred to me at the same time that I was not really expected to fly this low-level mission, whatever the target was. But I was swept up in the preparation for it primarily out of loyalty to my crew and perhaps some curiosity that caused me to want to see it through. For almost two weeks, B-24s in small groups were crisscrossing the desert in all directions, practising low-level formation flying.

'Tommie' Holmes wrote:

While practising in the desert we flew very low, which we enjoyed but I am sure some of the crew were somewhat upset or nervous about flying into the ground. We did hit two hawks, one hitting the No. 2 engine prop governor and a second hawk coming through the Plexiglas window in the nose, leaving blood, guts and feathers through the entire airplane, even to the tail. Luckily, no one in the nose was injured.[2]

Bill Cameron recalls:

Eventually the groups became larger as the training progressed toward a full-dress rehearsal involving the total force of B-24 Liberator bombers. Five bomb groups were to be involved in our still-undisclosed mission – three groups in their dull green-hued aircraft from England and two units stationed in Africa. The airplanes of the latter groups were dust coloured, almost pink and were easily distinguished from the England-based B-24s. All of these were B-24Ds – lighter and faster than the models that came later with the nose turrets and other modifications.

Target models had been set up in the desert. When we were considered ready, the entire force of 175 bombers took off, assembled in group-formation and lined up one group behind the other. Proceeding just as we would against the actual targets in Romania, we arrived at the practice IP and each unit then swung approximately 90° to the right. This manoeuvre put five units of aircraft flying side by side at very low level and racing toward our simulated target. In this manner, all our aircraft were streaking over their small targets at nearly the same moment: The units were then to turn to the right, which meant that once again the five groups would be lined up one behind the other, as they left the target area. A day or two before the mission, we were brought into the briefing room and the great secret was unveiled. The presentation was quite elaborate and included movies of models of each of the several refineries we were to attack. The movies simulated the view of the target, as a pilot would see it approaching at very low altitude. Everything would depend on surprise and exact timing. It was explained that the defences were relatively light and we would not have to concern ourselves too much about Romanian anti-aircraft because Sunday was a day of rest for Romanians – even in time of war. Some of the edge was removed from this optimism by Major General Lewis E. Brereton, who addressed us all at an open-air meeting in the African sunshine, where he stressed the importance of our target by saying that our success would justify the loss of every aircraft! He did not mean of course that such losses were expected but it gave us something to think about.

'Tommie' Holmes recalls:

We continued to practise low level flying and in between, flew about fourteen missions over Sicily and Italy. We had no ice in the desert so we took great pleasure in returning from these missions, drinking ice water frozen at altitude, eating K or C rations and listening to 'Axis Sally' on the radio. It may not have been Standard Operating Procedure but to keep from perspiring so much and to keep our clothes dry, we would remove them for take-off and dress as we ascended! To keep the sand from being drawn into the air scoops, we always had to be careful before take-off to keep our engines at low RPM or turned sideways to the wind.[3]

On 2 July the B-24Ds of the 8th Air Force flew the first of ten missions in support of the Italian campaign and the Allied invasion of Sicily with a bombing mission to enemy airfields. It was not an auspicious beginning. Three Liberators, including two in the 'Flying Eightballs' who lost their third 68th Squadron CO when Tommy Cramer was shot down and killed over Lecce airfield, failed to return. Captain John Diehl was promoted to command the 68th Squadron and 'Tommie' Holmes became operations officer. The former pilot of *Victory Ship* had finished his missions and hence did not fly many of the missions while at Benina. On 6 July twenty-six of the Group's Liberators flew a mission to Gerbani airfield in Sicily. Two of the 'Eightballs' returned early with mechanical problems but the rest of the formation successfully dropped their 500lb bombs from 25,000 feet, hitting the western end of the runway and the perimeter. There was no cloud but sever haze was evident and visibility was four to five miles.

Tech Sergeant Donald V. Chase, who was from Jersey City, was the radio operator on *Heaven Can Wait* flown by Charles Whitlock from Corsicana, Texas, whose crew were making their combat debut. Chase recalls:

It was a duty of the radio operator to leave his regular position behind the co-pilot's seat, go to the belly of the B-24, straddle the narrow catwalk of the bomb bay and activate a push-type lever. This prevented the bomb doors from creeping, once the doors were opened preparatory to a bomb-run. Secondly, he watched the bombs fall and to the best of his visual acuity, assessed the bombing results after the bombardier activated the bomb release switch in concert with the lead or first aircraft in the squadron. So there I was, on our first mission, poised in the belly of our ship waiting for our load of 12 × 500lb bombs to drop, when I noticed the bombs of our sister ships plummeting earthward but not ours. Could it be my fault? Did the bomb doors creep in? I pushed the anti-creep lever as hard as I could. No, there was no creep-age. There was nothing more I could do in the bomb bay, so I returned to the cabin area and plugged in my headset and tuned in to the intercom.

'Use the backup release, Whit,' bombardier Harold Schwab said on the intercom. Charles Whitlock nodded to his co-pilot, William Phipps, who reached down to the console between the pilot and co-pilot seats and grabbed hold of a T-shaped handle and began pulling upwards. I looked back into the bomb bay. The bombs were still cradled in the racks. Phipps, seated as he was and using his left hand, his arm at an awkward angle, apparently didn't have enough pulling leverage to activate the release handle. Standing between the pilot and co-pilot, I tapped Phipps' arm and pointed to myself then to the handle. When he moved his hand away, I squatted, grabbed the handle with both hands and pulled straight up with all my strength. Immediately, the plane lurched upward as 6,000lb of metal left *Heaven Can Wait*. The bombs of course landed far from the target area and splintered hundreds of trees.

It took all the next day to track down and repair the bomb release malfunction. We were, more or less, on stand-down till *Heaven Can Wait* was again serviceable. We six enlisted crew members took advantage of the stand-down by boarding a supply-run truck that was making a trip to the nearby city of Benghazi. The Allied Forces had only recently forced Field Marshal Rommel and his *Afrika Korps* out of North Africa and it was still thought necessary to be armed while away from base. Consequently, we roamed the bazaars of Benghazi with .15 calibre pistols holstered at our hips. One of our crewmen, tunnel gunner Ralph Knox of Chicago, appeared to be no more than seventeen. He was small of frame and sparse of beard. We called him 'Billy the Kid', as he swaggered through the fetid-smelling bazaar section, his gun hanging low and forward on his hip, the holster slapping his thigh with each step. A few of the vendors cried out, 'Viva Roosevelt, Viva Roosevelt.' Prior to our arrival, I'm sure, as battles raged back and forth across North Africa for four years the cries must have changed with the flow of battle – 'Viva Mussolini...Viva Churchill...Viva Hitler...' We trucked back to base, almost gladly, leaving the rag-tagged, alms seeking children and impoverished merchants to their dismal, war-scarred surroundings.

On 8 July the 'Eightballs' and the other B-24 groups bombed telegraph and telephone buildings at Catania, Sicily. As they flew over Sicily 'Tommie' Holmes and the others saw 'the largest armada of naval vessels assembled just off shore that we had ever seen.' For Don Chase and the crew of *Heaven Can Wait* it was their second mission, as he recalls:

Heaven Can Wait behaved well. Our bombs salvoed on schedule and we returned to base without incident. Upon landing and parking at our improvised hardstand, two or three ground men – mechanics and armourers – gave us the thumbs-up greeting and hastily removed canteens of water from the bomb bay section. The men in the late-afternoon desert heat would soon savour the water, still frozen from its five-mile high ride. Portable water was tanked into base and very little was allowed for personal use. Each man, however, did receive an allotment of one can of beer a day. We often carried many canteens of water and several men's hoarded beer, festooned to bomb bay struts, on missions, secure in the knowledge that, back at base, men were prayerfully awaiting our safe return.

There was little variation of food at base: pancakes, spam, powdered milk and eggs, Vienna sausages. The worst of all was a congealed, wax-like butter substitute called desert butter. Even under a punishing African sun it retained the viscosity of axle grease. Our waist gunner Edwin Stewart, a Californian, dubbed it a medicant for loose bowels.

Ken Matson was a first pilot in the 389th as it was formed at Davis Monthan field in Tucson. Second phase was at Biggs field in El Paso and then it was on to Denver at Lowry Field.

I was told to go out on a ramp and pick out one of the new modified B-24s (which had a retractable belly turret). We christened the plane *Wolf Wagon* and flew it to Hethel via Bangor, Goose Bay, Greenland, Iceland, Stornaway in the Orkney Islands (Prestwick was weathered in) and finally, Prestwick. Ten days later we left England for Africa via Land's End, through the Straits of Gibraltar where the Spanish Moroccans used up some of their monthly supply of anti-aircraft shells and landed in Oran. Next day on to Benghazi where living in tents in the desert, I flew most of my missions (eight). On 9 July, the night before the Sicilian invasion, we made our first raid. Our group alone (thirty planes) bombed the German aerodrome on Crete

(Maleme) with the loss of one plane. This was a feint to draw attention away from the attack on Sicily. We bombed Reggio de Calabrai twice. It was across from Messina where the Germans were ferrying their troops over to the boot of Italy. We also hit Bari and Foggia where the 15th Air Force later was based. We had flown every mission so far so we had a rest trip to Alexandria, Egypt, in the whiskey ship: *Bucksheese Benny Rides Again*. While we were enjoying ourselves, *Wolf Wagon* went on a mission with an inexperienced pilot. He weakened the rubber gaskets on the supercharger. We were climbing to altitude over Bari when two superchargers gave out. With a bomb load we soon fell behind the group. We were below them and soon bombs would begin to fall. Four Me 109s came at us from below. Sergeant Strasemeyer, the top turret gunner, set one of them smoking and Sergeant Bob Driver, the tail gunner, hit the second. The other two planes turned away. We saw one plane hit the ground and claimed it. The group above us saw the second 109 crash and confirmed it. The bombardier screamed, 'Get the hell out of here, they are about to release their bombs on us.' We managed to get back to base. We painted two Swastikas on the side of our plane.

Don Chase recalls:

On 10 July twenty-eight B-24s of the 'Flying Eightballs' departed Benina Main at 1230 to attack the marshalling yards at Catania. We reached target area and dropped 285 × 500lb bombs at 1637 hours from 23,000 feet. Thirty-six 500lb bombs were brought back with disposition of twelve bombs unknown. There was a heavy concentration of hits on the target where fires were still burning from previous raid. Fires were also seen at Syracuse and Augusta. Three aircraft returned with their bombs due to mechanical failure. The weather was clear and AA was moderate. Several aircraft were damaged by flak. One B-24 landed on Malta at 1900 hours. While en route to a target and over the Mediterranean, all ten of our .50 calibre guns were test fired. Flight engineer Charlton Holtz, a Minnesota lad, manned the top turret. When he test fired, spent shells cascaded out of the turret onto the cabin floor next to my radio position. Occasionally a shell or two would bounce off his leg and land on me. The casings were hot. One landed on my neck and left a burn welt. However, I preferred ducking hot shells to flying in a ship with a malfunctioning turret. Later model B-24s would include two added turrets, one in the belly, one in the nose, replacing four hand-held guns, giving improved firing power. Also, newer ships would have added armour plating to protect the pilots and incidentally, the armour plates would benefit me, too.

Two days later we bombed Reggio Di Calabria, Italy. Allied invasion troops were overrunning Sicily and our Group's attention was now diverted to pre-invasion strikes on mainland Italy. When we landed and parked our Lib, one of the ground crew went into the bomb bay to retrieve his cache of beer. He came out of the plane with his prize. Looking grieved and speaking with false sternness, he pointed to several small flak holes in the bomb bay doors and said, 'Dammit fella', you gotta be more careful; they almost shot my beer.' Banter and levity helped relieve the strain of missions, especially when all crewmen returned unharmed. With each mission the crew of *Heaven Can Wait* gained confidence and improved intra-coordination. We discussed water ditching and crash-landing procedures. Each crewman had at least a few minutes flying time – enough, perhaps, to maintain her in a reasonably level flight attitude. We kept interphone talk to a minimum and regarded each other as competent and reliable at his duty station. We were fusing into a proud ten-man unit. Yes we had some conflicting personalities and on the ground, spirited arguments arose but once aloft all differences ceased.

On 15 July we attacked Foggia airfield in Italy, dropping 260 × 500lb bombs from 23,000 feet. The flak, somewhat heavier on this mission, was inaccurate. Aimed flak, as it suggests, was fired at a particular target, usually a lead group or squadron aircraft. Barrage flak, however, was not targeted on a selected plane. Rather, it was a boxed pattern of ack-ack fire into which the enemy hoped the B-24s would fly. At our base were several British-manned ack-ack units, one fairly close to our tent area. Theirs was a boring task. For the two months of our stay no enemy aircraft came within range of their low to intermediate range of fire. Instead, only stripped down, extreme-altitude German photo-recon aircraft penetrated the desert airspace. Occasionally, one or two of us would visit the two-man ack-ack units, exchanging small talk and cigarettes and flicking ever-present locusts off our clothes. The base was devoid of mosquitoes in this parched area but we used netting to keep the five- and six-inch long locusts from our canvas cots. One of the crewmen, waist gunner Hugo Dunajecz of New York City, got so irritated with the invasive locusts that he fired his .45 at one, scaring the hell out of the rest of us and puncturing a half-inch hole in our tent. Desist or move out, we told him. From then on, Hugo shot at crashed German and Italian Lighters and light bombers that lay broken on the desert, the losers of earlier shootouts.

Most missions were flown without escort and soon losses were assuming the proportions sustained at the height of the raids on the U-boat pens in France. On 17 July eighty Liberators raided Naples. Instead of the usual light defences of the Italian targets this day the 'Eightballs' encountered fierce Italian and German fighter opposition and the flak was heavy. During thirty minutes of constant attack the gunners on *Buzzin' Bear* claimed five enemy aircraft, including three Macchi MC 202s. Italian farmers killed Lieutenant Joe Potter, a member of Lieutenant Rowland Gentry's crew in the 'Flying Eightballs' after he had baled out of the doomed aircraft. For the first time with *Buzzin' Bear*, damage occurred on No. 3 engine from a probable 20mm hit that caused a loss of oil pressure and Cameron was forced to feather No. 3. At this point they began to drop behind the formation. In addition to the No. 3 shutdown, they had high cylinder head temperatures from the high power settings attempting to stay with the formation. The high power settings with rich mixture in attempts to keep the engines cool had depleted their fuel reserve. Additionally, they had lost the two generators. All things considered, the decision was made to attempt to reach Malta rather than a return to Benghazi. Sometime after setting course for Malta, they saw land ahead. While Tom Clifford, the navigator, who was from Upper Darby, Pennsylvania, argued that it was too early to have reached Malta, the fuel situation dictated a landing as soon as possible. With the usual Cameron luck, a long shining strip was sighted on the land, which they could identify as a landing strip. As they turned toward it, one engine quit. Staff Sergeant Gola G. Gibby the flight engineer from Medisonville, Tennessee, quickly transferred fuel and got it restarted. Cameron also restarted No. 3-engine and proceeded with a straight in approach and landing. Prior to that time the crew had donned their May Wests and parachutes and stood by to bale out if things got quiet. A safe landing was made and rolling to a stop, they were met by a British officer in a jeep who informed them that they had landed, not on Malta but Comiso airfield on Sicily just a few miles from the front lines. He advised them to remove their aircraft as soon as possible as it was a big target!

By loading 600 gallons of fuel by hand from British 5 Imperial gallon Jerry cans most of the day and into the twilight and lacking any food, the *Buzzin' Bear* was back in the air sometime after midnight, en route to

Malta. After landing, Cameron, 'Gentleman' DeVinney who was from Atlantic City, New Jersey and Clifford – fortified by two pieces of stale toast and a cup of tea in the Officers' Mess – attempted to sleep in chairs. A return to Benina Main was accomplished the next morning. When the near starving Cameron caught up with him Major Moore's greeting was 'Where in Hell have you been?' In the afternoon Cameron was instructed to attend mission briefing for a very important target. In the briefing he learned that he was to lead the Group in *Suzy-Q* against transportation targets in Rome on what was his twenty-sixth mission. (Half of 'Pappy' Moore's crew had dysentery and *Buzzin' Bear* was undergoing four engine changes by the ground crew and half of the flight crew). Although the Italian capital had been declared an open city, its railway yards had nevertheless remained the chief centre of supply for the Axis forces in Italy. Because of the city's cultural and religious significance the briefing for the raid was the most detailed and concise the combat crews had ever received. Lieutenant Colonel Jim Posey concluded the 'Flying Eightballs' briefing with 'And for God's sake if you don't see the target bring back your bombs'. Don Chase recalls:

Airmen of Catholic faith were given the choice of flying this mission or remaining at base. The Littorio rail yards were proximate to Vatican City. An errant bomb conceivably could inflict damage to the home of the Pope. Therefore, stringent bomb drop precautions were invoked. Fortunately, the bombing was affected as planned. We heard that not one Catholic in our Group, including Bob Bonham our tail gunner, declined to fly the mission. But the Catholics' decision to fly the Rome mission was not unexpected. All combat flying seemed to be voluntary. From the beginning, each man received specialized training to prepare him for combat. Even the gunners, for the most part, attended four weeks of gunnery school prior to assignment to a stateside combat training group. And whenever possible, airmen trained together as a ten-man unit for three months before entering combat. Somewhere along the progression line, in school or training, each man had the opportunity to fail a course, feign a disabling ailment, or perform so inefficiently as to render him unsuited for combat flying. Of course, some did. Those who did fly combat however, did so with self-determination, an unspoken pride in contributing to the effectiveness of the ten-man unit that each B-24 carried. I'm sure men of the 44th were not unique in this respect but it did make for a unit cohesion that was not equalled in civilian life.

Colonel Posey need not have worried about the bombing accuracy. More than 100 B-24Ds bombed the Littoria yards and the raid was declared an unprecedented success. Only one bomb 'got away' and slightly damaged a basilica. It was precision bombing at its best but the conditions had been kind. Don Chase concludes:

> Since arriving in Libya the 44th had flown ten missions and the crew of *Heaven Can Wait* had flown on six of them. Only three of our Group's Libs had been downed by enemy action in 280 individual sorties, resulting in a 44th operational loss of 1 per cent, although several aircraft had incurred severe ack-ack or enemy aircraft damage. But our next mission, Ploesti, was destined to end our loss rate.

Ken Matson and the crew of *Wolf Wagon* in the 'Sky Scorpions' had gone on the first Rome raid on 19 July and like everyone else, were through making missions until 1 August. Matson recalls:

> We began to practise low-level flying in preparation for our historic raid on Ploesti. At first we went out singly and got down on the deck. Legitimate buzzing, what every pilot dreams of. It was more fun when we went out in three-plane flights and hoped the lead ship would keep us out of hitting chimneys or other obstacles. Each bombardier had a low-level bombsight to play with. We had our retractable belly turret removed for this raid. None of the other groups were so encumbered. Since we had the newest planes we were given the most distant target, Campina. We had somewhat more range than the old war weary desert ships. We had one bomb bay tank to give us 3,100 gallons of fuel. This was a 13:25 hour flight round trip. Needless to say, we didn't conserve fuel over the target.

On 20 July the five Liberator groups were withdrawn from the campaign and twelve days' training for 'Tidal Wave' (the code name for Ploesti) began, with practice flights against a mock-up target in the desert. On 6 July Brereton had told his five group commanders that a low-level daylight attack would be made on Ploesti to achieve maximum surprise and ensure the heaviest possible damage in the first raid. Brereton had studied target folders for two weeks before making his decision. And so it was that 177 aircraft would depart Libya on Sunday 1 August to bomb the energy out of Hitler's war machine. Most of the crews were apprehensive. This was no ordinary mission and morale was not improved when Brereton told them that losses were expected to be as high as 50 per cent.

Don Chase recalls:

That Russian Roulette 50-50 figure aroused our apprehension. Nevertheless, all ten *Heaven Can Wait* crewmen willingly readied for the assault. But orders called for a crew of only nine, not the usual ten; the tunnel gun position to be unmanned because of weight restrictions for the 2,500 mile flight and because our low attack altitude and 200mph target ground speed would cancel the effectiveness of a single, belly-fired, hand-held .50. The four mid and rear section gunners drew straws to determine which one would remain on the desert on P-Day. Young waist gunner Ralph Knox drew the 'unlucky' straw. He complained and cursed and feeling abandoned withdrew from the rest of the crew, not to speak until just before take-off when, woefully, he wished us luck. Ralph was dejected by this fracture in the brotherhood of battle. There wasn't much reason to stash beer aboard or extra water for the Ploesti run; we wouldn't fly high enough to chill it. But one of the ground men fastened a canteen in the already crammed bomb bay. 'Just for luck, okay?' he punctuated his words with the universal, jabbing thumbs up salute.

'Tommie' Holmes recalls:

When we were ordered to go to Ploesti the mission was of such importance that we needed every available plane and crew, even though several crews had finished at least twenty-five missions. Captain Rowland B. 'Sam' Houston of Long Beach, California, and crew would be doing No. 32 [in *Satan's Hell Cats*]. Even though he was recuperating from a traumatic crash at sea a few weeks earlier, we needed pilots so badly that I had to ask Robert J. 'Bob' Lehnhausen if he would fill out a crew [and take *Natchez Belle*]. He graciously consented.

'Tommie' Holmes too would fly the mission, in a *Wing and a Prayer*. It seemed an appropriate choice of name for his part in the mission, to 'Blue I', the Creditul Minier refinery at Brazi five miles south of Ploesti, which was being led by Lieutenant Colonel James Posey in Holmes' former aircraft, *Victory Ship* flown by John Diehl.[4] Posey's formation comprised twenty Liberators. Colonel Leon Johnson would lead another seventeen B-24s to White V, Columbia Aquila and Bill Cameron would lead the second wave in *Buzzin' Bear*. It would be his twenty-seventh combat sortie. Cameron wrote:

The day finally arrived. There were to be fifteen bombers in our particular formation – first, a three-plane element led by Colonel Leon Johnson, with Bill Brandon as his pilot, flying the venerable *Suzy-Q*. Next would come six bombers trailing to the right, which we were leading in the *Buzzin' Bear*. Off to our left would be the remaining six aircraft, led by Dexter Hodge. Trailing behind would be a spare aircraft, piloted by Bob Felber. It was arranged that should *Suzy-Q* falter for mechanical reasons en route to Ploesti we would move into the lead. As it turned out, only one of our thirty-six aircraft failed to reach the target area, a tribute to our maintenance men. I think it was also due in some measure to our dedication to Leon Johnson.

The refrain, *Double, double, toil and trouble; Fire burn and cauldron bubble* chanted by the witches in Macbeth, was brought to mind, by the scene confronting Flight Officer John E. O'Grady co-pilot in 2nd Lieutenant Blevins' crew as they approached B-24 816X. The men of the ground crew huddled around a smoking fire, intent on the activity within the circle. A closer look revealed a burning, oil soaked rope formed in a close circle. The men were dropping the morning's catch of scorpions, one by one, into the ring of fire. Crazed by the heat and trapped within the searing inferno, the scorpion ended the agony by stabbing itself in the back with the venomous stinger on the end of its long segmented tail. O'Grady recalls:

> Eerie ritual indeed but it was a momentary distraction from the grim task of preparing for the toil, trouble and fire awaiting us, the raid on the Ploesti oil refineries in Romania when nine of us faced combat for the first time. Blevins had flown in combat with the 98th Bomb Group. 2nd Lieutenant Toles, navigator, was on loan from the 389th. My crew, No. 15, minus Paul Peloquin, navigator, and Raymond Michels, co-pilot, both grounded with dysentery, filled the remaining eight positions. I was a last-minute replacement for the scheduled co-pilot.

During the night of 31 July crews were briefed on the part they were to play in the momentous raid. The grey dawn revealed the Libyan airstrip that Sunday 1 August and disclosed the apprehension etched on the faces of the combat crews. Blevins' crew went to their stations. The two pilots inspected the plane, kicking the left tyre and patted the battle-scarred fuselage. From the port side around the nose to the starboard side and there it was! *Snake Eyes* was painted on the right side only. Under the name the nose art was dice showing 'crap'.

John O'Grady says:

> All we needed was to have a black cat cross our path. Crouching to enter the forward port bomb bay, I checked the bomb load, three racks full. A bulging 'Tokyo Tank' in the forward starboard bay, carried the additional fuel necessary for the long flight. Up the catwalk to the flight deck, I followed Blevins into the cockpit and settled into the right bucket seat. Check list completed, we were ready to start engines at 0655 hours. Tension increased with each routine task.

First away were twenty-nine 'Liberandos' led by the CO, Colonel Keith Compton, with Brigadier General Uzal C. Ent (CO, 9th Bomber Command) in the command ship, *Teggie Ann*. (Brereton had intended to go in the command aircraft but an order from General 'Hap' Arnold in Washington forbade it.) Compton would lead thirty B-24s to White I, the Romana American Refinery. Behind them was the 'Travelling Circus' with twenty-one B-24s led by Colonel Addison Baker in *Hell's Wench*. Baker, whose target was White II, Concordia Vega, said that he would lead his outfit to the target 'even if my plane falls apart'. In the co-pilot's seat beside him was Major John 'The Jerk' Jerstad, the Operations Officer from Davenport, Iowa. Jerstad had graduated with a Bachelor of Science degree at Northwestern University in Illinois in 1940 and taught in high school at St Louis, Missouri, before he enlisted as an aviation cadet in July 1941. It was said that he was worshipped by the young pilots of new crews and was as 'Tough as a mule-skinner and tender as your grandmother'.[5] Ramsey D. Potts, who in nine months had gone from lieutenant to major under Timberlake, would lead the balance of the 'Travelling Circus' (fifteen aircraft) to White III, the Standard Petrol Block and Unirea-Spiranza. Led by Colonel John 'Killer' Kane in *Hail Columbia*, forty-seven B-24Ds in the 98th formation followed the Circus formations. Their target was White IV, the Unirea-Orion and Astra Romana. Then came the 37 B-24Ds of the 'Flying Eightballs' led by Colonel Leon Johnson in *Suzy-Q*, which was pronounced fit to fly after a broken spark plug in No. 2 engine had been fixed overnight.

Bringing up the rear of the formation were twenty-six B-24s of the 'Sky Scorpions' led by Colonel Jack Wood in Captain Kenneth 'Fearless' Caldwell's appropriately named Liberator, *The Scorpion*. Caldwell was a ten-year service veteran. The 'Sky Scorpions' target was Red I, Steaua

Romana at Campina. Each Liberator could carry only four 500lb bombs because an additional 400 gallons of fuel had been stored in the bomb bay. The 'Sky Scorpions' carried bombs with ten-second delay fuses, while the other groups carried twenty-minute acid-core-fused bombs, which would not explode until the bombs dropped by the 389th created a concussion wave in the target area. Any that did not explode in the concussion wave would eventually explode by means of the acid core fuse.

At 0700 Lieutenant Brian W. Flavelle's *Wongo Wongo!* in the 98th, which included some 389th crewmen as fill-ins, lifted off from Berka Two. The other 174 Liberators followed them into the sky above the Mediterranean. Bill Cameron wrote:

> After approximately a minute at the end of our dirt runway, we followed three giant clouds of dust left by the lead element and climbed into the pink-gray morning skies over Bengazi. I was confident about the condition of the *Bear*. As we headed out now to join the lead element climbing just ahead of us, those engines never sounded better. As we circled to take our place in formation, a large column of black smoke and orange flame blossomed up from an airfield just below us. We knew someone had not made the take-off. It was a tragic end for one crew and it did nothing to relieve our tensions.

Snake Eyes was the fourth B-24 to take off in Section 4. Section 1 lost one plane that had crashed and was still burning on the edge of the Benina Main runway. The rest of the Pyramiders climbed into the Libyan sky to join Killer Kane. Blevins settled *Snake Eyes* into the diamond position, behind and slightly below Major Hahn, the section leader. On the bomb run we would take a position in a V formation off the left wing of 2nd Lieutenant Ward, the Major's left wingman. 1st Lieutenant Fravega was on the lead plane's right wing. The code name for Section 4 on this mission was 'Hawk'.

Johy O'Grady recalls:

> The Pyramiders formed above Benina about 0810 and was shaped up and on course heading north to cross the Mediterranean Sea by 0830. Blevins turned the controls over to me as he slid back, pulled out a paperback, flipped the pages, found his place and settled down to reading. He seemed unaware as I white knuckled it until I got the hang of flying formation from the right seat. The monotonous drone of the four Pratt & Whitney engines was interrupted by the test firing of the twin .50 calibre guns in the top turret. Suddenly the war

became a reality. My eyes were riveted on Major Hahn's plane as I held *Snake Eyes* in the diamond slot. Since the sections of ten planes each were stepped up, we were hundreds of feet above the lead section with Section 5 above and behind us.

As the five-mile formation flew on to the German occupied island of Corfu the inevitable malfunctions reduced the numbers and seven of Kane's 'Pyramiders' were forced to abort. Three more B-24s from other groups also returned early. Nearing landfall at Corfu, *Wongo Wongo!* began to go out of control. It veered up, fell over on its back and plunged into the sea. Black smoke billowed up into the beautiful blue summer sky. *Brewery Wagon*, piloted by Lieutenant John Palm, took its place at the head of the 'Liberandos'.

Bill Cameron continues:

Shortly afterward we settled down and began the long, silent ride across the Mediterranean, barely visible in the hazy skies below and around us. Ahead of us were the 376th, 93rd and 98th – in that order. Behind us flew the 389th Bomb Group, only recently arrived in England and almost immediately sent off to Africa to join us.

The intercom cut into my concentration. Jim DeVinney, our bombardier, called attention to a column of smoke rising from the sparkling sea below us. Although we hadn't seen it, the lead aircraft of the 376th had suddenly gone down and with it the lead navigator. That crash has never been explained, to my knowledge. Had I known at the time that the alternate leader had followed the leader down to look for survivors, I would have been even more concerned. At the time, however, I did not realize that we had lost the two crews that had been especially briefed and trained to lead the entire formation to Ploesti. What a moment that must have been for Brigadier General Uzal G. Ent and Colonel Keith K. Compton – flying in the third and remaining aircraft of that lead element – to suddenly find that command of this vital mission had been so unexpectedly thrust on them. We were still puzzling over the smoke rising from the sea below when a bomber well in front of us swung out of formation and turned back toward us. As he passed under our flight, we could see that he had two engines feathered on the port side. All in all, these beginning omens were not good but in general the mission appeared to be going very much as planned.

John O'Grady continues:

The formation turned north-northeast over Corfu on a heading to cross the southern lands of Albania and Yugoslavia and the north-western area of Bulgaria en route to Romania. We were well above 10,000 feet leaving Corfu and soon encountered clouds ranging from 8,000 to 14,000 feet. At the Greek border the Pindus Range, rising to a height of, at most, 11,000 feet ruled out flying under the clouds and the absence of oxygen in the 98th Group's planes left Colonel Kane one option. He circled the formation in preparation for a frontal penetration. Blevins knew this procedure and took over at this point. The formation opened up to establish a safe distance between planes and each plane held a constant airspeed and heading as the sections ahead disappeared one by one into the mist. *Snake Eyes* nosed into the soup and suddenly we seemed to be alone. Blevins flew on instruments while I kept my head turning to spot any plane that might get dangerously close. A wing on the right, a wing on the left or twin vertical stabilizers ahead were the objects I strained my eyes trying to see but they remained hidden in the opaque mist. Suddenly we squirted out of the cloud bank and saw the group scattered before us. It took precious time to gather the formation, which would delay our arrival over the target. We finally got back on course to Pitesti, our Initial Point.

Compton meanwhile, had elected to climb above the cloud tops to save fuel and time and the 'Travelling Circus' followed him. The 'Eightballs' and the 'Sky Scorpions' adopted the same tactic as the 98th, entering the cloud in threes and after crossing the range, repeating the manoeuvre before setting course again and followed the 'Pyramiders'. This delay caused the 'Liberandos' and the 'Travelling Circus' to become separated from the rest of 'Tidal Wave' by sixty miles.

One of the 'Eightball' Liberators that was destined not to make the target was *Heaven Can Wait*, as Don Chase recalls:

There was only one other more saddening mission for our crew than this one. We aborted some 125 miles short of the oil complex, near Craiova, Romania. Fuel transfer problems and as proved later, oiling difficulties, caused us to shut down No. 1 engine and feather the propeller. We were tail-end Charlie, eating everyone's prop wash. We kept lagging farther behind. Then No. 4 engine lost power. We fell farther back. We had no choice. Navigator Robert Ricks from Richmond, Virginia, as was co-pilot William Phipps, gave Whitlock a course heading to the nearest friendly landing field, Cyprus, five flying hours' distant. Flying southbound we re-crossed the Danube at a point where people were wading and swimming. We didn't want to hurt them, so we dumped our bombs farther down river. Then we overflew Bulgaria into the Aegean Sea and skirted west of Turkey. Twenty minutes from the Cyprus coast No. 4 engine quit entirely. We were running out of altitude. At 500 feet and still dropping, Whitlock turned and asked if I was set up for a distress call. 'Yes Sir.' I knuckled out repeated SOS Morse signals, giving our code and holding the transmitter key down for fifteen to twenty seconds so air-sea-rescue could home in on us. Meanwhile, the crew threw out clothing, radio tuning units, ammunition and canteens to lighten our load so we could make landfall. The coast loomed and luckily we were lined up to land on the East-West runway. No turning; straight in. I fired red flares to ward off pattern aircraft. It was a good landing.

As they neared Ploesti Compton prepared to take the 'Liberandos' over the refineries alone. He overtook *Brewery Wagon* and nosed *Teggie Ann* into the lead slot. Events now began to overtake the B-24s. Owing to a navigational error the 'Liberandos' turned south too soon, at Targoviste, instead of at the correct IP at Floresti and the 'Travelling Circus'. Only *Brewery Wagon*, which was on course, took the route as briefed and was shot down soon after. The 'Liberandos' error led to the 'Travelling Circus's subsequent tactical mistake in bombing the 98th's and 'Flying Eightballs' targets and caused approximately twenty ineffective 'Liberandos' sorties. When the mistake was realized, Compton and Ent decided to make the best of the situation and head for the Astro Romana complex. The 'Liberandos' saw the 'Travelling Circus' already desperately fighting its way through to the target area and split to attack targets of opportunity instead. John R. 'Packy' Roche, who hailed from a farm near Davenport in Iowa, flying *Ready & Willing* in Ramsey Potts' B Force, recalled that 'the smoke stacks were 125 feet high. I was flying so low I had to look up to see the tops of them. There were high tension power lines at the end of the refinery. One of my engines was on fire over the target. I didn't have time to climb above those wires, so I flew the plane under them.' Roche emerged with five men wounded.

As the 'Liberandos' passed Ploesti and began climbing up the foothills east of the city they saw the 'Pyramiders' coming towards them. The plan was in ruins. Groups came in from the wrong directions and bombed any target, which presented itself. The 98th, led by 'Killer' Kane in *Hail Columbia* and the 'Eightballs' crossed Ploesti from the north-west. John E. O'Grady recalled:

The formation was descending as we neared the target area and the sections were forming the attack formations. Blevins eased back and slid left to take a position off John Ward's left wing. Speed increased to over 200mph as most of the planes dropped to tree top level. The crew kept us informed on the run to the target over the intercom.

'It's on fire! Look at that black smoke blowing to the right! It's like hell up there!'

'Bombs are going off and blowing stuff into the smoke and fire!'

'What happened? Some group hit it by mistake?'

'There's puffs of black all around us!'

'That's flak, boy and its heavy!'

'I heard about flak you could walk on. Hell! This stuff is walking on us!'

'That train off to the right – box cars with the sides down and some big guns blasting away at us! Somebody shot up the engine but the guns are still firing!'

'They've got balloons up too! Some planes are cutting through cables! Shoot at those babies! Good shootin' somebody!'

'They've got guns everywhere! Guns in the haystacks! Gun towers! Gun pits! They're shootin' at us with rifles!'

Comments were punctuated by bursts of 50-calibre fire throughout the plane. The WURRUMPH WURRUMPHING of 88 shells bursting all around the formation was accompanied by the constant POOM POOM POOMING of smaller calibre anti-aircraft weapons. Eardrums seemed ready to puncture. *Snake Eye* shuddered and started a snap roll to the left. We were hit. Blevins yelled an order! I heard 'right rudder' and jumped on the right rudder pedal with both feet and jammed it to the wall. Blevins was trimming the rudder to take the pressure off our legs and at the same time he hauled back the wheel to climb sharply. Recovering from the hit delayed our climb to hurdle a tall chimney directly in our path.

'Lieutenant! Whew! We missed that stack by inches. What a roller coaster ride that was!'

'We got bounced around back here but we got rid of the hot sticks (incendiary bombs were thrown out the waist windows by hand).'

'Let's get out of here!'

'Tail gunner to pilot. Only one from Section 5 made it past the target!'

'24s were dropping like flies back there. Some pan caked in the flat fields and seemed to be OK. Most of 'em blew up or went down in flames. Man! What a pounding we took!'

'Engineer to pilot. I'm at the left waist gun. Martin took a hit in the gut.' Staff Sergeant Martin was the armourer and left waist gunner. 'A burst hit under his window.' T/Sgt Knotts broke off as the 50s went into action during a fighter attack. He came back on during a lull. 'I gave Martin a shot of morphine.'

'Anybody else hurt back there?'

'This is Clemens, sir.' S/Sgt Clemens was the assistant radioman and right waist gunner. 'I got hit in the left ankle and my left arm. I bandaged them so I can stay at my guns. We've got some company!' Every gun in the plane cut loose!

'Sir!' Clemens again. Number 4 got hit and gas is spraying out past my window. I can smell it!'

Blevins nodded when I moved to cut off and feather number 4 engine. We re-trimmed as Blevins took us down to roof top level where we hedgehopped over trees and tall buildings. Once we reached the open fields we were skimming the ground. This action frustrated the Messerschmitts. The fighters pounced on the planes that failed to hit the deck. Ward's plane fell prey to the fighters because he stayed up about 1,000 feet.

Knotts filled us in on the damaged left vertical stabilizer. There was a jagged hole in the upper leading edge that had caused the drag that nearly caused us to spin in on the approach. The hole under the left waist window did not affect the performance of the plane. T/Sgt Weber, the radioman, checked the bomb bay and shocked the crew with his message.

'The bombs! They're still in the racks!'

2nd Lieutenant Hal Moore the bombardier, had flipped all the switches and grabbed the salvo lever to follow through. When he pushed the lever, to assure the drop, it broke off in his hand. The violent action when we were hit could have warped the hangers and jammed them. Blevins agreed with Moore's suggestion that he safety the bombs and release them manually into the Danube River. The fighters had broken off their attack as we approached the Danube River. Hal opened the bomb bay doors and waltzed down the narrow catwalk. The turbid water swished by beneath his feet as he safetied each bomb and tripped it out with a screwdriver. The consensus of the crew was that this river, immortalized by Strauss, was not blue.

Major Hahn's plane, with Fravega on the right wing, was the only part of the original section intact. Blevins caught up and completed the element by easing into the left wing position. Flight Officer Salyer joined us in the diamond spot, our original position in the formation. Two other B-24s, from Section 4, survived the bomb-run. Morgan and Sternfels took a beating from cables and anti-aircraft yet they were able to get back to Libya. Ward was shot down by a German fighter and the three planes to the right of Fravega, Dore, Thomas and Hussey, fell victim to flak, fire and/or explosions at the target. Weisler's plane was the lone survivor, of the six that made it to the target in Section 5. Sections 4 and 5 sustained 50 per cent losses.

Our mini-formation survived another fighter attack. A biplane, that must have been a trainer, got caught up in the air war and dove right through the middle of the formation. The foolhardy little plane spun on down in one piece. If by chance the pilot did land the plane, it was well ventilated by .50 calibre bullets. That was our last encounter with the fighters and it led us into what turned out to be a false sense of security.

'Hey! Isn't that a Ju 88 out there at 3 o'clock?'

I was at the controls, staying in close to the lead plane and dared not take a look but the rest of the crew craned their necks to verify the sighting. Someone remarked, 'That's an 88 all right, at our altitude and air speed, but he's out of range of our .50s.'

'He can't hurt us from there!' A sharp explosion punctuated the statement!

I saw the bright flash on our left out of the corner of my eye and felt the impact as the plane vibrated from the hit. She was still handling OK and I was able to hold our position. Blevins reported the hit to the crew. The innocent Ju 88 off at a distance was calling one or no re German bombers above us, giving them our altitude and air speed. The information helped the plane(s) above aim their aerial bombs at the formation. They either missed other tries or ran out of bombs. Our plane was the only one to sustain a hit. The bomb tore out a piece of the trailing edge of the left wing behind number one engine. The left flap was welded to the wing; the oil pressure on number one was dropping slowly. Blevins voiced concern about the condition of the left landing gear. We crossed our fingers.

Gas consumption was our main concern now. Knotts, the engineer, was switching valves to drain the last drop in each tank. Suddenly, we reached that 'Maxwell House' drop and all three engines quit cold. *Snake Eyes* started to drop like a rock. That instant before the three engines sputtered and roared again felt like an eternity. Knotts had been ready to switch tanks but the incident added a few more gray hairs to the day's crop. Major Hahn, with his number one engine feathered, headed the formation toward Sicily. We were forced to feather our number one engine when the oil pressure dropped too low. Number two was still running smoothly but number three was losing oil pressure.

The 'Travelling Circus' had followed Compton's force and trailed over Ploesti. Some Romanian fighters attacked the formation and the tail gunner of *Joisey Bounce* became the first casualty of the Ploesti battle. Baker and Jerstad turned *Hells Wench* left and headed for the smokestacks of Ploesti. Major Ramsey Potts in *The Duchess* and the second formation of B-24s in the 'Travelling Circus' followed. The flak batteries enveloped the 'Circus' with their fire and at only 20 feet the aircraft were sitting targets. During the five-minute bomb run the Group was torn to shreds. *Hell's Wench* was hit and caught fire. Baker jettisoned his bombs but he and Jerstad decided to continue to the target. At Ploesti *Hell's Wench* was enveloped in flames and surged up to 300 feet before falling back and crashing to the ground. Lieutenant Colonel Joseph S. Tate Jr, who was from St Augustine, Florida, and West Point '41, was flying *Ball of Fire Jr* 400 feet behind *Hell's Wench*. He said that when they got right on top of the target, the devil himself couldn't have held that ship together any longer. 'The cockpit must have been a blast furnace'. Tate could see the flames through the windows of as the doomed Liberator lost speed and he pulled up with it. Baker's right wing began to crumple and drop off but not before Baker had taken them through the target. And then he pulled *Hell's Wench* into a steep climb. Tate wondered God only knows how anybody inside could have still been alive but three men fell out the back before *Hell's Wench* crashed into a field. Tate was of the opinion that Baker could have saved himself if he had wanted to belly-land in a field before they got to the target when he was first hit but Baker 'stuck'. Seven men in Baker's ship had finished their tours of duty and had volunteered to fly with Baker.

Captain Walter Stewart, the deputy leader in *Utah Man* took over the 'Travelling Circus' lead. Despite severe damage to the bomber, Stewart, who came from Utah out near Salt Lake and had been a Mormon missionary to Scotland in 1938, managed to land again in Libya, fourteen hours later. His granduncle John M. Browning who used to sit around on the Stewart ranch in 1900 and who thought up the Browning machine gun would have been proud. Walt Stewart's mother had once written a letter saying she was so glad that her son was in 'one of those beautiful big Flying Fortresses'. Lieutenant Kenton D. McFarland from Galt, California, flying *Liberty Lad* on two engines was the last home by another two hours. Also safely home was *Red Ass*, flown by Captain Jake Epting, a veteran pilot from Tupelo, Mississippi. His tail gunner, Ben Kuroki, a Nebraska born Japanese finished his tour of duty. All he had to say was, 'To Tokyo I would like to do the same with Libs.' Nine other of the Group's B-24s, including two that collided in cloud, did not return. Among the survivors were *Joisey Bounce*, which made it home with a shattered tail, *Thar She Blows*, *Ball of Fire Jr*, *Bomerang* and *The Duchess*.

Bill Cameron continues:

In order to clear the mountains of Albania and Yugoslavia we had to make a long slow climb to 15,000 feet At that point; I felt a foreboding of trouble for the first time. As far as the eye could see across our flight path but still well ahead of us, there appeared to be a solid wall of towering cumulus clouds – beginning about where we judged the coastline to be.

The skies were clearer now, less hazy and we could see the aircraft of the 98th Group very clearly and beyond, numerous specks that would be the B-24s of the 93rd and perhaps the 376th as well. At any rate, the latter two groups were some distance ahead, not quite the way we had flown it in practice.

As we approached the clouds, they grew more menacing. It was vital that one group follow the other into the target area. Our success and our salvation depended not only on surprise but also on a simultaneous sweep across our various targets. We must arrive together, attack together and depart together. How would this be possible, we began to ask ourselves, if we were now to be separated penetrating the clouds? Would the mission now be abandoned? Would radio silence be broken to announce our recall?

Then one of the leading groups disappeared in the clouds and we had our answer. The only question now was could we find that same hole and follow through it?

As the 98th, leading us, came closer to that solid wall, we searched for the opening until it became obvious we couldn't find it. The formation veered off to look for another opening and at that moment, I knew that it was to be a new ball game.

The lead groups continued on course to Ploesti, while we lost time searching for a route through the clouds. It would not be a co-ordinated attack and from that time on we would be alone with the pink-colored airplanes of the 98th. Adding to our concern was flight engineer Sergeant Gibby's announcement that a fighter was approaching our formation. A fighter? Had we been spotted so soon? We were miles from the target.

'Hey, look!' someone yelled. 'It's a biplane.'

Strangely enough that's what it was and I agreed with co-pilot Bill Dabney's opinion that the pilot was a lot more startled to see us than we had been to see him! Nevertheless, we had been spotted.

Some minutes later we were clearing the clouds with only the aircraft of the 98th in sight ahead of us. Our own 44th was coming along in good shape. Even with this combined force of some seventy bombers, it felt very lonely.

Frank Maruszewski, our tail gunner, looked in vain for the 389th behind us. Nothing. I think we must have all felt threatened now and the formation began to tighten up. We began our slow descent that would eventually take us below the treetops in the vicinity of a city named Ploesti.

We had now descended the Balkan east slope. It was almost peaceful as we droned on a straight course, mile after mile. Because of the relatively few bombers we could see, the skies seemed strangely empty and nothing appeared to be moving on the green hills below. Tom Clifford, our navigator, said we were fairly well on course but I didn't know how our timing was and it couldn't matter much now since we were obviously separated from the two groups in the lead. The 98th formation was still stretched out in front of us and the 389th now appeared behind us and very high.

We were down to about 3,000 feet as we crossed the Danube and had a very clear view of the Romanian countryside. Ploesti was still more than 160 miles away. Pitesti, the first of three checkpoints before we began the turn on our bomb run, was now less than 100 miles ahead. We didn't know it then but the two lead groups were some sixty miles ahead of us. They had reached the first checkpoint on time but turned on the second checkpoint and streaked on a correct course for Bucharest. It was a correct course but for the wrong target!

What we did not know then was that the groups were very widely separated. As far as I knew the 98th and the 44th were alone, although the 389th was actually nearby and behind us. The 376th and the 93rd were twenty minutes ahead of us. After mistakenly turning east at the town of Targoviste, which closely resembled the correct checkpoint at the town of Floresti, the two lead groups realized their error and turned back to the north. As a result, the 93rd laid their bombs on the Astra Romana, Phoenix Orion and Columbia Aguila refineries, which were the intended targets of the 98th and the 'Flying Eightballs'.

The 376th had continued eastward somewhat further and then turned northward behind the attacking 93rd. Observing the heavy losses suffered by the 93rd as it attacked targets intended for the other groups; the 376th swung wide and abandoned the attempt to strike its targets. Considering that a successful attack against such a small target required precise navigation on the bomb run, this was not surprising. It was obvious that the vital elements of surprise and precise timing had by now been lost. All I can say, in hindsight, is that I am glad we didn't know what had happened. We were keenly aware of the smoke and the flame that was now becoming visible in the target area. We could begin to guess what was happening but we did not know that those huge fires came from the very targets we had been assigned to attack at near ground level!

With the aircraft of the 98th stretched out before us, we had passed Pitesti and Targoviste and were nearing the turning point at Floresti. As Floresti came in view, with our altitude approximately 1,500 feet, things began to get very busy. By now, it was clear that our target had already been bombed and was in flames. What followed was probably the most action-packed thirty minutes of my life.

The 'Eightballs' arrived at Ploesti at 1515, immediately plunging into a hail of flak and ripping tracers, smoke, fire and explosives. Several parts of the extensive plant were already ablaze and to reach the specified target Johnson led his formation directly over this fiery and bursting cauldron of oil and through a veritable forest of anti-aircraft guns. Modest barns and harmless-looking haystacks now revealed themselves as emplacements and from everywhere, including the handcars on the sidings, flew a barrage of steel. Colonel Johnson headed for the Columbia Aquila plant but through an error another group had already bombed the target assigned to the 'Eightballs'. Johnson decided to seek an alternative target. He changed course and headed straight and low through the smoke, flames and the floundering B-24s for a plant as yet untouched. Bombers went down on all sides and one, caught in the blast of an exploding bomb, pointed its nose upwards and soared about a hundred feet before falling helplessly onto its back. *Lil' Abner*, leader of the third wave, crashed forty miles from the target. Altogether, nine of the sixteen aircraft in the 'Eightballs' first formation were lost.

Johnson's *Suzy-Q* came through the maelstrom, as did his wingmen. Bill Cameron, leading the second wave in *Buzzin' Bear* also got through safely.

The long gaggle of pink-coloured 98th B-24s began a wide descending turn to the right and there we were, turning on the bomb run to the target labelled 'White Five,' the Columbia Aguila refinery. Colonel Johnson and Bill Brandon in the *Suzy-Q* turned their three-ship element inside the 98th and all together fifty bombers began to drop rapidly to their assigned bombing altitudes, flying parallel to a railroad on our right, which led directly toward our target. As we made the turn, we pulled our six-ship flight into position directly behind *Suzy-Q* and the remaining seven bombers fell in line behind us – sixteen 44th bombers in all. The last element numbered four Liberators instead of three because Bob Felber in the spare B-24 refused to go home and stayed with us all the way. The remaining twenty-one bombers from our group led by Colonel Jim Posey split off at this point to attack the Brazi refinery.

In the meantime the 389th had proceeded on alone from the first checkpoint, Pitesti, to attack the relatively isolated Steaua Romana refinery at Campina, eighteen miles northwest of Ploesti. It was called 'Red' target. Later reconnaissance showed that they did an outstanding job of precise bombing – equalling the performance of Jim Posey's formation against the Brazi refinery far to the south. Although the most destruction was inflicted on the White Five target by our formation, together with the earlier bombs left there by the 93rd, the two groups assigned to the 'outside' targets did the most precise work. The 389th and Jim Posey's formation were the only two units with clear shots at their objectives, flying on their briefed routes. The 93rd did have a clear shot but attacked the wrong target on a course 90° off the assigned axis of attack.

As we approached the target area, several B-24s were coming in straight for us from our left but there was no time then to try to figure that one out! It was just one of several unexpected happenings that had to be accepted. Later, we learned that these were Liberators from the 93rd and 376th. Some of these aircraft had unfortunately dropped their bombs a few minutes earlier on the very target we were now rapidly approaching.

As we raced toward Columbia Aguila, levelling off at our bombing altitude of 250 feet, my eyes were glued on the *Suzy-Q*. Her target would be almost exactly in line with the spot where our own bombs were programmed to go. We were expected to place our load into a low profile building some 210 feet wide and 600 feet long. I was conscious of three specific situations. First, we were edging in toward a train rolling side by side with us along the tracks on our right. It appeared to be exceptionally well equipped with anti-aircraft weapons of all calibres. By this time it seemed that almost all our own .50-calibre machine guns were in action and judging by the excited chatter on our intercom, they were directed toward the train. Second, the sky was becoming unusually crowded with pink aircraft sliding in on us from our left. Perhaps no moment of the entire episode worried me more than did the chilling knowledge that we were suddenly sandwiched between two bombers, one directly above us and one below! I could not have lifted either wing during those few seconds without bringing sure destruction to the three of us. Even now, I can visualize the rivets of the bomber above us, which I could see all too clearly. I could occasionally glimpse the bomber below but could only concern myself with the one above. Miraculously, both of our large neighbours slid away from us. We were now heading toward a point where the railroad disappeared into a great mass of smoke and flame – the Columbia Aguila refinery. By this time, I am quite sure that green and pink B-24s were mixed together as we neared our targets. I will always believe that a few pink bombers crossed through our formation just about the time we penetrated the smoke over the target area!

The third thing I became increasingly aware of was the flame and huge columns of smoke just ahead of us. There were two raging areas of destruction. These were close together with a narrow tunnel of light in between. The wind was from our left and the smoke from the towering flame on the left stretched high and over toward the fires on the right side, forming a top to the tunnel I have described. It seemed to me that bombers were converging toward that one small area that was free of flame and explosions. And then the Suzy-Q disappeared in that smoke and we were right behind. Below me in the nose section I could hear DeVinney and Clifford frantically trying to pinpoint our target. Then we were in the smoke – and then out of it. To this day, Bill Dabney maintains that our outside air temperature gauge reached its most extreme temperature reading as we sailed through the awful heat of those great fires that seemed to surround us!

If you have ever flown an airplane through a lone fleecy white cloud, you will remember how suddenly you pop out on the far side. It was just like that and just as abruptly I pushed hard on the control column and headed for the ground, all in a split second and I am sure this near spontaneous action saved our lives. Staring up at us were numerous shirtless anti-aircraft gunners in gun emplacements with long, black gun barrels pointing directly at us.

We levelled and began a flat turn to the right. By flat I mean that I pushed hard on the right rudder but kept our wings from banking with opposite aileron control. It may be that the skidding turn threw the gunners off but whatever the reason, we escaped destruction.

Unable to find our building in the smoke (augmented by smoke pots), flame, exploding tanks and the general confusion of that instant our bombs were held too long. I can only hope that they fell in an area that contributed to the general destruction in the target complex.

Few if any aircraft came off that target lower than we did – at least at that moment. Every Liberator I saw was above us. The abrupt pitch down from 250 feet dislodged the gunners in the rear, Sergeants Jerry Grett and Ernie 'Mac' McCabe, but they were on their feet again in an instant.

Everything was happening awfully fast now. The *Suzy-Q* and her two wingmen, Reg Carpenter and Ed Mitchell, were in the turn just ahead. My own two wingmen, Charlie 'Punchy' Henderson and Jim Hill, had dropped down with us and were doggedly hanging on in formation as we skidded around that turn.

A B-24 ahead pulled straight up and then fell out of the sky. Two doll-like figures popped out of the waist windows, barely two or three hundred feet above the ground. I learned later that both men survived that fantastic jump. As this was going on and we were still in our turn, a V-formation of five to seven Me 109s swung headlong into us, going from our left to our right. I didn't know it but both Charlie Henderson and Jim Hill had received damage by this time. I have always assumed that Henderson was hit by those oncoming Me 109s, because the damage was in his nose section where both his navigator and bombardier were wounded. However, more official records give credit to a Ju 88. Jim Hill hit a barrage balloon cable that put a rip in his wing but otherwise came though okay.

We took a hit somewhere along the line, ripping out hydraulic lines and putting our tail turret out of operation. There was a pretty fair-sized hole in the *Bear's* tail but no one was hurt. The loss of the tail gun turned out to be a great disadvantage during the next few minutes. In the meantime, there was a rather wild mixture of bombers and fighters and then we were levelling out and heading on the long road home. But we were not out of it yet.

The way things were developing; it had become almost a matter of individual survival, with little time to account for our companions. In fact, because of the personal nature of our targets, the three-ship elements were separated to enable each aircraft to attack its own aiming point.

The smoke, flame and the tremendous barrage of anti-aircraft fire we encountered in the target area further widened the formation. And because we were using high – though not maximum-power settings, ships to the rear could not readily close up, especially if they were damaged. Nevertheless, the formation was beginning to assemble when all the fighters in Romania seemed to descend on us. From all directions came Me 109s, '110s and '210s. All this took place not more than three to five minutes after leaving the target area.

The chatter on the intercom was pretty frantic by now but in all the excitement I understood that a Liberator off to our right was fighting for its life against repeated fighter attacks. Then in a cloud of dust it was on the ground and skidding to a stop. The war was over, apparently safely, for that crew. Nearby, a Me 110 went down and exploded, joined almost immediately by a Me 109, which crashed, leaving a fiery trail through a field of wheat.

I was pulling about thirty-two inches of manifold pressure and indicating 220 to 225mph as we closed in toward the lead element, when I noticed a twin-engine Dornier 217 just above and to our right. I usually left such matters to my eagle-eyed crew, who had scored five confirmed fighters over Naples not long before but I yelled to Gibby on the intercom to bring this one to his attention. He called back that we could quit worrying about that one if we were to do anything about the several other fighters on our tail! With the tail turret out, both Gibby and the waist gunners were busy warding off a number of single and twin-engine fighters that were to stay with us for the next fifteen to twenty minutes. In the meantime, we saw other fighters overshoot us in their pursuit of bombers ahead. It was what could accurately be described as a running fight!

We were flying at about 100 feet now because I intended to pull into close formation directly behind and under Colonel Johnson and Brandon. To elude the fighters, if we could, we went back down below the level of the scattered treetops. We followed the terrain, once lifting slightly to rise up over a man ploughing a field directly in our path. He never left his plough and acted as though American bombers flew over those fields every day. I especially recall two well-spaced trees that I deliberately flew between, thinking to myself under circumstances that seemed very unreal, that I might never have the chance to do that again, legally.

Now the fighters appeared to have turned off and we could begin to look around cautiously and take stock of our situation. As it turned out, the battle was over for us but we learned later that the fighting went on for many of the other crews. Fighters were still attacking some after they had reached the Mediterranean. By now, we had lost track of Henderson and Hill, who had taken up a direct route for Malta. It was a long, lonely trip but they made it. Ed Mitchell, who had been flying on *Suzy-Q*'s left wing, peeled off to land in Turkey. Worden Weaver, who was leading the flight behind, was hit very badly over the target and crashed about forty miles away – about the time we passed over the man ploughing the field. Hit severely with gaping holes in the fuselage and a missing vertical stabilizer was the airplane flown by Bob Miller and Dexter Hodge, leading the fourth flight. Luckily, three of their engines were spared and miraculously they made it safely 1,100 miles back to Benghazi. Both of their wingmen were lost.

Some distance away, Colonel Jim Posey was leading the other half of the 44th – twenty-one B-24s to the Creditul Minier refinery at Brazi. They had turned on a heading of about 70 degrees across the mountains of Yugoslavia and clouds which gave trouble but did not stop them. Later, they began a slow descent down the east slope to the Blue Danube River – which was a muddy brown from rains. As they flew lower, they could see the countryside cities, animals and people dressed in bright colours, as if it were a pleasant Sunday afternoon drive. 'Tommie' Holmes, piloting *Wing and a Prayer*, recalls:

Before we knew it, we arrived at the IP where we changed course and flew southeast for approximately 25–30 miles to the target. At this time we were flying very low, passing a downed B-24 on my right. It appeared to have landed wheels up, but fairly well intact.

The crew was standing beside the plane, waving as we flew by. How I did wish we could land and pick them up.

Next we came upon a power line and I remember pulling up to get over it, thinking of the planes on my wings. By this time the anti-aircraft guns were in full swing and many shells were exploding all around us. This was the first time we had ever been this close to 88mm guns and the impressive thing was the rapid rate of fire and the flames and bright flashes which seemed to be 30–40 feet long out of the muzzle.

We were now able to see many of the other targets burning – B-24s were coming back, over and through us. One plane – Bar D – flew directly over the top of our planes. I looked up about 100 feet and saw a hole about six feet across between #1 and #2 engines burning fiercely with the metal burning brilliantly around the outer edges. I'm sure he did not go far before crashing. The sky was full of B-24s returning from the other targets. They flew over the top of our planes as we were approaching the target, flying extremely low. Our target was less than a mile straight ahead. There were numerous guns around the refinery and they were all firing. We had one or two fixed .50 calibre guns in the nose for the pilot to fire, but I do not recall firing them. I was too busy flying toward the target to concentrate on a target for the nose guns. I remember seeing a ground soldier literally explode when hit by some of our .50 calibre guns. He was less than 400 feet away.

We had the target in sight from about 10–15 miles away and now we were rapidly approaching at a very low level – less than 50 feet high. I remember very clearly pulling up to get over the smokestacks on the power house, which was my assigned target and I feel sure we put our bombs directly over target. The bombs were delayed action bombs and they exploded at intervals of 30 seconds to 72 hours. This was to keep fire fighters away from the refineries.

After releasing our bombs we continued on a course which led us to the southwest and toward home. The fighters jumped on us on the retreat and several of them flew into the ground, as we were still at a very low level. Our gunners were well trained and experienced at shooting enemy planes and they did an excellent job.

I noticed one B-24 [G.I. Gal' flown by 1st Lieutenant Elmer Reinhart] trailing heavy black smoke from the tanks in the bomb bay. He was flying very low and about 200–300 yards in front of me. The smoke got bigger and I knew he could not last much longer. I never did understand why he did not gain some altitude in order to bale the crew out. After about 20 miles he pulled into a steep climb to about 700–800 feet. I was so close behind that I had to observe the direction of his nose in order to dodge his plane. I turned to the right as he veered off to the left. When he stalled, the nose fell abruptly and three chutes opened as the men in the tail were thrown 15–20 feet above the tail section. I felt sure they landed okay and probably made their way to the wreckage. The plane passed under our left wing and exploded, which I believe ended in the deaths of all the men at the front – six, probably. I never heard anymore about this plane or crew.

We lost #3-engine as our fuel ran out because of a faulty pump. We were not far from the target when this happened, so we transferred fuel and restarted the engine until we were off the coast. In the meantime I ordered the crew to throw everything overboard – guns, ammunition etc. I remember the long strings of .50 calibre ammo snaking through the air and into the mountains of Yugoslavia. We saved 100 rounds for the top and tail turrets, in case we ran into enemy planes. We dropped behind after crossing the coast, in order to save fuel. All engines were reduced – both RPMs and manifold pressure. Our flight across the Mediterranean was uneventful. We encountered a number of low cloud banks and felt that each one would be over landfall, but was not to be until about the fourth or fifth cloud bank. It was nearing dark as we finally crossed the coast and our field was now only about 20 miles ahead. We proceeded directly to the field and landed promptly, as we knew we were extremely low on fuel.

'Sam' Houston was shot down by a Bf 109 flown by *Hauptmann* Willie Steinmann of 1./JG 4, who had already shot down *Brewery Wagon* in the 376th Bomb Group formation. Steinmann picked up *Satan's Hell Cats* at about 150 feet from the ground, attacking from the rear. Steinmann recalled:

The American machine guns were spatting all around. I cut back on the throttle and gave the Liberator a good raking from wing tip to wing tip. I could see tracers walking across the width of the plane and flames coming out everywhere. The top turret and tail turret were shooting me up. I closed to within 70 feet. My engine caught fire and there was a tremendous quivering. My speed carried me under the left wing as the Liberator went out of control. I was caught between the ground and Liberator with no control. I slid open the canopy and loosened the harness. I don't remember crashing. First thing I knew, I was seated on the ground, trousers torn and cuts on my legs. Near me the two planes burned. I got up and walked away. No one walked away from Houston's ship.[6]

Despite the two losses, the performance of those twenty bombers was one of the few success stories that can be told about the attack on Ploesti.

Bill Cameron continues:

Eventually, we were well out over the Mediterranean and headed home. Where was everybody? I had taken a position on *Suzy-Q's* right wing and Reg Carpenter was trailing somewhat behind us. We were throttled back, maintaining about 145mph at minimum airspeed to conserve fuel but primarily to permit Carpenter to keep up with us. '*P for Peter – R for Robert,*' he had called, 'Keep it slow. We've got some problems.'

Dabney told me later that Carpenter's airplane looked like a battered wreck even in the twilight. We didn't hear anything more from Reg and he continued to drop behind.

I could see wounds in *Suzy-Q's* tail and wing tip but otherwise it was in good shape and so were we. However, Reg Carpenter and his crew failed to make it that night. They had slowly dropped back and below us. Eventually, they had to ditch. After twenty-nine very difficult and painful hours in a dinghy, they were picked up by a RAF launch in a rare night rescue operation.

It was dark now and at last we could see scattered points of light below, as trucks and jeeps and bombers manoeuvred into their parking positions on our home field. Colonel Johnson and Brandon wasted little time; we could see their wing lights peeling off into the traffic pattern. We were right behind, as we had been for the past thirteen hours and twenty minutes. As we pulled into our parking area and cut those four great engines, Howard Moore and a number of our flight-line people – Sergeants Gilbert Hester, Ed Hanley, Marion Bagley and others – extravagantly greeted us. And so it ended up that only two of us were back out of the formation of sixteen assigned to attack White Five. It had been a long day.

In the 'Sky Scorpions' formation *Wolf Wagon's* first problem was a thunderstorm over the Greek Alps as Ken Matson recalls:

We climbed in formation above it. Came out and began letting down as we approached Romania. We were maintaining complete radio silence (useless since the Germans had broken the Allied code and were reading the 9th Air Force transmission). Colonel Keith Compton of the 376th made a turn (wrong) too soon and was headed for Bucharest. The radio silence ended with many screaming 'Wrong turn not here!' Fortunately for us we were the last group so we had broken away from the other four groups and headed for the mountains above Campina. We also made a wrong turn and started down a valley. Colonel Wood and Caldwell realized their error and did a 180° turn in the valley. Our flight (three planes) was the second in line. I was flying in the right seat as I flew on Elmer Rodenberg's left wing. We made a steep turn at low altitude. Major John Brooks, leading the second element, had realized we were in the wrong valley but fortunately followed us and didn't turn until he saw we had turned. If he had been turning we would have run into him as we came up over a ridge. John Fino [Compton's bombardier on the raid] sent me a combat film showing my plane over the target, a powerhouse with three smokestacks. I cleared the 200 feet chimneys by 50 feet and then dove down to join my flight leader. The two of us joined the lead flight and the five of us headed for Benghazi. We were down on the deck until we had to climb over the Greek Mountains. My gas gauges began to show that we were about out of gas. We waved goodbye to the other four planes. My navigator Jack Englehardt gave me a direct heading to Benghazi. I began going over ditching procedure in my mind. We were on the ground when the other planes returned.[7]

The greatest success, however, went to the 'Sky Scorpions', which brought up the rear of 'Tidal Wave' and struck for its target at Campina, although there were some anxious moments when the formation turned down the wrong valley. Led by Colonel Jack Wood and Major Caldwell, the 'Sky Scorpions' pulled up and flew on for perhaps three or four minutes before turning to the right. They started down towards the refinery, which was marked by a great pall of smoke and split into three sections to hit the target from three different directions. The target was completely destroyed but four Liberators being shot down marred the success. Another nine were forced to land in Turkey and Cyprus and seventeen returned to North Africa. The B-24s flew so low over the oilfields that enemy fighters hit the ground when they failed to pull out of dives after making their attacks on the bombers. The bravery and determination of the men of the 'Sky Scorpions' was exemplified by the courage displayed by 2nd Lieutenant Lloyd D. 'Pete' Hughes of Alexandria, Louisiana, piloting *Eager Eagle*, who refused to turn back after shells had ruptured the left fuel tanks. The twenty-two-year-old pilot has been described by Major Philip Ardery, his squadron commander who was flying with Lieutenant Edward L. Fowble[8] in the central column, as a 'laughing, youngish, handsome lad and a much-better-than-average pilot'. Although fuel was streaming over the fuselage, Hughes and his co-pilot, Lieutenant Ronald H. Helder, piloted *Eager Eagle* low over the blazing target. Heat engulfed the bomber and flames licked at its fuselage as the fuel ignited. Hughes struggled to complete the bomb run but after Lieutenant John A. McLaughlin got the bombs away the starboard wing dipped, hit the ground and cartwheeled before exploding in flames killing the two pilots and Lieutenant Sidney Pear, the navigator, a New Jerseyite from Weehawken, 'whose skill was exceptional' and four of the enlisted men. Incredibly, two gunners managed to scramble from the wreckage. McLaughlin, who had knocked around New York City most of his life in a variety of jobs, among them bar tendering in Greenwich village for a year or so, was partially thrown clear of the burning Liberator but he was mortally burned and died in a Romanian hospital two days later.

Next morning the results of the mission were pieced together. Unfortunately, the plants the Liberators had sought to destroy were soon repaired and were operating at pre-mission capacity within a month. The 'Pyramiders' suffered the highest casualties of all five groups, losing twenty-one of the thirty-eight B-24s that started out from North Africa. At least nine were destroyed by the blasts from delayed action bombs dropped by the 'Liberandos'. Of the 177 B-24s that had set out, eight were interned in Turkey and 45 were brought down. Twenty-three had landed in Cyprus (including Kane's *Hail Columbia*), Malta or Sicily.

As *Snake Eyes* and the three other B-24s approached the south-eastern coast of Sicily, three Spitfires came in close to look them over as John O'Grady explains.

The leader snapped us a salute, rocked his wings, pointed down and led us to an RAF base in the vicinity of Syracuse. *Snake Eyes*, the most battered of the four, made the first approach. The fighter strip looked very short. Running through the checklist, we found that we could not lower the flaps as we had feared. 'Gear down and locked! Check list complete.' Blevins lined up with the strip and nosed the plane down. I was reading the airspeed aloud as he kept it around 135mph. He was trying to use every inch of the short runway. The nose came up and as the wheels touched he pulled back the throttles to land at about 130mph. The crew had been briefed and had braced themselves for a possible crash landing. *Snake Eyes* dropped on the left and pulled left toward the trees that lined the airstrip. The aerial bomb had flattened the left tyre. Blevins reacted and advanced the number two throttle as he pushed the right brake. *Snake Eyes* responded sluggishly and started to turn right. A few hundred yards ahead, a man jumped out of the trees, his legs running before he hit the ground. He headed toward the runway but realized he was on a collision course with our corrected path and reversed his direction and dashed back to the trees. Blevins reacted to the first move and released the right brake as he cut the power on number two. When the man headed back to the trees a right turn was attempted but by that time the trees had caught the left wing tip and pulled us into the row of trees. As *Snake Eyes* ploughed into the trees the man made his final dash toward the runway. A rugged stone wall ran parallel to the tree line. The trees and the wall finally stopped us with our left wing over the wall and our nose up against it. Number two, our last good engine, hit the wall and the prop snapped off. 'Switches off!' Blevins and I were the last to exit the top hatch. Clemens, gasping for breath, told us that he had jumped out of the right waist window before the plane stopped. The flak wound to his ankle was forgotten in the near panic situation.

'Where is Martin?' I asked.

'He's still in the plane.'

'Well? Get him out of there!' I surprised myself; Flight Officer O'Grady gave a command with some authority. Even some of the British airmen sprung into action to assist. Martin was passed through the left waist window on a stretcher and carried to the waiting lorry. I told Martin that he would be back with us in no time. Clemens followed the stretcher-bearers after a last handshake. I was told by the crew that Martin had a severe case of dysentery but refused to go on sick call. He didn't want to miss the first mission with the crew.

Major Hahn, Fravega and Salyer landed safely. One of the crews came over and pirated the guns and ammunition. They had jettisoned everything they could to conserve fuel. The ground crews of the Spitfires were examining *Snake Eyes* with great interest. The RAF chap that had jumped out of the trees explained that he was running communication lines when he saw *Snake Eyes* heading toward him. 'Blimey gov'nor I t'ought you 'ad me!'

I assumed he was talking to me but he was looking at *Snake Eyes* as he spoke.

'Gentlemen, if you will please follow me, I will direct you to the mess.' An RAF officer led our hungry crew to the mess tent where we dined on a gourmet meal of beans and fried tomatoes. A few British eyebrows were arched, as I declined the milk and sugar proffered and drank my tea straight.

The friendly RAF sergeant collected our well-fed group and escorted us to our billet, which in this case was the hospital tent. Lined up in a neat row were our sleeping accommodations, a stretcher for each man on the dirt floor of the tent. The air raid shelter was visible through the open tent flap. The sergeant gestured toward the shelter and informed us, 'Jerry may be over tonight!' The German troops still held northern Sicily and were in the habit of bombing the airstrip every other night. The threat of an air raid was not enough to keep us awake after thirteen hours and twenty-four minutes in the air.

Hal Moore told us about the frantic activity that took place on the flight deck while *Snake Eyes* was jolting and grinding to a halt. Knotts, the engineer, was standing on the catwalk with his arms on the back edge of the flight deck leaning forward. The nose wheel buckled and the nose hit the ground. The underside was being chewed up and Knotts was running on the debris that was sliding under his feet. On the flight deck, the top turret had broken loose and was spinning erratically. Moore braced himself to help Knotts as he jumped forward. The turret was spinning and the foot rest was about to smash Knotts in the head when Hal threw one arm around Knotts' neck and pulled his head down. The headlock saved Knotts from a nasty blow on the head but it also caused him to lose his purchase and slip back onto the moving junk. Knotts struggled to keep his footing for another try. The scenario was repeated two more times before Hal was able to clamp on a good hold and pull Knotts onto the flight deck under the spinning foot rest. The menacing foot rest whipped around until *Snake Eyes* jolted to a halt.

Major Hahn's flight plan included our crew as passengers for the return flight to Libya. Repairs held up the flight, which gave us a chance to visit a nearby farm to dicker for some lemons. We gave the farmer the equivalent of one dollar for all the fruit we could carry. One of the other crews followed our example but they equipped themselves with every container available. They returned with twice the amount that we had. We had not mentioned our sharp deal and one of the other crew boasted, 'We gave the old farmer an American cigarette and he was all smiles.' Our deal suddenly became 'Top Secret'.

The lead plane was airworthy but the RAF could not spare enough of their precious fuel to get us back to Benghazi. They sacrificed sufficient petrol for the short hop to Malta, a supply base, where the planes were serviced. At 2247 hours, on 2 August, Major Hahn made a perfect landing on Benina Main and taxied past the empty spots that attested to the heavy losses. Paul and Mike, our navigator and co-pilot, met us in the mess where we were interrogated and fed. Back at our tent there was no chance to sleep until Hal and I related the events of the past two days in detail.

Martin, the armourer, who was seriously wounded, died after clinging to life for six days. Clemens was recovering from an operation that removed the flak from his left ankle. The fragments in his arm were left to work their way out. This information was sent to me by the American Red Cross.[9]

Of the eighty-eight Liberators that returned to North Africa, fifty-five had battle damage.

Don Chase recalls:

On Cyprus *Heaven Can Wait*'s fuel transfer and oil problems were remedied by engineer Holtz and by personnel in two days. But then pilot Whitlock came down with an intestinal disorder and we couldn't leave. British infantrymen befriended us five sergeants and provided lorry transportation to their mountain rest camp. There we met scores of Ghurkha soldiers. Born in the foothills of the Himalayas and fighting for the Crown, they, with their sword-like *kukri* knives – preferring them to guns – had created panic among German *Afrika Korps* men, beheading rather than shooting, as they stealthily penetrated the Axis battle lines. They were barrel-chested, short, sombre and visually impressive as combatants. Each morning the Ghurkhas would serve us tea before we got out of our cots. Naturally, as they served, we thanked them for the extra service. After two or three mornings they returned our signs of respect with tight smiles and retreating, bowed to us. We were glad they were fighting with the Allies. Whitlock regained his strength and our weeklong hiatus ended as we flew over the British encampment at low altitude and rocked our wings in salute to our kind hosts who had been at war for nearly four years. Just before we left Cyprus the UK troops presented us with a ceremonial *kukri*. Somehow I became custodian of the curved ten-inch blade set in a beautifully wooden-engraved, silver-banded handle. We landed at Devasoir Airbase in Egypt. For two days we toured Cairo, checking back at our hotel late in the morning and again in the afternoon awaiting word from Group HQ as to our disposition. Orders received, we boarded a C-47 and flew back to our Libyan base, never to see *Heaven Can Wait* again. At base we learned that nine of our Group's thirty-seven aircraft were lost to enemy action or fell into the sea. Two others, forced to land in neutral Turkey, were interned for the war. It was a 30 per cent Group loss.

In North Africa the 'Sky Scorpions' waited in vain for nine Liberators, including the one piloted by Lieutenant Harold L. James, *Vagabond King*, piloted by Lieutenant John McCormick, and *Hitler's Hearse*, flown by Captain Robert C. Mooney.' McCormick poured out the story when he finally returned to the 'Sky Scorpions' and wrote about it in a letter home.

We got up early, the morning of our take-off, ate and got out to the ships for a final check-up on our gas, oil, oxygen, bombs, rations and ammunition. We were well prepared. We thumbed-up to Sergeant Frank Chowanski and Pfc Eddings and got off, last plane in our Group. Nerves were a little on edge because one plane just ahead exploded on take-off and worried some of the boys who knew about it. A small last-minute repair had delayed our take-off so that my wingman had taken off shortly before I did. That was James, our bad-luck kid, since he joined the Group back in Texas. My left wing man lost a carburettor on the runway and had to abort. That was Lighter. He certainly looked sad to be left out of it and I didn't particularly like losing a damn good wingman for a blank space of enemy sky.

We got into formation and headed across the bluest Mediterranean you can imagine. Things were running smoothly. The air was full, from starboard to port, from top to bottom with the Libs. Everything looked good. Things never look dangerous when you have so much company. We even felt secure in the rear guard. We called ourselves 'The Cluster On The Purple Heart Squadron'. James' plane was even the 'Right Leaf On The Cluster'. Then out of a blue sky, without warning, the leading plane of another group up front spun sickeningly out of formation and exploded against the sea, burning, so as to leave a black tomb marker. The second ship down, before we had even touched enemy land. Immediately, all gunners got itchy looking for a possible fighter and the pilots stood by silent radios waiting for a Change Order or explanation but there was nothing, except the continuous drone of our four giant engines. We passed through the sickening black smoke, into the blue skies beyond. There were no survivors. Then another B-24 peeled off, heading home, one engine feathered. That was the hot desert putting in its two cents worth. We looked to our giant engines but they gave no indication of weakening under the heavy load we carried.

Finally, land! Greece, our maps said. Enemy territory. Tension was relieved; a new excitement gripped us now. The enemy was man and his threat was tangible and at hand. We were at 10,000 feet and were working up towards our objective, against a little more head wind than anticipated. Clouds were becoming heavier but still no opposition. Then, through gaps in the clouds, we could make out the mountains, marking the time for us to turn south for our letdown to the target. An intercom call: 'Fighter at 5 o' clock!' It was an antiquated biplane. He couldn't even catch us as we began dropping down the mountainside. Slowly changing our formation from the protective one we travelled in, to one designed to allow us good individual runs on the target. We could see the lead plane down the valley in which lay our target.

'Good Lord! Mooney, we are too high!'

'Lord Almighty! I can't recognize the refinery stacks!'

'What kind of camoufleurs are these boys?'

'Mosco, open the bomb bay doors!'

And down we dropped, to silhouette our target against the sky, just like Mosco and I had practised on the model area, simulating Ploesti, they had built for us on the desert in Libya. Then the lead plane, realizing he had turned too soon, worked back in a big 'S' to the next valley. 'By Johosaphat if fighters were to hit us now!' We were spread out but I stuck to Mooney. James came in close as we turned to the north again; ready to make the final approach and bomb run. I warmed up my fixed nose-guns with a loud burst that startled Mosco so much he almost jumped out of the nose. We were ready for strafing now. For the first time in history B-24s were going to be used on a strafing run. We turned south down the valley. The lead plane had already started his bomb run. Christ! His plane was already burning and he was carrying thousand-pound bombs with delayed fuses! Then it was 'Gunners, keep your eyes open for fighters and ack-ack batteries.' 'Don't shoot civilians unless they're throwing bottles at us!'

'OK Mosco, bomb-bay doors open.

'Start the camera, Van.'

Bang! What the Hell? Here we go anyway. Down on the carpet… We get right behind and under Stan Podalak's plane… Mooney's left wing… We line up our two chimneys, which will put our bombs right through the windows of the boiler house. We can't drop far behind Mooney's plane 'cause he's carrying 45-second delay fuses same as we are. Above us, we could look into Stan's open, bomb-bay doors. We could see the bombs hanging ready, willing and able. Tracers… red… white… were streaming up at the boys ahead hitting them, too! Then our cockpit exploded with sparks, noise and concussion… tracers spat out over my head. Luckily, George and I crouched down, making ourselves as small as possible.

The tracers melted away into the smoke and fire of the refinery. Murphy cut loose in the top gun turret, with the twin 50s. I wanted to shoot him… he was ruining our bomb run!

Wham! More bullets through the cockpit! The emergency windows blew open, giving us a 225mph blast of air in the cockpit. But now, we were down to almost ground level, lined up and anxious to go. We came up to the target chimney height and through the smoke over the other bomb explosions… then… BOMBS AWAY! Our plane was now 4,000lb lighter.

In front of us, Mooney's bombs had released beautifully but he was veering off to the right and we were supposed to hit the same building![10] Through the smoke… down on the deck we scooted. Mooney and Stan and Sparrier were above us… too high. 'Come on down, Boys. Fighters can't dive on you when you're on the deck.' We hang right below them with or Heimie's plane so close. He was sticking his right wing through my waist window. Then we noticed Bob's engine was feathered but then he started it 'windmilling' to fool any fighters looking for cripples. Sure enough, there was a Me 110 circling over us. He had already shot down two 24s but for some reason he didn't close with our tight-flying 'Purple Heart Squadron'. Neither did any of the other fighters. We knew we'd never be able to re-form with the main group and we were afraid to break radio silence for fear of drawing fighters so we followed Bob as he headed home, sticking close together, to protect us against fighters.

Three minutes after 'bombs away' the boys told me we had been hit pretty hard [and] that Sergeant Martin Van Buren was bleeding badly. An anti-aircraft cannon shell had hit his knee as he was turning on the automatic camera. Miller, in the tin-can, tail-turret, called to say that the bombs we dropped, had exploded and our target was flattened and burning fiercely.

Finally, Mooney's #2-engine was feathered but his bomb-bay doors wouldn't close so the boys began tossing out everything that wasn't permanently nailed down. They had to get rid of all excess weight in order to keep the big bird flying. They even tossed out most of their 50-calibre machine guns and ammo. It was the only way they could keep flying and save gas. It would be a long haul to any safe-haven and they knew it but at least we were sticking together and that must have cheered them some.

James broke radio silence after about ten minutes and told me he wouldn't have enough gas to get home, so I told him to head for the nearest neutral landing spot. He was afraid to mention places over the radio so I asked him if he wanted to go to 'gobble gobble land'. I dropped back and flew on his wing so he could save gas. He was so slowed down that the other three crates were almost out of sight. While this was going on, navigators on both planes were busy making our courses for Turkey. We realized that Mooney was making for Turkey, too. So I told James to pour on the coal and catch up with them. This was when James' plane started doing acrobatics. I didn't know what was up but I followed him and all of a sudden, I saw a lot of flak puffs. We were passing over Bucharest, inadvertently, and they had blood in their eyes.

We didn't get hit as we continued our chase after the other three… Van was being cared for with morphine and tourniquets. All he said was, 'Here's where I get one medal you guys won't get.' He was right. No one else did get hit except the *Old Vagabond* itself. After about forty-five minutes we were back in formation heading for Turkey in a strange procession. Fighters were our big worry. We expected them every mile of the way and we had climbed high enough, to about 8,000 feet, to be 'duck soup' but no fighters came.

Finally we hit the Sea of Marmara and since the country was neutral from then on, we decided it was best to let the others do as they please. We were going to friendly territory and get Van to a hospital. We turned for Cyprus and the navigator began working in earnest. We were right in the Turkish mountains, busy transferring fuel, when all four engines cut out at the same time. I damn near died! We had only about 1,000 feet of clearance and there wasn't a flat spot within fifty miles, big enough to park an L-5 in.

Van couldn't jump and we weren't about to jump without him. I figured I'd have to put down somewhere the best I could and take our chances but with a roar and lurch, those good old Pratt & Whitneys took hold again. But just as a big smile jumped across our faces, all four engines died again. Dave Shattles moved faster than any man I'd ever seen. He jumped down into the bomb bay and switched gas valves to break the air lock in the lines. And this time, those wonderful engines roared back to life, as we scooted between the peaks and resumed our course to the Nicosia Airport on the island of Cyprus which was still 300 or 400 miles somewhere to the South.

Our nerves were sure taking a hellava beating. We'd been in the air for ten hours already. Now we were all alone, over rough, unfriendly, terrain, even if it wasn't 'the 'enemy'. And now, we had to sweat out our gas supply. Mendy called to tell me we had just run off the edge of his last, good Air Corps' map. From now on, we would have to figure by time, distance, compass and dead reckoning. Nobody bothered us as we flew over Turkey. At least, they didn't hit us! So we made it to the seacoast and wondered if we'd be able to find Cyprus. It was getting late in the afternoon, haze was forming and our only map was an old, schoolbook Mercator Map.

We finally reached the blue water of the Mediterranean Sea. I looked longingly at the flat sand beaches of the Turkish Coast. I considered plunking her down there but I wanted to get medical help for Van and I knew none of us wanted to be interred in Turkey for the length of the war. Anyway, I thought if we failed to find Cyprus and if we had enough gas, we could come back and find a nice soft beach to set her down on. A big if. As I looked at the needles of the gas gauges hovering near zero. I headed for Cyprus.

Mosco was taking good care of Van. We swung out over the water, squeezing every mile, out of every drop of gasoline. We were flying slow to save what little gas we had left. But still, it shouldn't have been this long 'til we saw some solid land out there. Cyprus was a big island but we couldn't find it!

'Mendy, let's turn in on our ETA. Maybe it's just off to our right in that haze.' So we turned and holy smokes there it was just off our left wing! We made a direct course for Nicosia. Our gas gauges showed we were on our last 100 gallons. Ten precious, gas-eating minutes went by and still no Cyprus! It had suddenly disappeared... ten minutes wasted chasing a mirage. Our 'Cyprus' had been nothing but cloud shadows and now we were really lost, to boot. We listened to our radio, hoping to get in touch with the airbase at Nicosia, the only airport on the island. We could hear other planes in distress. One was going down near us, into the sea but we couldn't help.

We continued on, looking for land any beach or any piece of good solid dirt. A B-24 doesn't 'ditch well' if you have to put her down on water. It breaks up and you don't have much chance of getting out. I wanted to land at Nicosia Airbase. It was growing dark when I finally saw the airport beacon. There were three other planes milling around the area, trying to find the field and to get up enough nerve to go in and land, in their damaged condition. I gave the tower my call letters with 'wounded aboard' and was immediately cleared to land. The gear came down OK then the flaps came down without faltering. Props OK. Turbos OK. How are the brakes? Check. It was all coming out OK. All controls working fine. It was getting dark but I could still make out the runway so I lined up and sailed in. The damn runway was uphill and almost fooled me but the tyres screeched and I 'stuck' the landing. We were down in one piece! I coasted to the end of the runway and turned down a little road off the runway, to keep it clear for the other planes trying to land. No one came out to meet us so we taxied up the road. 'Cripes,' I thought, 'this is sure good camouflage but that ditch was real enough,' so I pulled up onto an embankment and cut the engines. The silence was deafening. We were back on the ground! We were alive! We were safe! I unfastened my safety belt. It had been 14 hours and 30 minutes since I'd sat down in the pilot seat and started out in that cold damp morning which now, seemed so long ago.

As soon as we had cleared the runway, Colonel 'Killer' Kane, the CO of the 98th Bomb Group, came in for a landing in his shot-up crate, with one engine feathered. He misjudged the uphill runway and didn't have enough power left to pull it up. He washed out his landing gear, nosed up and smashed up his plane... No one was hurt and Colonel Kane beat us to Tel Aviv, leaving his wrecked plane to be salvaged by us.

Now, finally, safe on the ground, we were the happiest, tiredest, hungriest boys you've ever seen! We all kissed the ground we landed on. There was a doctor working on Van when I got aft and soon, he was taken to a hospital. He's OK now and back in the States. I haven't seen or heard from him since. We worked on *Old Vagabond* using any scavenged parts we could find and soon had it flyable, barely but flyable. We lumbered down the bumpy runway, pulled her into the air and headed back to Libya.

Well, that is the story of my part in the big Ploesti air raid. What others did must remains secret for a while longer. I'll tell you all about it when I get back home. I can tell you, there wasn't a man among us who will ever be the same, after that fourteen-hour jaunt to Ploesti. I am happy to be able to tell this story. But, I am sad for the many who were there, on that mission to Ploesti, who'll never be able to say they were even there.[11]

On arrival at Benina Lieutenant 'Jack' Martin had taken the place of a co-pilot who was in a truck accident three days before the raid and he flew with 1st Lieutenant Donald G. Westerbeke. Martin's engineer-top turret gunner, Tech Sergeant Lowell Vick, went along on Ken Matson's crew for a man who was in the hospital. Staff Sergeant Albert Bailey, Martin's tail gunner, volunteered to take the place of another gunner who was in the hospital and did not return.[12] Martin wrote to his parents about the mission.

We haven't heard a thing from them but believe that they're all right. I saw them come out of the target in fine style and make their get-away. They must have force landed somewhere in occupied territory. Although it was the biggest and most effective job we ever undertook it almost kicked the heart out of me. We were down low when we dropped our 'eggs', giving us a grandstand seat on everything that went on, both on the ground and in the air. It got plenty hot there for a while. I couldn't keep up because I had an engine shot out over the target and had to come home on three. The song 'Coming in on a Wing and a Prayer' fitted nicely that day. As for the raid, that's about all except that we knocked out an enemy fighter. It was a Me 110. We know we got him because my tail gunner saw him force land.[13]

For men like Clarence W. 'Bill' Neumann in the 'Travelling Circus' anxiously waiting at the bases in North Africa, news of their crews either brought relief or pain. The young bombardier from Portsmouth, New Hampshire, had been up very early to watch the take-off at 0730 for the big mission. His pilot, Lieutenant Donald R. Dahl, was originally slated to fly with Lieutenant Enoch M. Porter in *Euroclydon*. Dahl finally flew as a second co-pilot aboard *Bomerang* flown by 1st Lieutenant Roy G. Martin, a Texan rancher from Cotulla, and his co-pilot, Luther S. Bird, a fellow

Texan, from Bryan.[14] The crew were known as 'Martin's Red Caps'. *Bomerang* flew off Joe Tate's (leader of the second wave of lead element) left wing. *Bomerang* had no wing tip fuel tanks, so they had two bomb bay fuel tanks in front and two 1,000lb bombs in the back. *Bomerang* made it over the target and back without a scratch but the crew chief, George Ewall, could drain only a cup of gas from the fuel system. Dahl, who worked *Bomerang*'s engines while Martin and Bird flew the aircraft, related the following to Neumann after his safe return from what turned out to be the roughest mission to date.

> One aircraft from our Group [*Kickapoo*, a 93rd ship that was on loan to the 98th] crashed on take-off [when an engine failed]; Lieutenant Russell W. Polivka and Sergeant Eugene Garner (who later joined our crew) were the only survivors. Approximately 175 aircraft were assembled out over the Mediterranean and headed north. Saw one of our aircraft suddenly dive out of control and crash into the Adriatic Sea. Later learned there were no survivors. Arrived over the target at approximately 1455 hours and due to faulty navigation on lead group's part we were led into our oil refinery target right over flak corner. They threw so much flak the sky was black with it. We were flying at about 50 feet all in tight formation going 220mph. Saw Colonel Baker and Lieutenant Porter, with whom I was first going to ride, both go down in flames and explode in front of us.[15] Every haystack was a machine gun nest. We got our bombs into a cracking plant. An exploding tank missed us by seconds. It got the plane right behind us. Bombs were thirty-minute fused. Somehow we managed to get outgoing like hell. In all, I saw seven planes go down in flames and explode. On way home two more collided and spun in. Saw no fighters on return flight. However, fuel was a big problem. Sweated it all the way home. Touched down at 2100 hours, exactly thirteen and a half hours after take-off. Only twelve planes of thirty-two dispatched returned to home base. Some may be safe elsewhere.
>
> Lieutenant Dahl told me 'God was with me on this one.' Amen.

'Tommie' Holmes thought that he had flown about 14 hours, but later records showed 13 hours and 26 minutes.

> The next day I was told by the crew chief on our ship *Wing and a Prayer* that we had less than ten minutes of fuel. He drained the tanks to be sure. We were very tired but elated at the excellent results of our mission – 'Blue Target' which was the Brazi refinery – the largest and latest American built refinery in Romania – 100 per cent

destroyed. We were all saddened by the loss of fifty or more planes in the five groups making the raid, but especially touched by the loss of 'Sam' Houston. All of us felt the importance of this raid and had practised long and hard to make it. Patriotism was very much alive in America on 1 August 1943 and most certainly in our crews as well. The experience was something we endured with hope and gratitude, but never desired to repeat.[16]

Back home 'Sam' Houston's wife, Maria, waited for news in Long Beach, California.

Clarence W. 'Bill' Neumann wrote in his diary:

No happy faces about today. Yesterday was a bad day for Army Air Corps. Word thru the grapevine has total losses were fifty-five to sixty aircraft. A blow to any Command. Ploesti will surely take its place in history. We were blessed as Hinchman and Dahl both made it back safely, though both aircraft had moderate to heavy battle damage. God really took care of Dahl as they took him off Porter's plane and sent him on another. Porter never made it, as he went down at the time our *Hell's Wench* was lost. Found out Lieutenant Polivka was badly burned and will be hospitalized till stabilized and then returned to the States. Rumour also has it that all survivors of Ploesti mission will be awarded the Distinguished Flying Cross. They sure earned it.

All participants did indeed receive the DFC; and all five groups received Presidential Unit Citations. Posthumous Medals of Honor were awarded to Lieutenant Colonel Addison T. Baker[17] and Major John Jerstad and to 2nd Lieutenant Lloyd H. Hughes in the 389th. 'Addison Baker had a total disregard for his own life. Every one of us would have followed him through hell,' said Alfred Asch who as a young lieutenant fresh out of flight school had served under Baker before the raid. Colonel Leon Johnson and Colonel John R. Kane each received the Medal of Honor. In addition, there were fourteen Silver Stars and Distinguished Service Crosses awarded. One of the DSC recipients was Major Ramsay Potts, who later would make no bones about how he survived the raid. 'Both of my wingmen were shot down. They shielded me from getting shot down,' he reflected. 'I was just one of the lucky ones.' Bill Cameron, described by General Leon Johnson as 'one of the best combat leaders we had in World War II', was also awarded the DSC for his part in the low-level Ploesti mission.

As soon as Leon Johnson knew of the award of the Medal of Honor he wrote to the family of every man in the 44th who went down on the Ploesti raids to tell them that he did not feel he had exclusive ownership of the medal but that he was accepting it for very man in his outfit who took part in the raid. 'I didn't do anything that every man behind me didn't do,' he said. 'The higher the rank you have the easier it is to get a medal.' Although the order was cut seventeen days after the Ploesti raid Colonel Johnson was not presented with the Medal of Honor until 22 November 1943 when General Devers put the blue ribbon and the medal around his neck at an awards ceremony at Shipdham. Colonel Johnson was not upset that the presentation was delayed. On the same order the Silver Star was awarded to a man for heroism performed in the Spanish-American war in 1898!

Following a well-earned leave, the Liberator groups resumed raids on Axis targets in Austria and Italy. On 13 and 14 August the Liberators bombed the Messerschmitt factory at Wiener Neustadt in Austria. Howard Moore, having completed his combat tour, turned over command of the 67th Squadron to the newly promoted Major Bill Cameron. 'Pappy' Moore and Cameron, who had once had 'serious doubts on the probability of a long life' were the only two of ninety original combat men to complete a tour. Bill Cameron was making preparations for the return of the 'Eightballs' to England when they were ordered to mount a raid on the German-held satellite airfield at Foggia North in southern Italy, despite reports that the Axis had been moving its defences and concentrating them there. General Dwight D. Eisenhower was working on the goal of capturing Rome, which would be the first capital city to be taken on the European mainland. Troops had already taken Salerno, but he needed an airfield close to the port of Naples. Foggia was the best solution. So on 16 August, one day after taking command, 'with great, great pride', the new commander with some new crews having arrived, scheduled seven aircraft. There was Jim Hill and Charlie Henderson, the veterans. There was the Cameron crew with 'Gentleman' Jim De Vinney as bombardier and two new pilots, Lieutenant Leighton C. Smith from San Antonio, Texas, and Flight Officer Joseph S. Milliner[18] in *Buzzin' Bear*. And there was a veteran crew from the 506th; Walter Bunker with Dick Butler, who had been transferred to the 67th as co-pilot. Lieutenant Walter R. Bateman and crew, on their first combat mission, were in *Suzy-Q* and the new crew of Lieutenant Carl S. Hager were in their new plane, *Black Sheep*.

Charles 'Joe' Warth from Cincinnati, Ohio, who was the hatch gunner on *Southern Comfort* in the 506th Squadron, piloted by Lieutenant Horace W. Austin from Virginia Beach, recalls.

We were told that the raid would be a 'milk run'. We were 'fat, dumb and happy' to go there. But conditions change rapidly in a combat zone and the German High Command, getting word we were returning, laid a little trap for us.

Foggia was to be the Austin crew's twelfth mission of the war.
Bill Cameron continues:

Because of their experience I scheduled Walter Bunker and Dick Butler to lead the 67th. Previous missions to targets in this area, as well as the one I had flown to Foggia, had been made without loss and not much opposition. So on 16 August I proudly watched them take off – the first mission of the Squadron under their new commander. It was a heady feeling!

In all, twenty-five B-24s departed Benina Main by 0430 hours to attack Foggia. Only six of Lieutenant Whitlock's crew flew the mission in a ship named *Timba-ah*. Co-pilot Phipps, bombardier Schwab, engineer Holtz and Don Chase were grounded by respiratory and ear infections so their places were taken by replacements. The Liberators' propellers whipped up great sandstorms as the bombers taxied from their dispersal points. Two Liberators developed mechanical troubles shortly after take-off and were forced to jettison their bombs in the Mediterranean and return to Benina. The twenty-three remaining aircraft continued to Foggia North, which was reached at 1033 and the Liberators released their forty-five-second tail delay and fragmentation bombs from 20,000 feet. Flak was accurate and several B-24Ds suffered minor damage. Light scattered clouds over the target area afforded no protection at all. Using the unlimited visibility to good advantage, upwards of fifty Bf 109s, Ju 88s and Bf 110s tore into the 'Eightballs', as Joe Warth recalls.

Our Liberator took an uncountable number of direct hits from the German fighters, which came at us from every direction. I know we shot down at least three of them when we heard the bale-out klaxon sound; three of our engines were shut off and on fire and the bomb bay was a blazing inferno. In the rear of the aircraft we were completely cut off from the rest of the crew. I made it to the camera hatch, turning round to see the door to the bomb bay vaporize in the flames. The four of us in the rear wasted no time in getting out, Staff

Sergeants Lee and Purcell going out of their waist windows. *Southern Comfort* was a mass of flame as she spun down, crashing into an Italian hillside. There was a final blast of flame and noise as if she had but one desire left; to return to the earth as the ore from which she came.[19]

2nd Lieutenant George Temple, navigator on *Natchez Belle* in the 68th Squadron, flown by 1st Lieutenant Eunice M. Shannon, who was from Cranbury, Texas, recalled the attacks of twenty-four yellow-nosed Bf 109s.

The first 20mm shell hit the flight deck near the radio, setting the upholstery and other flammable materials on fire. The next thing I knew, two engines were burning and we started down on a long glide. All the way down we were under attack; the waist and belly gunners were killed by enemy fire. At 18,000 feet the pilot gave the signal to bale out. He did a good job of trimming the ship and giving everyone a chance to clear before abandoning his post. We all jumped except the two dead men and the co-pilot. (Temple learned later that George Hersh, the co-pilot, who joined Shannon in the bomb bay had forgotten his chest 'chute and could not return to the flight deck to get it because of the flames. He refused the offer to share a 'chute with his pilot because it would harm Shannon's chances of survival.)

I opened the nose wheel and baled out. I figured I needed a minute before opening my chute and I was afraid that I would get excited and open up too soon. As I fell, I followed the second hand on my watch with my finger. When it had been around once, I pulled the cord and she opened up nicely. I was coming down in a valley with mountains all around me, but the last fifty feet seemed to come up in a rush and I miscalculated the slope on which I landed, so I broke my left ankle. It seemed only a moment until an Italian farmer with a shotgun appeared over the top of the hill. He got me on a mule and took me to a main road where a truck was waiting. The truck took me to the local police station in the town of Atella.[20]

At Benina Main Bill Cameron waited for the formation to return.

The first hint of trouble came when the veteran lead crew returned early with engine trouble. Later, when it was all over only Hill returned! Our men had run into an estimated 75 to 100 German fighters, which had been recently moved down to Italy. Our Group lost seven planes and crews including my own *Bear* and the *Suzy-Q*.[21] It was very hard to take. From that day on, I never sent a crew out on a mission that was not absolutely required, or a crew that I did not consider tried and ready for combat.[22]

Don Chase, two officers and a second enlisted man waited in vain for the return of *Timba-ah* and their six fellow crewmen and the four replacements, as Chase recalls.

Long after the last ships returned and the sun had set we trekked mournfully back to our tent area. It was a night of angst. Eight of our Group's B-24s including *Timba -ah* failed to return. If I had been older, instead of twenty-two, perhaps I might not have searched for a symbolic reason, which governs fateful events. But regardless, I picked up the Ghurkha *kukri*, walked into the desert and threw the knife across the sand into the darkness. It had brought only bad luck. More than half my crew was gone, probably dead. I cried. Without loss the 44th flew another two missions after losing 60 per cent of the strike planes in just two raids, Ploesti and Foggia. Late in the month, 44th personnel returned to our base in Shipdham. Only twenty-two aircraft made the trip back, whereas forty-one plus four replacements had come to Africa two months earlier. Costly (about $300,000 each) as the loss of our twenty-two bombers may have been, more importantly and personally grievous was the loss of more than 200 airmen. And several of those 'airmen' were ground crew fellows who volunteered to fly as gunners when attrition slashed the number of available regular gunners. I returned to England in mid-September after being hospitalized with fly fever in Marrakech, Morocco, for two weeks. I never saw Holtz, Schwab or Phipps again.

Following the bombing of Cancello on 21 August, the three 8th Air Force groups were ordered back to England to continue the air war against Germany. Their sojourn in the desert had been a harrowing experience and life on their bases in Norfolk would never be the same again for the survivors. For the next three months Don Chase flew an occasional weather reconnaissance flight and made several rail trips to various RAF and AAF airfields throughout southern England to help return damaged or fuel-starved B-24s to Shipdham that had earlier failed to make base following a mission. He recalls:

New crews arrived frequently. In fact we now had more crews than planes. It was not unusual for two different crews to alternate flying missions using the same Liberator. Sometime in late October I transferred from the 506th Squadron into the 67th Squadron. In mid-November, to my surprise, Ralph Knox [the well gunner on *Timba-ah* that went down on 16 August] limped into my Nissen hut. He had spent many weeks in hospitals recovering from shrapnel wounds. He related the grim facts of the Foggia mission. Gunners Bonham, Stewart and Dunajecz were KIA. Whitlock and navigator Ricks were taken prisoner by Italian troops. Of the four replacement crewmembers flying that day, two were KIA and two PoW. Knox was in an Italian hospital when advancing American troops secured the area. Shortly after visiting me, Knox returned to the States for further medical attention.

Perhaps I could have avoided further combat. Squadron Operations certainly didn't pressure me to fly. I was in a non-assigned state of limbo. Maybe it was guilt or pride or shame. Whatever; I decided to or tried to complete my tour of combat, twenty-five missions but not, if I could help it, with an inexperienced crew. My opportunity came toward mid-December when, on his fifteenth mission, the radio man of Lieutenant James Hill's crew fell, or was blown, from the foot-wide bomb bay catwalk during the bomb ran and parachuted into France. This crew had survived the 90 per cent Group loss suffered by the 44th in just three missions – Ploesti, Foggia and Wiener Neustadt (another 30 per cent loss mission) and had several enemy aircraft credited to their gunners. Top turret gunner, John Pitcovick had, I think, tallied six enemy aircraft. It made me feel almost comfortable flying as radio operator with John manning the turret above me. So, fortunately, I flew the next ten missions with Lieutenant Hill and his battle-experienced crew.

In England, during the Liberators' absence, the loss of about 100 Fortresses and men during 'Blitz Week' had been made good and on 12 August the 390th Bomb Group at Framlingham helped swell the ranks of 330 bombers heading for targets in the Ruhr. Once again, adverse weather was to dog the mission and it caused many groups to seek targets of opportunity. Groups became strung out and the *Luftwaffe* seized the opportunity to strike at the widely dispersed formations. They hit groups time and again, inflicting heavy losses, including twenty-three Forts in the 1st Wing. The 379th lost six Forts including two that crash-landed on return and the 91st, 92nd and 384th each lost four aircraft. The anti-aircraft guns also found their mark, as Howard Hernan in the 'Hell's Angels' relates.

The flak was terrific and at no time had we encountered more attacks from fighters. I sweated out the whole trip. We lost number two supercharger before reaching enemy territory, then number one engine began throwing gas and oil badly from the oil cooler vent. Number four engine also began running roughly. Campbell had to feather the number one engine to prevent it from burning out. We lost oxygen on the right-hand side and had flak holes in several places.

We were leading the second flight of the 303rd, which was leading the 1st Wing this day. Our hut-mates' aircraft [*Old Ironsides* piloted by Lieutenant Arthur H. Pentz] was off our left wing. When we were this close together I could see my friend John Dougherty in his top turret and we would help one another. I was basically patrolling forward before we got to the target. There was quite a bit of flak around, as there always seemed to be over the Ruhr Valley. I turned my turret around and looked over at Pentz's ship. It looked as though it was on fire from wing tip to wing tip. I just could hardly believe what I was seeing. I was actually yelling at them to bale out but they were still flying along as if nothing had happened. Pentz's ship had all colours of smoke coming out of it. Although there were a few fighters on us at the time, it was flak that had got them. They flew along momentarily beside us and then dropped out of formation. I called one of the waist gunners who always had a pair of field glasses and he followed it as far as he could. The last time he saw it, it was still on fire.

About a minute later another B-17, flying about 200 yards away and level with us at 10 o'clock, started to make snap rolls. It would snap over, level out momentarily and then make another flip. They were all to the right. I counted each one and he made twenty-one! Each time he flipped over every gun position fired and the tracers would come flying out. The plane looked like a porcupine. Of course, this was because of centrifugal force: as the gunners tried to hold on they would press down on their triggers. I just could not believe that this plane was still holding together. After its twenty-first flip it levelled out and started to go down in a great big sweeping turn to the left. I often try to figure out what was wrong with this 'plane as there hadn't been any fighters homing in on him and he was a little too high for flak. I can only think the pilot was trying to set up the automatic pilot for the bombardier and somehow or other it had malfunctioned. It was certainly an empty feeling to look over the empty bunks that night. I vowed there and then that whatever crew replaced Pentz, I was not going to make friends. I would be sociable and as pleasant as I could but it was too hard when you lost them.

Next day Hernan dismantled the tandem he and Dougherty had built. Hernan learned later that Pentz had crash-landed his B-17 and that nine of the crew, including Dougherty, were taken prisoner.

Three days later VIII Bomber Command participated in the *Starkey* deception plan, which was created to make the enemy believe that an invasion of the French coast was imminent. In theory it would relieve some of the pressure on Russia and halt troop movements to Italy. The Fortress formations roamed across France, Belgium and Holland, dropping their deadly loads of bombs on long-suffering German airfields. Friendly fighter support was generally described as 'excellent' and the *Luftwaffe* largely stayed on the ground. In the 390th *Phoenix* and another Fort collided over France, tearing the tail off one of them and they both spun in. Strikes against enemy airfields in France and the Low Countries continued on 16 August when 171 Forts in the 1st Wing attacked the airfield at Le Bourget. *Dollie Madison* was the only YB-40 to accompany the Wing and this was the last time that a Fortress 'gunship' appeared in combat.

Early that evening, operations staff stood by their teleprinters and awaited orders for the morrow; the anniversary mission of the 8th Air Force. At Grafton Underwood speculation had been rife on the base ever since late in July when the 384th had received an order from higher headquarters. Colonel Budd Peaslee, the CO, explains:

It said: 'Select one of the best of your lead crews; stand them down. Send them to headquarters, VIII Bomber Command, for special briefing, thereafter they will not leave the base nor communicate with other crews. They will fly practice flights daily and practise high altitude bombing on the Irish Sea bombing range whenever possible.

At Chelveston Louis Nelson, the twenty-one-year-old bombardier from Minneapolis, Minnesota, and twenty-three-year-old Malvern 'Mal' Sweet, the navigator from Livermore, California, on the crew of *Ex-Virgin* flown by David A. Tyler had been briefed for six weeks on the 17 August show. Tyler, the son of a worker in the City Department of Hartford, Connecticut, was a great swimmer in college. He travelled all over America in swimming meets and he could have gone to Yale on an athletic scholarship but he preferred to go to Trinity College because it was in Hartford. He trained for the Air Force all over America; he came to

England by way of South America, Africa and Northern Ireland. The Fort in which Tyler's crew had flown to England was called *Deadly Nightshade* and they had almost landed it in Southern Ireland, which was neutral, after wandering around in overcast until all the red lights were showing on their tanks. And then they got one called *The Vanishing Virginian*. They had not liked the idea of 'vanishing' and no one in the crew was from Virginia, so they just painted out everything of the old name except *The Virgin*. And then one day they came home with a flak hole just about dotting the 'V' and after that they called their Fort the *Ex-Virgin*. Tyler had flown on bombing missions over Germany, Denmark, Norway, Holland, Belgium and France. The more places he saw, the more he wanted to go home to Hartford. To him Hartford was Heaven.

Nelson's sister was in the WAC. His father was in the lumber business. A student in the University of Minnesota, majoring in history; Nelson wanted to be a teacher of ancient history. When the US entered the war, he had tried to be a pilot. He already had a white silk scarf and he wanted 'Uncle Sam' to give him a P-38. Sweet's father used to be a rancher but the ranch died when the spring dried up and he now drove a school bus. Mal's kid brother was in pre-flight training. Mal, who had been at San Jose State studying to be a teacher of manual arts, had also wanted to be a pilot but his eyes washed him out. The thing he talked most about at Chelveston was 'Blondie', a pony he had raised from a colt.

Nelson and Sweet did not know where the target was but they could draw pictures of what it looked like. And when they told them that they could recognize a certain five-storey building, they knew that were going to hit at less than their usual altitude.[23]

Notes

1. In June 1942 a detachment of twenty-three B-24Ds under the command of Colonel Harry H. Halverson, codenamed 'HALPRO', which was en route to join the 10th AF in China had bombed Ploesti with limited results. No further raids were made on Ploesti and then, on 6 March 1943, Field Marshal Erwin Rommel launched what proved to be his last offensive. It failed and he was recalled to Berlin. The path was now clear for another strike on the Ploesti oilfields. In April 1943 bomber chiefs in London pressed General Lewis Brereton the CO of 9th Bomber Command, for another attack but he was anxious to contain his bombing force for the Tunisian and Sicilian battles that lay ahead. On 6 May 1943 Operation *Husky* – the invasion of Sicily – began and the Liberators of the 98th BG and the 376th BG attacked Reggio di Calabria, the terminus of the San Giovanni-Messina ferry service to Sicily.

2. Walter 'Tommie' Holmes writing in the *8 Ball Tails; Journal of the 44th BG Veterans Assoc.* (Spring 2008).

3. Walter 'Tommie' Holmes writing in the *8 Ball Tails; Journal of the 44th BG Veterans Assoc.* (Spring 2008).

4. *Victory Ship* was finally lost on 21 January 1944 on the mission to Escalles sur Buchy on its fiftieth mission. Five members of Alfred A. Starring's crew were KIA. One evaded and four were taken prisoner. This mission was costly for the 44th; five B-24s being lost, twenty-eight men KIA, fourteen were captured and nine evaded.

5. *First of the Many* by Captain John R. 'Tex' McCrary and David E. Scherman. 1944.

6. Walter 'Tommie' Holmes writing in the *8 Ball Tails; Journal of the 44th BG Veterans Assoc.* (Spring 2008).

7. 'The history book credits the 389th as "one of the two classically executed performances of the day". The Steaua Romana refinery was totally destroyed and did not enter production for six years. We lost six of twenty-nine planes. We led the next raid to Wiener Neustadt, Austria. The group went back to England and pulled three raids. I had engine troubles and after stops at Algiers and Tripoli, ended up at Oran where my plane was repaired. General Jimmy Doolittle wired me to bring my crew and plane back to Tunis. On October 1st we flew out of there for what turned out to be my last mission, again to Wiener Neustadt. B-17s were supposed to hit Schweinfurt and Regensburg the same day but weather called off the raid. 389th again led the five group raid. We were attacked by sixty-five German fighters and lost fourteen or fifteen planes. I was flying on the lead plane's left wing when I was hit by 88mm flak. Flames were pouring out of the instrument panel and we were forced to leave our oxygen supply. T/Sgt Stanton A. Early, the top turret gunner, and his turret were blown out of the plane. Jack Englehardt, navigator, and Bob Driver, tail gunner, were also killed. I was wounded and bleeding in the radio compartment. I pulled the ripcord and lost consciousness. The Austrian with a rifle said, "For you the war is over." Nineteen months later Patton's 4th Armoured Division liberated me at *Stalag VIIA* Moosburg.'

8. Fowble was killed in a night crash at Marrakesh on 1 October while returning from a second deployment in North Africa.

9. 'Ploesti – August 1 1943' by John E. O'Grady writing in the *2nd AD Journal*. The two other members of the crew were S/Sgt Dietrich, assistant engineer, and S/Sgt Propst, tail gunner. Crew 15 was taken off DS (detached service) with the 98th BG and assigned to the 567th BS, 389th BG, as per their original orders. After flying one mission with the 'Sky Scorpions', to Cancello, Crew 15's orders sent them to the 409th BS, 93rd BG. Home at last, they unpacked their toothbrushes and settled down to complete their combat tour of twenty-eight missions (twenty-five was increased to twenty-eight) with Ted's

Captain William B. Cameron in the 67th Bomb Squadron, 44th Bomb Group, at Shipdham which he later commanded. (*Bill Cameron*)

Smoke rises from direct hits on the boiler house and powerhouse of the Steua Roman refinery at Campina 20 miles northwest of Ploesti on 1 August 1943. Damage was considerable. (*USAF*)

Post attack reconnaissance photo of the Columbia Aquila refinery at Ploesti shows the distillation and cracking plant completely smashed. Smoke still rises from one of the many burnt out oil storage tanks. Damage is also visible on railway sidings and among buildings alongside. (*USAF*)

Black oil smoke from burning storage tanks at the Columbia Aquila refinery on the southwest edge of Ploesti. In the background flames can be seen spreading among the structures of the cracking plant and still, which were vital target in the oil refinery. (*USAF*)

Left: Close-up view of the Columbia Aquila refinery showing burning oil storage tanks. (*USAF*)

Below: Oil storage tanks at the Columbia Aquila refinery in flames. The tangled mass of pipes, tubes and towers of the distillation cracking plants was an important target. (*USAF*)

B-24D Liberators pass low near the burning Ploesti oil refineries. (*USAF*)

B-24D over the burning Astra Roman oil refinery. (*USAF*)

Through clouds of black smoke B-24s are seen coming over the Astra Roman oil refinery, which had already suffered direct hits. (*USAF*)

B-24D-1-CO 41-23711 *Jerk's Natural* in the 93rd Bomb Group at Hardwick in August 1943 after returning from North Africa where it was flown on the 1 August raid on Ploesti by Major John 'The Jerk' Jerstad. *Jerk's Natural* was lost on 1 October 1943 flying from North Africa. (*USAF*)

B-24Ds in the 93rd Bomb Group over Norfolk in late August 1943 after their return from North Africa where 'Ted's Travelling Circus' were part of the Liberator force that bombed Ploesti and targets in Italy. Nearest aircraft is B-24D 41-24228 *Joisey Bounce* in the 328th Bomb Squadron. This aircraft was lost on 13 November 1943. The top aircraft is 41-23729 *Shoot Luke*, which was lost with Lt Charles R. Hutchins' crew on 18 October 1943, and 'C', the leading aircraft in the vic, is 41-23722 *Bomerang*, which returned to the ZOI in May 1944. (*USAF*)

Waist guns with hundreds of spent shell casings on the floor. (*USAF*)

A scene from *Twelve O'clock High*, the classic movie that was based on Beirne Lay Junior's novel published in 1946. Lay and Major Sy Bartlett, who as a major had been General Carl Spaatz's aide, wrote the screenplay for the film, which was largely based on the factual events surrounding the 306th Bomb Group. Lay created the fictional '918th Bomb Group' by multiplying 306 by 3. The 306th suffered particularly heavy losses early in its career and in the movie the 918th believe that they are going to be sent home but Colonel Savage (aka Gregory Peck) tells them: 'You're not going home, you're going to die; in fact consider yourselves already dead!' (*USAF*)

B-17F-60-BO 42-29553 *Arkie II* in the 366th Bomb Squadron, 305th Bomb Group (which was named by Major Sydney R. Smith after his wife) was lost with 2nd Lt Wright F. Gerke's crew on 12 August 1943. Eight men died and two were taken prisoner. The first *Arkie* was lost with Captain Everett E. Tribbett's crew on 26 February 1943. *(via Bill Donald)*

Contrary to popular belief, *Memphis Belle* was not the first heavy bomber to complete an 8th Air Force tour of twenty-five missions. This honour went to B-17F-25-BO 41-24577 *Hell's Angels* in the 358th Bomb Squadron, 303rd Bomb Group, which completed twenty-five missions between 16 October 1942 and 14 May 1943. *Hell's Angels*, which completed forty-eight missions on 19 May 1943, all without an abort, was autographed by hundreds of members of the 303rd Bomb Group at Molesworth early in 1944 and flown stateside. *Hell's Angels* was broken up for scrap at Searcey Field, in Stillwater, Oklahoma, in August 1945. *(USAF)*

An armourer attends to the bombs in the bomb bay of a B-24. *(USAF)*

B-17F-120-BO 42-30758 *Rosie's Riveters* with Robert Rosenthal (kneeling, second from left) and his crew with ground crew members. Rosie got the badly damaged *Rosie's Riveters* back to Thorpe Abbotts after the raid on Bremen on 8 October 1943 when the 100th Bomb Group lost seven B-17s. *Rosie's Riveters* was repaired and Ross McPhee's crew took over the famous Fortress. In early February 1944 they renamed the aircraft *Satcha Lass*. The name lasted barely a week because on 4 February *Satcha Lass* was heavily damaged on the mission to Frankfurt and

McPhee crash-landed the plane near Mönchengladbach after trying to reach Holland. On 10 October Rosenthal flew *Royal Flush* to Münster and they were the only one of thirteen crews to return to Thorpe Abbotts. *(TAMM)*

B-17F 42-5816 *Judy* in the 527th Bomb Squadron, 379th Bomb Group, which saw long service and returned to the ZOI (Zone of Interior or the USA) at the war's end. *(USAF)*

Captain Adrian Poletti, group Roman Catholic chaplain, leads the crew of 1st Lt Edward J. Hennessy Jnr in the 368th Bomb Squadron, 306th Bomb Group, in prayer in front of B-17F-25-BO 41-24560 *Little Audrey* at Thurleigh. Captain Hennessy finished his tour on 29 June 1943 when the 306th Bomb Group flew their fiftieth mission. *Little Audrey* transferred to the 544th Bomb Squadron, 384th Bomb Group, on 5 September 1943 and returned to the ZOI in June 1944. (*USAF*)

B-17F-30-BO 42-5077 *Delta Rebel No. 2* in the 323rd Bomb Squadron, 91st Bomb Group. The original *Delta Rebel* was assigned to Lt George Birdsong's crew, but after diverting to Mitchel Field, New York, due to poor weather during a long training flight transient maintenance taxied the *'Reb* into two other aircraft, badly damaging all three! *Delta Rebel No. 2* carried on into 1943 until Birdsong went home to Mississippi. This aircraft and 2nd Lt Robert W. Thompson's crew FTR from Gelsenkirchen on 12 August 1943. (*USAF*)

B-17 being rebuilt in a hangar on an 8th Air Force base. (*USAF*)

Ground crews taking a break. (USAF)

B-17F 42-5830 *Hag of Harderwyk* in the 524th Bomb Squadron, 379th Bomb Group, which was later re-named *Al Jo Son*. The Fortress twice made forced landings, at RAF Odiham on 18 August 1943 and at Shipdham on 11 January 1944, but survived the war and returned to the ZOI in 1945, finishing its days at Ontario, California. (USAF)

B-17F 42-5736 (actually a retired YB-40) in the 379th Bomb Group at Kimbolton with English visitors on 2 October 1943. (*USAF*)

The crew of B-17F-10-DL 42-3002 *The Old Squaw* in the 359th Bomb Squadron, 303rd Bomb Group, at Molesworth. Back row L–R: Claude Campbell, Miller, Ririe and William A. Boutelle, bombardier. Kneeling L–R: Howard E. Hernan, top turret gunner; Wilson; Quick; Kraft and Backert. *The Old Squaw* was lost on 6 September 1943 when it was ditched in the North Sea. Lt Robert J. Hullar and crew were rescued. (*Howard Hernan*)

B-17F 42-29921 *Oklahoma Okie* and a crew member wearing a flak vest. The aircraft and 2nd Lt Baynard T. G. Dudley and crew FTR on 31 December 1943. Five men were killed, four were taken prisoner and one evaded capture. (*USAF*)

Lt (later Captain) Claude W. Campbell, pilot of *The Old Squaw* in the 359th Bomb Squadron, 303rd Bomb Group, at Molesworth. (*Howard Hernan*)

B-17F 42-5180 *The Black Swan* in the 427th Bomb Squadron, 303rd Bomb Group. (*USAF*)

'Travelling Circus'. John O'Grady salutes *Baggy Maggy*, in which they flew their last eleven missions, and sings praises to her crew chief, then T/Sgt Joseph T. Zak, who kept her in the air for sixty missions without an abort.

10. *Hitler's Hearse* had taken several direct hits. Captain Robert C. Mooney was killed instantly by ground fire.

11. On 18 November, *Vagabond King* and its crew were lost over the Skagerrak, approximately twelve miles from the Southern coast of Norway. Among the dead were McCormick and Marvin Mosco.

12. The crew of the *Bomerang* were shot down and Bailey was interned. My thanks to research provided by Lowell Vick's son Clyde L. Vick, who visited seventy-nine-year-old Jack Martin in Vacaville, CA, in 1997.

13. The *Oklahoman* returned to Hethel with its regular crew and went on to fly about twenty missions before being lost on 5 December 1943 with Lt Harley Mason's crew.

14. Altogether, fourteen crews in the 'Travelling Circus' carried an additional co-pilot.

15. *Euroclydon* took a direct hit in the bomb bay and became 'a fountain of flames'. Porter climbed in a desperate attempt to gain altitude to let his crew bale out but the B-24 stalled. Ray 'Jack' Warner, whose shoulder blade was shattered by flak, and Lt Jesse D. 'Red' Franks of Columbus, Miss, went down to the nose wheel hatch where Franks pushed Warner out. Franks' chute did not open. The only other survivors were two gunners. *Ted's Travelling Circus 93rd Bombardment Group (H) USAAF 1942–45* by Carroll (Cal) Stewart (Sun/World Communications Inc 1996).

16. Walter 'Tommie' Holmes writing in the *8 Ball Tails; Journal of the 44th BG Veterans Assoc.* (Spring 2008).

17. On 9 August Colonel Leland C. Fiegal, who was formerly with the 93rd during its training days in the USA, arrived from America to take over command from Lt Colonel George S. Brown, who had been acting CO since the death of Lt Colonel Addison Baker.

18. Milliner had flown to Ploesti with Charlie Henderson.

19. Lieutenants P. Singer, navigator, and S. Finder, bombardier, lost their lives. The Germans, who reported that their parachutes were bullet-ridden and had failed to work properly, later found their bodies. The rest of the crew were captured by the Germans and sent to PoW camps.

20. George Temple and the other prisoners escaped from Saint Carlo hospital on 10 September when American forces targeted the roads and railway junction in the town and one bomb hit the room and stairway next to Temple. The prisoners were re-captured but with Mussolini now removed from power, the new Italian Government signed a peace treaty with the Allies. Nine days after parachuting from *Natchez Belle*, Temple found transportation to Tunis

and then was able to get back to the 68th. *8 Ball Tails; Journal of the 44th BG Veterans Assoc.* (Spring 2008).

21. All ten men in Walter R. Bateman's crew were KIA.

22. Leighton Smith, Milliner, 'Gentleman' Jim De Vinney and Flight Officer Tom Clifford were taken prisoner. T/Sgt Leroy R. Winter, the engineer from Orland, California, escaped. S/Sgt Gerald A. Sparkes, the radio operator, and S/Sgt Ernest G. McCabe, the assistant engineer from Pontiac, Illinois, were taken prisoner but later escaped. S/Sgts Gola Gibby, Gerald L. Grett, the right waist gunner from Urbanette, Arkansas, and Frank A. Maruszewski from Uniontown, Pennsylvania, were KIA. The 66th Squadron lost *Lady Luck*, piloted by 2nd Lt Rocco A. Curelli from Biddeford, Maine. All of the crew, who were on only their second mission, except for the radio operator were KIA. 2nd Lt Carl S. Hager of Glasgow, West Virginia, and *Black Sheep*, flown by 2nd Lt Carl S. Hager, which was crash-landed on the beach at Cape Stilo was the third 67th BS B-24D lost (five PoW, five KIA). Also, *Baldy And His Brood* put down on Malta so that three wounded men could rapidly get medical treatment. In all, thirty-three men were KIA; six became PoW; twenty-five were PoWs but escaped. Bill Cameron signed on for another tour and took the Squadron back to England, then the return to Africa and back to England. He relinquished command of the 67th when he was promoted to Lt Colonel and replaced Bill Strong as Group Operations Officer where he remained, with the exception of a stint as Vice Group Commander, until the end of the war. In his post-combat crew service, Bill Cameron flew nine more combat missions as Command Pilot without mishap.

23. Adapted from 'Hartford Is Heaven' in *First of the Many* by Tex McCrary.

CHAPTER 2

Consider Yourselves Already Dead!

*The scene is a Fortress field. Even in the early fog light of English dawn,
you could tell that this Fort had a new wing. And on her nose there was a
familiar name: 'Our Gang.' Remember what happened to the old wing?
That was the one that got chewed up at Hüls weeks ago. This was the
dawning of August 17, first birthday of the brazen, bloody daylight
storming of Hitler's Fortress Europe by the Flying Forts of the US Eighth
Air Force.*

Captain John R. 'Tex' McCrary, 8th Air Force Public Relations[1]

Captain John R. 'Tex' McCrary, war reporter for 8th Air Force Public
Relations, could feel that 17 August was going to be a rugged day . The
Texan, who had once worked on the *New York Mirror*, which always
specialized in 'Rape, riot and ruin', was no desk-bound war reporter.
When he wanted to hitch a ride aboard a Flying Fortress he normally
headed for Bassingbourn. The Cambridgeshire base became famous for
drawing press and photographers from London to its portals like a siren.
It was more easily accessible from London than most bases in far-flung
East Anglia with its poor road and rail links. It was the station that
McCrary had done most of his 'hitch-hiking' as he called it, flying three
missions with Captain Oscar O'Neill's crew, and he had 'got to know
them pretty well'. McCrary had flown the mission on 23 June to Hüls
aboard *Our Gang* piloted by 'Smitty' Smith. Tex had been so sure that the
raid would be scrubbed and his initial nervousness had ebbed away but
the raid had gone ahead and he flew the mission in Smith's ship. As fate
would have it McCrary was down to fly the Schweinfurt raid aboard
Harry Lay's ship, *Bad Egg*, but this was changed just before take-off to *Our
Gang*, which this time was being piloted by Bill Wheeler.

Captain Harry T. Lay of Denver would be flying the last of five additional missions that he had volunteered to do. So too, would his engineer-top turret gunner, Tech Sergeant Roy Cameron, a blue-eyed, pink-cheeked stocky Oregon boy who held the Air Medal with two Oak Leaf Clusters for meritorious achievement in combat against the enemy. But they had not had their fill of combat. 'I like combat - I don't know why – but I like it' Harry smiled. Maybe I've read too many books and seen too many movies, but I've always liked thrills. I like skiing and mountain climbing and at one time I was an electric linesman. I always wanted to fly. Piloting a heavy bomber is almost like driving a big truck.

Lay was a happy-go-lucky fellow with blond curly hair and a contagious smile, the son of Mrs H. T. Lay. He attended Denver East high school and Colorado University and worked for the Rocky Mountain Engineering Co. in Denver as a surveyor. Two days after Pearl Harbor he applied to the Air Corps and in March 1943 he came overseas to take a hand in the 8th Air Force's aerial offensive over Europe. In the course of more than seven months of operations, Harry had more than his share of thrills. On a flight to Hüls in June his squadron lost four of six ships. He had an engine shot out over Hamburg and fell behind the formations. His Fortress was attacked by persistent fighters until he found some clouds in which to hide. Coming home from Stuttgart his fuel gauge registered zero and one engine ran out of gas as the wheels hit the runway. There was not enough fuel left to taxi the plane to the hangar for repairs. Only once in his combat career did he turn back because of technical failure.

'As a combat man, Cameron can't be beat,' said Lay. 'I've had him with me on all my missions and wouldn't fly without him. He is cool and calm and knows the airplane.' Roy Cameron and his pilot did not know why they asked for an 'extra five'. They both said that they had had their share of thrills; their nerves were worn as thin as the next combat man and they 'want to go home'. Cameron was tired, his smile came a little slower than when he landed in England; his eyes did not sparkle as bright as when he joined the Air Forces in Marshfield, Oregon, on 12 March 1942. High-altitude combat matures a boy rapidly. Cameron was the son of Mrs M. J. Laird of Charleston, Oregon. He graduated from Salem High School in 1936, worked for the Hipper Dairy of North Bend and the Darling Logging Co. of Portland, Oregon, and before joining the Army Air Forces he was a machine tool operator for Western Oil Filter Co. at Glen Cullen near Portland. He went into the battles over Germany well prepared. His first combat mission on 13 May 1943 was preceded by over a year of study to fit him as a gunner and engineer. After a brief stay at the Presidio of

Monterey, California, Cameron spent four months at Air Mechanics School at Sheppard Field, Wichita Falls, Texas; one month at Advanced Air Mechanics School at Boeing's Seattle plant; six weeks of gunnery school, Las Vegas, Nevada; then a long session of 'training phases' when the ten-man B-17 team work for the final polish and shakedown in bombing runs, night flying and high-altitude work. Cameron recalled:

> The Stuttgart raid was a tough one. We had our share of anxiety – sweating it out – or whatever you want to call it. The red lights on the fuel gauges started flashing over France. As we came over the French coast Captain Lay put the ship into a gliding angle, throttled the four motors back and high-pitched the props. We came over our home field okay – but when we hit the runway, one motor starved. There was not enough fuel left to taxi the ship to the hangars for repairs. The trip to Heroya, Norway, made me homesick – the coastal scenery reminded me of the Oregon coast. Then I remember that raid too, because it came on my 27th birthday, July 24th.

Harry Lay, Cameron and the top turret gunner's buddy, Tech Sergeant Donald Robertson of Drain, Oregon (the radio operator), would remember Schweinfurt also. 'The raid "goes in the book",' Cameron said.

'Tex' McCrary was scared as hell when he pulled up inside the nose of *Our Gang* to tell Wheeler that he was carrying a hitchhiker. Fear had been piling up in the coils of McCrary's guts for days. He knew that this job would rank with the first raid on Berlin and the first night raid in drama, excitement and importance. He wanted to be ringside and he wanted to find out if he could 'cure' fear. McCrary found that he couldn't.

The Field Order for Tuesday 17 August called for ambitious and daring strikes on the aircraft plant at Regensburg and the ball-bearing plant at Schweinfurt. Brigadier General Robert Williams, commander of the 1st Wing, would lead his force to Schweinfurt, while Colonel Curtis E. LeMay was to lead the 4th Wing to Regensburg. To minimize attacks by enemy fighters, LeMay's B-17s would fly on to North Africa after the target. The 1st Wing, meanwhile, would fly a parallel course to Schweinfurt to confuse the enemy defences further, returning to England after the raid. Despite the planning, Eaker and his subordinates were under no illusions. They knew that the B-17 crews would have a running fight on their hands but hoped that four P-47 fighter groups detailed to escort the Regensburg force would keep losses down. Howard E. Hernan, top turret gunner in

Lieutenant Claude W. Campbell's crew in the 'Hell's Angels' at Molesworth, summed up the feelings of many.

> We had been briefed for this one three weeks before, so naturally the Germans knew we were coming. Since the previous mission had been scrubbed we were called in every day and told not to mention the target area. Intelligence seemed to think there were a lot of spies in Great Britain.

Crews realized the risks better than anyone and were made aware how important the targets were. His pilot added:

> Our target was the ball-bearing factory, or rather I should say, the elimination of Schweinfurt and all its inhabitants. It is predicted that this is the straw that will break Hitler's back. We were told that within three months from this date Hitler would feel the blow so seriously that he would throw in the towel.

At Kimbolton Tech Sergeant Johannes Johnson and the rest of Lieutenant Donald W. Merchant's crew would fly the mission in *The Bolevich*. Johnson, who was from the Bronx, recalled Maurice Preston's remarks after the Group's first mission, when the tough CO and strict disciplinarian had asked if anyone was scared. 'If not' said Preston, 'there's something wrong with you. I'll give you a little clue how to fight this war – make believe you're dead already; the rest comes easy.'[2]

At Bassingbourn the young men of the combat crews turned to Major Lawrence A. Atwell of Boston, the staff weather officer. Larry Atwell looked like a football player – and he was one. Before he was a professor at Princeton, he played halfback for Minnesota and captained the team at Brown. His job in the Army was a tough one. The changeable weather of the ETO is controlled by maritime air masses and with the exception of the Aleutians, it is the most difficult in the world to forecast accurately. In addition, wartime conditions handicapped the meteorologists. With the exception of occasional reports from submarines, there were no observations from ships on the Atlantic. With most of Europe occupied, the only stations providing the Allies with regular service reports were in Portugal and Sweden. 'It's like trying to forecast the weather for the state of Illinois without any reports from the other forty-seven states,' Atwell once remarked.

Before the war the average young man was interested in knowing whether it was going to snow the day of the homecoming game or whether there would be enough sun next week to ripen the tomatoes, or whether it was going to be warm enough on Wednesday for a picnic. But now they had sent him to England, given him a $350,000 Flying Fortress, or a pair of .50 calibre machine guns, or a Norden bombsight and told him to go over and blast targets within Hitler's *Festung Europa*, the weather suddenly became a vital factor in his life. He was no longer is interested merely in whether it was going to rain or shine tomorrow. He wanted to know whether there were going to be clouds over Schweinfurt and if so, exactly how many and at what altitude. And he wanted an accurate forecast of the weather every mile of the way from his base in England to the target and return. And how about the winds and temperatures and the moisture content of the air? These were things that never occurred to him before in his life, but now he turned to the weather men with these kind of questions because his life as well as the success of the daylight bombing raids over Europe depended upon the answers. A bombardier wanted to know if it would be clear over the target. He was also interested in speed and the direction of winds on the ground in order to estimate the effectiveness of smudge-pot smoke screens. Navigators had to have the same information on winds aloft in order to make allowances in charting the course.

The target briefing had held no new horror for McCrary but it was a jab into raw nerves. Colonel Ordway, McCrary's boss, had never ordered him not to fly again but he had told him that he would issue orders grounding him unless he promised not to fly. At the end of the briefing McCrary bumped into Ordway who said, 'You're not going to try to go today, are you? Remember what you promised. You are not to go. Get that. You are not to go.' McCrary laughed and said, 'I'll flip a shilling. If it's heads, I won't go' but only because it took more nerve to admit in front of the other crewmen that he was scared than it took to go on the mission. Ordway looked straight at him. Tight-lipped, he said 'You are not to go' and walked off to the club, to sleep until breakfast.

Wheeler's position in the formation would be in the Composite Group, low flight, a better place for pictures but a dangerous spot nonetheless. Over breakfast Bill Hearst had tried hard to talk McCrary out of going on the mission. 'Just why do you want to go?' he asked. McCrary did not have an easy answer and at 5am over pancakes and thick bacon it was too early to reason things out. What he said was: 'Because I want to.'

McCrary went out to *Our Gang*. He was wearing the boots of a pilot who had finished his missions and Smitty's helmet. The Texan noticed that the Fortress had one new wing to go with its whole new crew. Bill Wheeler, who came from Scarsdale, New York, was already up in his seat when he got there, running up the engines. He pulled up inside, and stood up in between the pilot and the co-pilot. The regular co-pilot, Clive Woodbury, from Fresno, was off that day. Sad-faced, dark Louis Bianchi, from Bakersfield, California, was riding his saddle. McCrary told Wheeler he was hitch-hiking. Wheeler looked 'worried, cold and unfriendly'. 'Okay, if Operations say okay. Take off is at dawn.' That was that.

At station's time, the crew was kidding around – there was a little too much laughter. McCrary sensed that every man in the crew knew that *Our Gang* would not come home from this raid and he knew that they knew it. It hit him suddenly, sharply, like a kick in the groin. They knew it and he knew it.

As taxi time ticked on, they crawled into the ship. Bill Hearst tried once more to get McCrary to stay on the ground. McCrary never searched so desperately and so fast in his life for a reason for an excuse as he did then. But now the difference between him and combat crews was too sharply drawn – they had to go. He had a choice – and so, he had to go, too.

McCrary recalled:

We sat there in the nose. The engines rose and fell in their rumble. The ship quivered. There was a chill sitting beside me and around me and in the bottom of my pockets when I stuck my hands there in search of warmth. Still there was the joking that could not hide the strain. And now the brakes were off and we were creeping out of the hardstanding, out on to the taxi strip, nosing toward the runway that was our 'point of no return.' And then suddenly the engines died. The flash came over the intercom that there was a delay of thirty minutes. Instantly, speculation was hot. Will they scrub it? Nobody said he hoped there would be a scrub – instead, Joe Newberry said: 'Goddamn it, I hope they don't scrub this one today. We're flying in a good position. I'd like to get this mission behind me.'

We were flying lead of the low flight, the 'Purple Heart Corner'. And Joe Newberry did not hope this mission would not be scrubbed. I know that everybody in that plane hoped it would be scrubbed.

When Death creeps into a Fortress, you feel it. I'm not kidding. You feel it as surely as you feel the chill of dead air in a refrigerator.

We didn't get out of the ship. Not worth it for thirty minutes. We settled down and tried to wriggle up a little warmth against the grey fog that still clung to the field. The sun was trying to burn a hole in it. No luck.

There can be no tension contrived by Man alone to equal the strain of waiting to see whether or not a 'delay' will turn into a complete 'scrub' on a tough mission. All the special weaknesses that have been inherited from generations protected against Man's original struggle for survival, each crack in the armour of insulation against panic, widens as the pressure grows.

At the end of thirty minutes, engines whined and peevishly coughed and angrily roared all over the field again. There was no scrub. There was no laughter now. We taxied a little further out from our hardstanding, only about twenty yards. And then, once more, the engines choked and died. Once more there was the flash: 'Delay thirty minutes.'

At first, there was relief. Now, surely, the mission would be scrubbed. But then the relief was routed by fresh nerve-strain.

Each delay only snafus all the carefully worked out plans for attacks – further loosens the timing of the diversions and the fighter escort – bet the Jerries know what we are cooking up by now – bet they'll be waiting – Yep, fears were fulfilled. At the end of thirty minutes, the same routine: Engines, whine, cough, roar. And the taxiing begins again. Once more the engines die. This is too much. Nerves snap. Rich cussing crackles over the intercom, through the ship. This time, the zero hour is delayed two hours. By now, the navigator has made so many changes on his forms that he can't figure out exactly when the take-off will be.

This much is certain: this time, we do not sit inside *Our Gang* for whole hours. This time, we tumble out to fight the chill that has clamped our spines. And quickly, I prayed that Colonel Ordway was awake by now, that he would find out that I was in the plane and order me out, the way he did that time when I was heading for Vegesack. Bill Hearst had heard back at Control Tower that Zero Hour was shoved back; he drove down and together we went back to the officers' mess and sat out in the rising warmth of the sun, as it wrestled with the morning fog.

Finally, McCrary gave in. Sure, he went out to the Fortress, inventing a lame story about being sure that they were going to scrub it. He collected his cameras and flying clothes out of the nose and drove back to the Officer's Club. Then Ordway, Bill Hearst and McCrary drove over to Duxford where they watched the Thunderbolts take off after the briefing. The P-47 pilots were not told where the bombers were going. The three visitors stayed at the base through lunch, heard the fighter pilots' interrogation, heard them tell how the Germans had ducked tangling with them, how 'Jerry had flown on to stalk over our Forts beyond the range of our Thunderbolts'. And then Bill Hearst and McCrary drove back to Bassingbourn to join the rest of the 'sweaters-in'.

Early on Tuesday morning the aircrews at Thorpe Abbotts finished breakfast at the Combat Crew Mess and groped their way through the eerie blackout to the briefing hut. Inside, dozens of voices were heard chatting in rapid short bursts while trying to get a grip on the anxiety and dread that always haunted mission briefings. The 'Bloody Hundredth's'[3] Commanding Officer, Colonel Neil B. Harding, and his briefing staff arrived about 0400. Harding was a famed football coach for the Army and a graduate of West Point but the Group was not well organized. He drank with his fliers and saw liquor and fistfights as acceptable forms of release. His men he would say, were made of 'flesh and brains; not unfeeling iron. He did little to enforce tight discipline on the ground or in the air and his Group had become known for being 'a rowdy outfit filled with characters'.[4] Harding's great West Point team had included Bud Sprague, Blondy Saunders, 'Light Horse' Harry Wilson, Moe Daly, Tom Trapnell, Art Meehan, Chuck Born, Gar Davison, Bill Wood and Tiny Hewitt. In this war some of them had been killed in action or taken prisoner. The team that Chick Harding now quarterbacked sat in stunned silence when the curtain covering a huge wall map of Europe was pulled back. A red string stretched from England to Regensburg, Germany, and then south over the Alps to Italy and across the Mediterranean to North Africa! 'My gosh, we'll never make it!' they murmured. 'Who dreamed up this one?' 'I feel sick!' 'This trip ought to count as two.'

'There was downcast disbelief and hushed attention as we listened to the briefing officers,' recalled James P. Scott Jr, radio operator on *High Life* in the 351st Squadron flown by Lieutenant Donald Oakes and which was named for the High Life beer brewed by the Miller Brewing Company in Milwaukee.

> Our target was the Messerschmitt 109 fighter factory at Regensburg. After bombing the target, the crews would fly to airdromes in North Africa. Fuel capacity was not sufficient to risk returning directly to England under combat conditions. At least that is what we were told. The briefing staff stated that if the factory could be pulverized, it would be a major blow to the *Luftwaffe* and one of the most important missions of the war.
>
> There was little said on the way to hardstand number five where *High Life* was parked. Aircrew losses were running about 10 per cent

and we pondered the odds of making it back from a raid so deep into Germany without fighter escort. We knew that the 'little friends' would have to turn back just short of the German border. We would be flying on our thirteenth mission. After a long delay caused by local weather conditions, we lined up for an instrument take-off with the belly of *High Life* full of 250lb incendiaries. As she raced down the runway and thundered into the cloud draped sky, our ship responded to every demand made by our pilots, Don Oakes and Joe Harper. The mission was on!

After what seemed like a lifetime of flying through one cloud layer after another, we assembled in our tail-end position behind a massive air armada that stretched for miles across England. There were about 160 Fortresses scheduled to bomb Regensburg. Our flight was in the tail end of the formation in the high squadron. This position was called 'Tail-End Charlie', better known as 'Coffin Corner'. We were flying off the left wing of the flight leader in *Piccadilly Lily*. Lieutenant Colonel Beirne Lay, who would later write *Twelve o'clock High*, was flying in the right seat of that plane as observer-pilot. As we left the coast of England and headed across the Channel, we manned our battle stations, double checked our equipment, test-fired our guns and kept a sharp eye out for enemy activity. I glanced at my watch. It had now been eight hours since we had been roused out of bed at two in the morning.

The long, straggling formation stretched for fifteen miles and this presented the fighter pilots with an awesome responsibility. Up front were the 'Snetterton Falcons' with Colonel Curtis E. LeMay at the helm. Behind came the 388th and 390th, followed by the 94th and 385th making up the 2nd Combat Wing. Lieutenant Richard H. Perry of New Jersey, co-pilot of *Betty Boop the Pistol Packin' Mama*, flown by Lieutenant Jim Geary in the 390th, recalls:

Just after we reached the Dutch coast we were attacked by several FW 190s. A .30-calibre armour-piercing shell entered the waist gun area and went right through the steel helmet of Sergeant Leonard A. Baumgartner and struck him in the head. The bullet also shattered a rudder control cable that made our landing in North Africa very difficult later. I went to the back of the aeroplane to administer to him. Baumgartner took his last breath in my arms.

Bringing up the rear of the formation were the 95th and Colonel Harding's 'Bloody Hundredth', each carrying incendiaries to stoke the fires created by the leading groups.[5] To add to the problems, only one P-47 group rendezvoused with the bombers as scheduled. When the *Luftwaffe* attacked in strength the overburdened Thunderbolts could not possibly hope to protect all seven groups in the 4th Wing. Fortresses in the rear of the formation were left unprotected and the 95th and the 'Bloody Hundredth' bore the brunt of the ferocious attacks, which were mostly made from head-on.

James P. Scott again:

A large number of enemy fighters swarmed on us as we crossed into Germany south of Aachen. The fighters came at us like jackals. It is difficult to describe how terrifying it was to watch the German fighters in pairs and foursomes swooping in toward our formation with their wings blinking as the dreaded 20mm cannons were fired. I felt like an old man whose nerves had become petrified. This feeling was short-lived as a fighter came whizzing through our flight. As the German pilot rolled by *High Life* I could feel his arrogant eyeballs dancing across my frozen face. It was an unforgettable experience. We were under constant, brutal fighter attacks for an hour and a half. During this onslaught we had our number two engine damaged and then received a direct hit on number three from a Me 109. With two engines dead and one of them windmilling, our effective power was reduced far below normal. The pilots struggled to keep up with the formation, but we began to fall behind. In order to stay with the formation, the pilot had the bombardier jettison the bomb load in a forest near Heilbronn. Even so, the gap continued to increase.

The 'Bloody Hundredth' lost two B-17s and the 95th lost five – *Little Hell*, *Assassin*, *Mason's Morons*, flown by Lieutenant Robert C. Mason Jr, *Piccadilly Commando* and *Our Bay Bee*, which was hit by ground fire over Belgium. Losing engine power, *Our Bay Bee* dropped helplessly out of formation and became an easy target for two German fighters whose pilots set the Fortress on fire. With the front of the aircraft burning out of control, Lieutenant Walter A. Baker, the pilot, gave the order for the crew to bale out. All ten crewmen made it out of the burning B-17 and parachuted to the ground. Seven men were quickly captured by German troops. Henry Sarnow, the bombardier, and the badly burned co-pilot, Marty Minnich, hit the ground near the small town of Mol, Belgium. Hank was born in 1920 and raised in Chicago, Illinois. In 1942 he enlisted in the Army Air Corps. He married his sweetheart, Regina, soon after being promoted to 2nd Lieutenant. Soon after landing in the wooded area,

Sarnow and Minnich were approached by Emiel Joris, a fifteen-year-old boy. Sarnow gave the boy his dog tag, presumably in an effort to get word to Hank's family that their son was alive. The dog tag had Hank's name, that of his mother, Mary Sarnow, and the family address in Chicago. Hank and Marty were directed to a canal and told to swim to the other side and hide among the bushes growing at the water's edge. They both hid in the canal for over nine hours, breathing through grassy reeds, while the German patrols and their dogs frantically searched for the downed flyers.[6] Later that day, with the help of Gus Fruythof, Hank and Marty were taken to a farmhouse nearby. The Fruythof family gave them a change of clothing and nursed Marty's severe burns. Eventually, both men were moved to Brussels, where they were hidden from the Germans and cared for by Anne Brusselsman and her husband, Julian.[7] It took over two months to get Hank and Marty back to Allied lines. During their time of hiding in numerous safe houses, a young nurse, who had smuggled medicine for the treatment of Marty's burns, was discovered by the German military authorities. She was put to death in front of a firing squad. She never gave up the information about Anne's hidden airmen.

In the 1½ hours preceding the bomb run seventeen Fortresses were shot down. 'Van's Valiants' lost three bombers while others, badly shot up, barely made it over the treacherous snow-covered Alps.

The 2nd Combat Wing was forced to swing around in a 360° turn and make another bomb run after the target had been obscured by smoke from the leading wing's bombs. The bombing was extremely accurate and this might well have been due to the presence of Colonel LeMay, an exponent of high-level bombing techniques, in the first wave.[8] Six main workshops were hit, five being severely damaged. A hangar was partially destroyed and storerooms and administrative buildings wrecked. All production at the plant came to an abrupt halt and thirty-seven Bf 109s at dispersal were damaged, if not wrecked. Although it was unknown at the time, the bombing had also destroyed the fuselage jigs for a secret German jet fighter, the Messerschmitt Me 262.

The surviving 128 B-17s, some flying on three engines and many trailing smoke, were attacked by a few fighters on the way to the Alps. LeMay circled his formation over Lake Garda to give the cripples a chance to rejoin the Wing. *Battle Queen-Peg of My Heart* in the 390th glided down toward the safety of Switzerland, about forty miles distant. On board *High Life* Don Oakes was about to order the crew to prepare to bale out but before the bell was rung, Hiram Harris, the navigator, advised that Switzerland was only thirty-forty minutes away. Oakes decided that they should try to make a run for Switzerland and he swung the Fortress on a course that Harris had plotted.

Jim Scott continues:

Fortunately, the fighters did not come in for the kill. One lone fighter followed us for a time, lobbing cannon rounds at us, while staying out of the range of our .50 calibre guns. Bursts of tracer bullets spewed out of George Elder's top turret toward the fighter. This put him on notice that we were still full of fight. Apparently he was convinced and disappeared without engaging us further. It was another streak of good luck and a timely one at that. The top turret had started to malfunction. Leonard Goyer's tail guns were out of ammunition and Nolan Stevens and Vincent McGrath, in the waist, had only a limited supply. Leslie Nadeau, who had been in the ball turret, was now able to leave that cramped position. About this time I was able to leave my machine gun and sit down at my position at the radio desk. Since I wasn't able to make contact with England, the pilot gave me permission to send out an emergency message. The following message was decided upon and was pecked out on the radio key: 'SOS. SOS. SOS HIGH LIFE 180.' The message was sent several times. There was no acknowledgement. I knew that if the SOS message did get picked up in England, it would tell them that we were out of formation and on a heading of 180 degrees.

Our crippled Fortress was now down to about 10,000 feet as we came in sight of Lake Constance (Bodensee). We continued to lose altitude as we neared the lake. Suddenly, a barrage of flak appeared all around us. The bursting flak shells and the dreadful sound of shrapnel hitting the fuselage played a horrible tune on our eardrums. We learned later that Friedrichshafen, which we were passing over, was the location of a training station for anti-aircraft gunners. Each battery used a different coloured smoke to aid in scoring. The sky was filled with bursting shells displaying every colour in the rainbow. We failed to see any beauty in this deadly display.

Our pilots took evasive action and *High Life* acted like a leaf tossed by the wind. We made it across the lake without further incident. The pilots looked for a flat piece of land and spotted one that was open except for a lone farmer loading hay. The landing gear would not go down so we cranked them down by hand only to discover that a tyre had been ruined by flak. Hastily, we cranked the wheels up again and assumed our crash-landing positions. As we came in for the belly landing, there was a terrifying shock from the initial impact, together with the awful sound of tearing, ripping and crushing metal. The fuselage filled with dirt and debris before shuddering to a stop. We scrambled out of the various exits and welcomed the feel of good old Mother Earth under our feet. We were shaken up but not hurt. We considered ourselves lucky just to be alive. Swiss soldiers, in battle dress and armed with rifles, appeared from out of nowhere and surrounded us. The Swiss officer in charge told us in flawless English, 'For you, the war is over. You are in Switzerland.'

High Life was the first B-17 to land in Switzerland. My watch indicated that it was about twelve o'clock.

The *Battle Queen* also crash-landed at Lutzendorf and all ten members of 2nd Lieutenant Stephen P. Rapport's crew were interned, as were Oakes' crew. *All Shot To Hell* and *Madie* in the 390th had been shot down in the target area and the crew of *Princess Pat*, almost out of fuel, headed for Spain. 2nd Lieutenant Dale A. Shaver got as far as Hyères, twenty kilometres east of Toulon, and force-landed. An unidentified Fortress crash-landed in northern Italy and five more eventually ditched in the Mediterranean. Red lights were showing on all four fuel gauges in every aircraft and it was a ragged collection of survivors that landed at intervals up to sixty miles along the North African coast. Two 390th ships, *Blood, Guts & Rust* and *Purgatory Pete* ditched off the coast to take the Group's losses to six. 2nd Lieutenant Wade H. Sneed's crew were picked up but three men in 2nd Lieutenant Raymond A. Becker's crew on board *Pete* were killed and seven taken prisoner. Nine of the 'Bloody Hundredth's' two dozen Forts failed to land in North Africa; the highest loss in the 4th Wing. Ninety of Chick's boys had gone.

The 4th Wing had encountered so many fighters en route because the 1st Wing had been delayed by thick inland mists for 3½ hours after the 4th Wing had taken off. This had effectively prevented a two-pronged assault, which might have split the opposing fighter force. The delay gave the *Luftwaffe* time to refuel and rearm after dealing with the Regensburg force and get airborne again. They attacked the Schweinfurt force with the same ferocity, shooting down thirty-six Fortresses. Colonel Maurice 'Mo' Preston, the 379th CO who led the 103rd Provisional Combat Wing, recalled:

I was positioned toward the front of the column and the 303rd from

Molesworth flew the low box. The top box was a composite furnished by the 303rd and the 379th. The 379th provided the top element of six planes in this composite box. We began to encounter enemy fighters when we were about half way to the target and had them almost constantly with us from there until we left the target area on the way out. There was every indication that the Germans were throwing at us just about everything they had in their inventory. Probably as a result of introducing units that were not combat-seasoned, the tactics employed were most unusual. The fighters queued up as usual out to the right front and up high but then, instead of turn diving down for attack on the lower elements, they turned in more sharply and delivered diving attacks on the topmost elements. Woe be it to that 379th element in the composite box. That entire element of six aircraft was left in central Germany this day.

Worst hit was the 381st, which dispatched twenty-six Fortresses, twenty of which made up the vulnerable low Group and the remaining six flew in Composite Group in the high position. Over Belgium *Lucky Lady* and one other B-17 were the first to go down. Having crossed into Germany, *Sweet Le Lani*, *Strato Sam* and *King Malfunction* were the next victims. Near Frankfurt *Hell's Angel* was badly damaged and the crew baled out after they had salvoed the bomb load. The eighth and ninth B-17s in the Group went down over Schweinfurt. Seven were from the main Group and two from the Composite formation. *Chugalug Lulu* steadily lost altitude on the return and was finally abandoned west of Eupen. Four of Lieutenant Loren Disbrow's crew evaded capture.

Big Time Operator in the 532nd Squadron was flown by Captain Briggs, as Marvin T. Lord, the regular pilot, was flying as tail gunner to check the formation. Major Hall flew as co-pilot. Ken Stone, the twenty-year-old ball turret gunner who would usually tell himself that he was 'flying with the Lord and the Lord will protect me', recalls:

> Our P-47 fighter escort left us near the German border. As we entered Germany, we were protected only by our own guns. Ten minutes later enemy fighters appeared. There were over 100 of them. I watched from my ball turret as they circled our group, sizing us up. They separated and formed into flights of five. They lined up, five abreast, about 5,000 yards in front of us. The first flight came in head-on with their guns blazing. They flew underneath our plane and into our formation. I fired at the nearest one with short bursts as he went by. Four more flights went through in the same manner. The deputy

lead left the group formation with one engine blazing. The crew baled out. Three more dropped out and parachutes billowed. Fighters were going down right and left. Lieutenant George R. Darrow's plane [*Our Mom*] had one engine knocked out, but he managed to stay with what was left of the formation.

The fighters left after what seemed like hours of fighting. Our group had four losses already and the mission was only half over. We dropped our bombs and the target appeared well plastered with bomb hits. Smoke rose high and fast.

About fifteen minutes after leaving the target we saw fighters coming in again on the right. They circled once and lined up again, five abreast and attacked head-on, as before. This method of attack was new to us. It was very effective. They came in under our plane and I had many beautiful shots. I was too busy to notice if I was registering any hits, but I'm quite sure that I didn't waste all of my ammunition. They came in at one o'clock, three o'clock, six o'clock, nine o'clock, etc. Lieutenant Leo Jarvis [*Ole' Swayback*] on our right wing had his number three hit and it caught fire. His crewmates waved goodbye to us and they dropped out of formation.[9] I could see other Forts dropping out too. Chutes were all over the sky. The white ones were ours. The brown ones belonged to enemy pilots. It looked like a parachute invasion.

Major Hall, riding in our co-pilot's seat, took 16mm shots of the fighters attacking head-on. Sweat poured down my face even though the temperature was 30 degrees below zero. The fighters were persistent and kept attacking all positions. I was positive we would never see England again. The odds were too much against us. I saw more fighters on our left, heading our way. I really began praying to God and asking him for courage to see this through. These fighters came closer and closer and then began attacking the enemy. Our escort had finally arrived and just in the nick of time. They were angels from heaven.

There were dogfights all over the sky. Goering's 'Yellow-Nose Boys' were getting the worst of the battle. Now that our boys were taking care of the enemy, I turned my turret around to see what was left of our group. I counted ten planes, including ours. Darrow was now dragging along with only two engines and things looked mighty tough for him. He dropped out to our left and tagged on to the tail end of the 91st formation. The formations slowly proceeded across France and over the coast. I could still see Darrow's plane. It was descending slowly. It looked like they would have to ditch in the Channel. The White Cliffs of Dover were a beautiful sight to see. We reached base, circled once and were the first to land. When those wheels touched the ground, I was the happiest person in the world. We were safe once more in good ol' England.

The engines were cut off at about 1900 hours. We examined the battle damage and thanks to God, we got through with very little damage, a few holes in the wings and the tail, but nothing to worry about. *Big Time Operator* had pulled us through again. We had made the deepest penetration yet and hit one of the most important targets in Germany. We were told that it would shorten the war by six months. Our group had been hard hit. Twenty planes were dispatched and nine returned. Ten were shot down and one crew ditched. Darrow and his crew returned to the base the next day. We were lucky we had flown as the lead ship because all the flight leaders were shot down. After this mission – our seventeenth – our crew became a regular lead crew.

'Life will never be the same' wrote Chaplain James Good Brown in his diary from his small room inside the chapel at Ridgewell. He had left his wife and his church in Lee, Massachusetts, and had been with the Group since Pyote, Texas. While he was at Yale University Brown's class in Social Ethics took a trip to the New York City morgue. It was this that came to mind as he walked around Ridgewell airfield.

In the barber shop the usual flippant topics of conversation are not heard. Men sit in a stupor waiting for their turn, glad to wait so that they will not have to go out and face someone else. Men eat in silence. They arise and leave the table in silence. If they ask for anything at the table, it is a low murmur. Or they may go without butter in order not to talk. If any man were to walk boisterously into the dining room, throwing his conversation around loosely, he would be scorned. On the roads men pass by without acknowledging each other. If they smile it is forced. Why should we smile when we are getting no smile in return?

Ridgewell is like a morgue.[10]

Forrest J. Eherenman, the navigator on a replacement crew who arrived at Kimbolton in time to watch the bedraggled survivors return to base, was appalled at the sight that greeted him. He saw Forts coming in one by one, 'some weaving and bobbing'. There was a belly landing, 'with lots of wounded aboard'. On 7 December 1941 Eherenman was playing saxophone with the Red Roberts Band in Buffalo, New York. Navy Shore Patrol entered the ballroom where they were playing and rounded up personnel. This had given him uncomfortable feelings. He gave the band two weeks' notice, enlisted in the Army and completed training to become an aircraft mechanic. Eherenman had never been very 'handy' around machinery so when an opportunity arose he entered navigator training. Nine months later he was a member of Lieutenant Corson's crew and they went off to war by ship to England. If Pearl Harbor day had given him uncomfortable feelings, Eherenman would remember the name, Schweinfurt and on 14 October he would hear that name again.

The 'Hell's Angels' flying in the low box also had its problems as Howard Hernan in *The Old Squaw* piloted by Claude Campbell remembers.

On the way over we had two abortives from our squadron, leaving it under strength. It looked bad. We had a P-47 escort part of the way in who were to pick us up on the way back. By this time they were using belly tanks and pilots would tell crews over the intercom when the fighters were due to leave. Quite a long while before we reached the target there were a lot of Me 110s. The Thunderbolts were supposed to leave us about ten minutes previously. Out on the right of us, flying at about 2,000 yards were six Me 110s, flying in a stacked up formation with the lead ship low. Occasionally, there would be a German fighter calling out our altitude to the ground for the flak gunners but I'm sure these were not doing that. All the time I was watching these Me 110s I suddenly saw the sun glint off four wings of planes above us. Right at that moment I couldn't identify them so I kept my eye on them. When they got above these Me 110s they dived down and I could see that they were four P-47s which were supposed to have been gone ten minutes before. Flying a finger-four to the tight, they came down at a 70 or 80° angle, made one pass and got all six Me 110s. They were just sitting ducks. The rear gunner in the last Me 110 evidently spotted the P-47s commencing their dive and baled out!

Immediately afterwards three enemy fighters came in at us from about 1 o'clock. A FW 190 was in the lead and right behind him were two P-47s on his tail. The FW 190 was making his turn to attack us and all six turrets were pointed at him. I'm sorry to say we got the FW 190 and the first P-47. The other Thunderbolt peeled off and headed for home. We felt bad about it and I doubt whether the P-47 pilot realized he was so close to the bomber formation. There was little flak from the target, which was battered from the bombs of other B-17s. We loosed our incendiaries into the middle of the town and as we left, huge fires were burning. The trip out was a long one and fighters were many.

The coast of England was a welcome sight for the survivors. At bases throughout eastern England anxious watchers counted in the returning Fortresses. Eighteen had taken off from Grafton Underwood but the watchers in the control tower counted no further than thirteen. *The Old Squaw* landed safely back at Molesworth.

Claude Campbell recalls:

For some unknown reason there were no losses from the 303rd. The lead bombardier was hit in the stomach forty-five seconds from the target and the waist gunner was killed and the other wounded. It was the longest, most impressive, toughest and the most important raid of the war. We got a bullet hole through our left aileron and one through the fuselage, which went under Miller's (the co-pilot) seat and a fragment struck my hand. Following the raid the 8th got the biggest letdown of the war by the RAF. The British night bombers were to follow us and do most of the damage. Our job was merely to start fires so they could saturate the area with blockbusters. But they assumed the target was hit and enough damage done so they failed to follow. It was discovered later that Schweinfurt was not hit as terrifically as supposed. We sacrificed 600 men, sixty planes and many injured men to start those fires.

The total loss of sixty bombers was more than twice as great as the previous highest, on 13 June, when twenty-six bombers were lost. Hardest hit Groups in the 1st Wing were the 381st and 91st, which lost eleven and ten B-17s respectively. The third highest loss of the day went to the 'Bloody Hundredth', which lost nine Fortresses. One of the replacements who arrived at Thorpe Abbotts was Robert 'Rosie' Rosenthal, who after enlisting on the day following Pearl Harbor, had been sworn in on 1 January 1942. The crew were relatively informal around one another; there was no saluting and rarely any military protocol but then Rosie was never the 'military type'.

At Bassingbourn there had not been a sweat like this one in a long time on the station and McCrary and the others watching patiently, saw other whole groups fly past to other fields. The 91st had been the first over the target and they should have been the first home. Long minutes after other groups had gone by, straggling ships, first one then only two more, circled Bassingbourn and dropped their wheels and flaps to land. *Oklahoma Oakie*, the lead ship, with Colonel Clemens L. Wurzbach, the young CO who had trained in mediums and Colonel William M. Gross of Wing Headquarters, came in. McCrary watched them climb out as the ground crew pushed close around their Fort to look at battle damage. Without asking a question, McCrary knew that the mission had been 'rugged'. He noted that in seven hours, Wurzbach, whose boys all liked him and said that he was a 'raunchy guy', had aged at least one year. There was a great exhaustion in his walk, in his face, in the way his arms hung at his sides.

Lieutenant David Williams, lead navigator, recalls:

> Our group had lost ten aircraft and we were one of only two aircraft, which were able to make it back to Bassingbourn without an intermediate landing. At that, we had part of our left wing shot off from a 20mm frontal attack, which resulted in our left wing man being completely shot out of the air. We discovered after landing that we also had an unexploded 20mm in out left main wing tank. A bullet of unknown calibre (I hope it was not a .50) came through the top of the nose, passed through my British right-hand glove, through my left pant leg and British flying boot without so much as breaking the skin, then out through the floor. It paid to be skinny at the time!

'What a hell of a way to celebrate an anniversary,' 1st Lieutenant Eugene M. Lockhart moaned as he swam away from his sinking bomber and climbed into an inflated rubber dinghy. Exactly one year before, Lockhart, a blond, twenty-five-year-old boy from Hilsboro, North Carolina, had flown to Rouen as a pilot on the first Flying Fortress raid over Europe. There were only twelve B-17s and three enemy fighters that day. Since his injury on his fourth mission he had been forced to abandon combat until mid-June. Schweinfurt was his nineteenth raid and he was piloting *Hitler's Gremlin* when he ran into trouble on the way to the target. A 20mm cannon shell hit the left wing tip and blew that to pieces. There was a large hole in the right stabilizer and then another cannon shell hit number three engine in the intake manifold. The pilots did not feather the prop but let the motor wind-mill and trusted to luck that it would not get hot and start burning. A feathered prop was always an invitation to enemy fighters.

Lockhart managed to keep the ship near the formation and flew over the target. On the way home they were hit again by swarms of fighters, which they successfully beat off without further damage. Staff Sergeants Chester W. Raphoon, of Clarksburg, West Virginia, and John Husick, of Broadtop, Pennsylvania, the two waist gunners, claimed he destroyed an enemy fighter.

When the *Gremlin* reached the Belgian coast, number one engine 'conked out for lack of gas' recalled engineer, twenty-six-year-old Tech Sergeant Ted Cetnarowski, of Milwaukee, Wisconsin. 'By luck the fighters left us. We feathered the props on the two bad engines and started a long power glide toward England from five miles up. I guess we had about a hundred miles of water to cross.' Cetnarowski and Lockhart and co-pilot, 2nd Lieutenant Clive M. Woodbury, of Fresno, California, knew that they were not yet out of danger. They had been watching the fuel gauge and knew that their efforts to keep the damaged bomber in formation had used too much gasoline and that they would not be able to make England.

Captain Lockhart had us throwing out guns, ammunition and unnecessary radio equipment to lighten the ship, our radio operator was calling the English monitor stations so that they could get a location 'fix' on us. Slowly we came down to 2,000 feet and held her there for a time over the North Sea. Our two overworked engines were fading. All the crew, except the pilot and co-pilot, were in the radio room huddled and braced against the forward bulkhead.

Soon the two good engines sputtered and stopped – out of gas. They prepared to ditch. Up to this point the radio operator, Tech Sergeant William C. Dardon, of Rotan, Texas, had stayed at his desk sending out the distress signal. Cetnarowski continues:

Lockhart made a nice landing; first our tail hit. Then the ball turret sent out a shower of spray. We were skimming beautifully until we hit the front side of a swell and came up short. The radio room door broke under the impact and two of us landed in the bomb bay. The bomb bay doors were smashed inward and the ocean was pouring in. My Mae West was inflated and held me up. I looked up through the radio door and saw the rest of the crew scrambling out the radio hatch. We got two back into the radio room and I pulled the release handle for the two dinghies.

Husick, Cetnarowski and the bombardier, 2nd Lieutenant Robert Sherwin, of 570 Park Avenue, New York, were thrown through the closed door of the radio room into the bomb bay where they found themselves in water shoulder deep. By pushing and pulling each other, the four managed to get out the open hatch in the radio room ceiling before the big bomber sank a few seconds later. When Ted Cetnarowski got outside, one dinghy came floating by. 'I grabbed on to it and it pulled me along through the water. The Fort was sinking. The dinghy got caught under the sinking tail and I was pulled under with the dinghy. The crew got into the dinghies okay.'

The ten-man crew piled into two dinghies where they sat for three hours before being sighted by a Spitfire. Earlier they had shot a flare to attract a group of 'planes', which turned out to be a flock of birds. Within an hour, guided by a searching Spitfire, a Walrus flying boat landed alongside, took the men aboard and began taxiing toward England, unable to take off because of the load. It was not an exactly smooth ride. By this time it was dark and when a rescue launch arrived, they thought at first that it was a German E-boat. Three of the men were transferred to the launch with difficulty due to the high sea. The others stayed with the Walrus, taxiing for nine hours and reaching England early the next morning. They were taken to British Air-Sea Rescue headquarters and given tea, brandy, cigarettes and dry clothing.

Cetnarowski must at one stage have begun to doubt the value of the good luck charms he always carried. He recalled:

I had several. I carried a rosary given me by Chaplain Regan at the base. Then I carried a St Christopher medallion given me by my sister, Marty. When we ditched, the chain broke. Hours later, when I changed to dry clothing, I found the medallion plastered to my wet skin. Another funny thing was that when I got back to base I found a white scarf waiting for me at the mail room. It had arrived before I had taken off the day before. But I was too busy getting ready for the raid to go to the mail room. It was from the folks and written in it in ink was 'happy landings' and their seven autographs. I've had happy landings ever since.

On New Year's Eve Cetnarowski flew his twenty-fifth combat mission.

That Schweinfurt mission absolutely was my roughest. In the seven months I was over the Continent I saw the 8th Air Force grow from a small group of fifty or seventy Fortresses until this winter we were punching Hitler with hundreds of bombers. A fellow sees a heck of a lot on a mission. You don't look forward to making the trip, but you go because it is a job to be done. When you get back to your English base, you just forget about what happened that day. You go to your barracks, clean up, loaf around and write a letter home. The day's impressions are on the other side of a curtain, one just doesn't think about them and you josh the folks in your letter that you are learning to drink English tea.

My Prayer flown by twenty-three-year-old 2nd Lieutenant James D. Judy, a former railroad inspector whose wife lived at Seattle, was enveloped by fire and went out of control. On the nose of the Fortress formerly known as *Heavyweight Annihilators No.2*, Tony Starcer's provocative, reclining brunette in a silky negligee had become a biblical scroll bearing the words: 'Yea though I fly through the shadow of the valley of death, I fear no evil, for Thou art with me.' Judy recalls:

> Thirty to forty fighters were attacking our ship, pouring in ten and fifteen at a time. I dodged most of them with evasive action, but one came straight at us and I couldn't seem to get away from him. Then there was a big explosion. He must have got us with a 20mm shell, which hit our oxygen and batteries. Flames and smoke poured into the cockpit. The electricity went out. The canvas around the bottom of my steering wheel burst into flames. One of the control cables to the rudder was severed and the ship started spiralling down in a half-hearted spin.

All except the pilot, co-pilot and the top turret gunner, thirty-five-year-old Tech Sergeant Earl W. Cherry, who was wounded in the leg and whose chute was damaged by the flames, baled out. Cherry, of Little Rock, Arkansas, who used to work in the legal department of Sears Roebuck at Memphis, Tennessee, was on his second mission. He had been painfully wounded in the leg by shrapnel. Grabbing a fire extinguisher, he put out the fire around the pilot's feet. Then he went to work on the big fire behind the cockpit, beating it with his legs, his gloves and anything he could lay his hands on. He and 2nd Lieutenant Roger W. Layn, the co-pilot, a former farmer from Bristol, Vermont, managed to put out at least fourteen fires. By this time Cherry's parachute was burned so he could not jump and Judy had regained control of the plane and had discovered that all four engines were running smoothly, so they decided to drop down 'on the deck' and make a run for home. Layn went back and handled the two waist guns while Cherry, burned and wounded, crawled into the nose. Between the two of them they repelled enemy attacks until they got down to an altitude of 50 feet and the fighters abandoned the chase.

Judy flew *My Prayer* back at tree-top height with Cherry working the nose guns and Layn manning the waist guns. Judy said:

We came home at 210mph buzzing cities, factories and airfields in Germany. It was the first legal buzzing I've ever done. We drew some fire but I did evasive action and we escaped further damage. The people in Germany scattered and fell to the ground when they saw us coming but in Belgium the people waved and saluted us.

Passing over Belgium, Layn was throwing things overboard to lighten the ship. He came across a pair of shoes that he tied together and dropped to the next Belgian he saw waving. The ship was running low on gas and they had no navigator to show them the shortest route home. Judy did his best to estimate the course. Layn cranked down the landing gear and eventually Judy crash-landed *My Prayer* at Manston. The crew told of their wounded gunner who beat out the flames and then took over the nose guns to repel enemy attacks. They laughed as they described 'scaring hell out of the Germans' who threw themselves to the ground as the Fortress zoomed overhead and waving to friendly Belgians who came out in the streets to cheer as the B-17 flew over at 50-foot altitude. And they told the incredible story of being guided home to the nearest point in England by a large 'V for Victory' on the ground in Belgium formed by laundry laid out to dry. Judy forecast that after two weeks of repair work the gallant Fortress would be back in the air. It wasn't; *My Prayer* was salvaged.[11]

Tex McCrary and the rest stayed on the field at Bassingbourn a while longer.

Two more ships came in, then *Lady Luck* with Brigadier General Robert B. Williams in the co-pilot's seat. Williams, a Texan who was a stickler for military discipline usually carried a swagger stick and was easily recognizable by his moustache and only one good eye; the other lost while serving as an observer during the Blitz on London. He had won his wings and commission in 1923 and in 1936 at Langley Field, Virginia, he had been operations officer of the first group to fly the Fortress. It was a moving sight to see him get out and walk around and shake each man warmly by the hand, each man in the crew. The pilot of his ship used to be the jockey of a Spitfire in the RAF – he finished his ops in Spitfires, then shifted to the 8th Air Force and now he was finishing up in Forts. The things he learned in Spitfires helped him fight Focke Wulfs with a Fort today.

Thirty-year-old Captain Vernon A. Parker was a quiet, mild-mannered fellow, who a few years back was flying a Cub and selling wholesale candy and bakery goods. In January 1941 he left his wife and baby daughter in San Antonio and joined the RAF because he knew America was going to get into the war and he wanted 'to get the jump on the other fellows'. He certainly got his jump because he probably was the first American to complete a tour on both fighters and four-engined bombers. The RAF considered six months a tour of operations but Parker flew fighters with the Eagle Squadron for ten months before laying off combat. When the United States entered the war Parker (then a flying officer) wanted to get into the Army Air Forces. He and Pilot Officer Don Macleod went to Ambassador John O. Winant as representatives of the boys in the Eagle Squadrons. The Ambassador told them that they would have to wait until arrangements could be made. Parker finally was transferred to the USAAF in November 1942 and was assigned to 'Wray's Ragged Irregulars'. 'Fighters were a lot of fun, but I had enough and I wanted to try the heavies' he said. 'I thought it would be good all-round experience.' He had never flown a heavy plane before. They gave him thirty-four hours and then sent him on his first mission, to Hamm, in which sixteen of the 'Irregulars' went over the target alone and were attacked by more than seventy-five enemy fighters. Four of the B-17s were lost. Vern Parker's Fortress tour covered more than 150 daylight combat hours. Vern had flown his Spitfire in dogfights involving 300 RAF and German fighters and he had seen as many as a dozen Focke Wulfs attack his B-17 simultaneously. In order to live through 550 hours of action in the world's toughest theatre of aerial combat, you had to have more than extraordinary luck.

'Tex McCrary continues:

> And then to the interrogation of the three or four crews who sat in the still emptiness of the interrogation room. The customary wild chatter was not there this day. Nobody wanted to make too much noise. Everybody had one ear cocked for the sound of Fortresses coming home.
>
> Dixie Tighe, the hardest working reporter in England, was there. She had watched the raid going out today from the waist of the old Fortress *Yankee Doodle* – the one that General Eaker flew in on the first raid just a year ago. Dixie knows the kids in this group better than their mothers. She was a barometer of their losses today, sad, solemn and silent.
>
> Captain 'Doc' Ross came in and reported on the first ship that had landed. She had fired two red flares. One boy had been taken out.

He was dead. The ship was Captain Harry Lay's – the one Major Alford, the Operations Officer from Rising Star, Texas had wanted me to go in. And the dead boy was the radio operator – just like the first raid I ever went on.

The 'dead boy' was Donald Robertson, Cameron's buddy. Robertson died in the radio room with a bullet through his throat. Cameron said:

My oxygen mask went haywire. I got woozy from lack of oxygen. That wasn't so bad, but I saw whole bunches of imaginary German fighters boring in. I was frantic – my guns wouldn't do anything to them. It was all an oxygen hallucination – even though I was throwing real lead.

'Tex' McCrary went back to the control tower and 'checked the list that had phoned in from other fields, where they had been forced down without gas. I studied the list – eleven ships were still missing, no word from them.One of the missing ships was *Our Gang*.[12]

I walked back over to Operations Room. A bunch of the guys were standing around, talking, quietly, the way you talk at a funeral or in an elevator – going down. Bill Martin looked up from behind the operations board and said:

'Hello, luck.'

Harry Lay and Roy Cameron were two of the first men in the ETO to complete thirty missions; five raids more than the number required to retire a man from combat. 'I'm ready to start on fighters now because that's real flying' Lay said. Every now and then Vern Parker had got an idea he'd like to do a tour of combat on medium bombers to complete his experience. But then he got to thinking about his wife and little Sandra Lou, who was four years old now, and he decided it would be nice to get back to the States for a while. Can you blame him? He unquestionably had done his share of combat and deserved a trip home. So too had Cameron and Harry Lay but the happy-go-lucky pilot with the blond curly hair and a contagious smile was killed on 17 July 1944 flying his beloved fighter aircraft.[13]

At Chelveston the 305th had despatched twenty-nine Forts and three had aborted. Just two – *Settin Bull* and *Patches* – were shot down and four more were overdue.[14] Word was received that three of the latter had landed at the fighter airfields of Martlesham Heath and Wattisham in Suffolk but there was no news of *Ex-Virgin* or David A. Tyler Jr's crew. The 305th had been about the fifth group over the target but by the time they had reached Schweinfurt, there was not enough left of the two preceding groups to make up a good squadron. The *Ex-Virgin* got hit hard at 1405 hours, just after the fighter escort had left them. Tyler's ship was in the centre of 'Purple Heart Corner' in the low squadron. Two 20mm shells holed the Fortress, blowing out all the oxygen system on the left side and killing William W. Frye, the left waist gunner, who never knew what hit him. A few of the crew had more of a reason for wanting to get home than some of the others. This was the last mission for Tyler and Nelson and Sweet and Cullin A. Lee, the radio operator from Sun River, Montana. It was the next to last for the twenty-two-year-old co-pilot Wayne Hendricks who was from Salt Lake City, Utah and Fred E. Boyle, top turret gunner from Reno, Nevada. Hendricks was born on a farm between Idaho and Utah; his father was the State Veterinarian. He was married to a Salt Lake City girl. He saw the sights in Brazil and French Morocco on the way to England and he did not like the smell. Ball-turret gunner, Hugh Johnson was from 'somewhere in Illinois'; right waist gunner, Jackson Daugherty used to be a second pilot for TWA and had transferred from the RAF. Tail gunner, Stan Salomon, was from Scranton, Pennsylvania.

The same shells that knocked the oxygen out blitzed the intercom too and the whole tail end was swirling with a strange white smoke. This is when the boys in the back of the ship started baling out. Tyler could not tell them to stick to the ship and he did not know what he would have told them if it had been put up to him. There was not enough oxygen for all of them to live and get to the target and then get home at altitude. And if they broke formation and tried to get home down on the deck by themselves, well, it would have been curtains for all of them. A few minutes later the Fort went into a spin. The first thing that would happen when a Fort went into a spin, the tail would snap off. Tyler guessed that Stanley Salomon figured that he did not want that to happen to him and he did not blame him. Tyler also remembered the time that they saw a Fortress go screaming by them after everybody had baled out except the tail gunner, still blazing away at the fighters on his tail. Salomon was the first to bale out in the back of the ship. Johnson, Lee and Daugherty went too. *Ex-Virgin* ploughed on. They added up the oxygen in the emergency bottles, set the indicator to 10,000 feet to make it last twice as long and moved around as little as possible to conserve their strength for the trouble ahead.

When the limping Fort had gone over the target, the bomb racks would not release their load. Flak had jammed all the controls and the crew were really mad. Louis Nelson told Fred Boyle to go back there and get to work with a screwdriver, see if he could not pry the bombs loose. He did. Boyle got them all set until they were going over another German target and then he kicked the bombs away. By this time most of the tail surfaces were shredded and flopping in the prop-wash; the power was failing; the red lights were showing. When they left the target Tyler started hoping that they would reach the coast. When they did they began hoping that they would reach mid-Channel so that Air-Sea Rescue would get them instead of the enemy. When they got to mid-Channel, they started hoping that they would reach the beach and when they crossed the beach then they started hoping that they would reach home. But they didn't. They crash-landed on a fighter field, and skidded in on the *Ex-Virgin*'s belly, smoking down the runway.

Tyler did not start to hate Germans until he lifted William Frye's body out his ship when they got back home.[15]

Flat Foot Floogie brought Joe Chely's crew home safely to Chelveston just as she had done during Blitz Week when the crew had flown three rough and tough trips: Hanover on 26 July, Kassel two days later and Kiel on the 29th as Ed Burford recalls:

Like a mother *Floogie* cradled Staff Sergeant Harold Conley in her room when he died inexplicably of anoxia. On 12 August she dodged walking barrages of flak at Gelsenkirchen in the Ruhr Valley and smiled when that murderous flak indiscriminately took out a FW 190. On 15 August she cried when her sister ship *Lady Liberty* was actually cut in half by those extremely accurate flak batteries at Flushing. On 16 August she clawed back in the Le Bourget scrap with the vaunted JG 26, which we respectfully called the 'The Abbeville Boys'. Then on 17 August she carried us home from the first Schweinfurt raid. I used to amuse our crew but not mon capitaine Chely, with my high pitched interphone serenade to *Floogie* with *I'll Get By ...as long as I have you...*

Colonel 'Mo' Preston concludes:

The first Schweinfurt was a matching of excessive efforts. We, for our part, put up a maximum all-out effort in an attempt to deal the Hun a telling blow and at the same time prove to one and all the decisive nature and the viability of the daylight programme. The Germans, on the other hand, felt themselves pricked at their sensitive heartland with their major industries threatened and the morale of their population in the balance. So they put up everything they had to stop the Yankee thrust and make it so costly it would not be repeated. The result was a mixed bag. Our effort fell far short of expectations but nonetheless achieved some of its purposes. But the losses suffered were certainly unbearable and could not be borne by us on a sustained basis.

The lack of facilities in North Africa ruled out any more shuttle missions in the immediate future and VIII Bomber Command continued flying missions to France and the Low Countries. One of these was to Villacoublay, on 24 August, when Joe Chely's crew were on pass, as Ed Burford recalls:

Glenn 'Red' Ellenberger flew *Floogie* through the maze of flak at the very unforgiving altitude of 16,000 feet attempting to knock out the fast developing rocket site at Watten. Don Moore went down in *Moonbeam McSwine*. Shortly before that he had passed out cigars as a very proud new father. Of all the 305th's planes, Lieutenant Ron Barstow flying *Kayo* encountered the most harrowing set of circumstances. Normally, he filled in the No. 2 slot of the low Squadron – more in the centre of our wing box and normally a good defensive position but exactly the opposite when ramming into a cloudbank. With planes converging on either side of him, Barstow and Lieutenant Kincaid chose to crash dive, even though the bomb bay doors malfunctioned and had not yet closed. *Kayo* now dived from 24,000 to 13,000 feet, with the centrifugal force playing havoc with the crew and the guns. Sensing that it was Valhalla time, navigator Townswick tried to get to the hatch but only managed to get himself pinned to the ceiling.

After levelling off, Barstow ordered Sergeant Brandemoen, the engineer, to crank up the bomb bay doors. When Brandemoen got down to the bomb bay catwalk to face his task, a flock of German fighters, sensing that several of the guns were inoperative, closed in for the kill. Defensively Barstow dived again and Brandemoen, without his parachute, was violently hurled toward the open bomb bay doors, just managing to grab the narrow catwalk and with a scissors hold, to hang on for dear life – half in and half out of the airplane. Barstow and Kincaid both pulled back on the control wheel and levelled off again but the hounds followed. So far

Sergeant Joe Kocher, the ball turret gunner, had not particularly enjoyed the roller coaster ride but what really infuriated him was that his guns would just not fire. Cranking himself out of the ball turret, Joe entered the radio room when a string of 20mm shells demolished the rack of radio equipment, wounding both Kocher and the radioman, Sergeant Hanson. When matters seemed a trifle out of hand, Townswick mustered all the calm he could and on the intercom briefly reminded the crew that survival depended upon each man giving his best effort. Since the navigator was on his twenty-fifth mission and seemed to possess all his faculties, others took heart, calmed down and continued firing. Townswick felt that was, 'his one real contribution' and that 'some damn good flying by Barstow and Kincaid and the veteran experience of the crew pulled them through'.

One of the guns consistently able to fire was the left waist, so the pilots, when faced with frontal attacks, would, always veer right to give Sergeant Long his best shot. The manoeuvre repeated over and over convinced the fighters to change tactics and go for the tail. The tail gunner, Sergeant James Frazier, already battered and bloodied by 20mm fire added:

> I was almost blinded, thought the ship was going down, thought everyone had baled out, thought I was alone. I opened the tail door and saw Long and Sweet. They were having plenty of trouble. I went back to my guns and ran smack into another 20mm explosion. I thought it was the end of the world. It blew me back against the door. I positively oozed to the floor and crawled back to the guns for another shot at those babies. A Jerry was coming in fast. I caught him, after missing with three bursts. He went down in flames.

Frazier maintained that throughout the engagement he did not realize he had been wounded, although conscious of a sting in his left shoulder. Later, three unexploded shells were found in his compartment. One whizzed past his head and through the door. Long was still busily engaging several FW 190s. After being wounded twice in the left shoulder, he got one at 8 o'clock swinging in from the left. Long remarked:

> I couldn't help thinking it was funny... the first slug flattened me and the second straightened me up. I had to get that guy and as I let my gun go at him I saw oil on his wings. Then the bullets upped into his cockpit and he started to break up.

Kincaid thought they had about had it when he spied some P-47s in the distance and with a whoop he shot off a red flare. Before the friendlies could arrive Kocher saw a Bf 109, undoubtedly out of ammunition, swoop in from the port side for his last close-up look-see at a B-17, which he thought should not be flying.

Practically home free, everyone in the ship truly became aware of the increasing vibrations of alarming proportions. When the crewmembers were again thinking exit time, Barstow cautioned against any rash moves until he could try to solve the problem, until he could throttle down to the lowest possible airspeed. No one in the ship could have known that a 20mm had taken off a chunk of propeller tip. Upon eventual landing three walking wounded and a stretcher-borne Frazier were hustled away by ambulance under the supervision of Flight Surgeon Bergener. Over twenty-five photos were taken of the damage to *Kayo* and all crew were recommended for the Silver Star.

Only one B-17 was reported as lost to enemy action for the day and Sergeant Spero, Lieutenant Cline's ball turret gunner, received credit for the only destruction of an enemy fighter by a B-17 gunner. The P-47s had a wild time and were credited with six victories. Over at Thurleigh, home base for the 306th; seventeen of their participating eighteen ships were flak damaged, which may have had something to do with their suspect lead. The last plane to land flown by Immanuel Klette of their lead squadron climaxed the long day. Flak had knocked out two of his engines before the IP. After limping home, one of his two remaining engines caught fire over the base. For the moment, the crippled Fort weaved crazily and after a semi-controlled dive, landed spectacularly on one engine and one wheel, flak having deflated the other tyre. The long 'sweating-out line' drew an appreciative sigh of relief.

On her last mission with the 305th to Amiens on 31 August someone in our squadron snapped the last known prized picture of *Floogie*. We almost bought the farm that day in 'Purple Heart Corner' and I mean the last and lowest ship of the 40th Combat Wing! Our ship and others stupidly allowed those sneaky white-nosed FW 190s to close from the left rear shamming P-47 tactics, suddenly flanking right and letting loose an unhealthy barrage of 20mm. After a prolonged fight, *Floogie*'s make-up was a mess. Thirty-calibre and 20mm holes cut up her frame. One 20mm made a gaping hole larger than head size in the inboard trailing edge with considerable damage to the flap. Shrapnel from the same shell penetrated the fuselage and entered the radio room, where the last remaining piece glanced off the oxygen bottle, neatly clipped the headset cord of our radio operator, Chester Voorhis, and came to rest in his thick glove. After cosmetic surgery, unknown to us she was transferred to the 381st on 11 September. The 305th was slowly beginning to get Fs with Tokyo tanks and Gs with chin turrets. We flew nine of *Floogie's* ten missions with the 305th and shot down three German fighters. No other crew could have known her better. We had some wild, exciting times – laughing joking singing cursing fighting and living on the edge of life. The constant danger of that bloody summer of '43 made all of our lives vibrantly intense. We never even had a chance to say good-bye but she knew we loved her in our own peculiar mannish way. She had flown in combat with the 305th for only a month and a half but she was part of us. Humphrey Bogart's *Casablanca* farewell to Ingrid Bergman said it all: 'Here's looking at you kid'.

It was on 31 August that Staff Sergeant Charles E. Allen in the 401st Bomb Squadron, in the 91st Bomb Group, was riding in the lonely tail-gun compartment of *Eager Beaver* shortly after leaving the Sussex coast on the way to the target at Glissy near Amiens when there was a terrific mid-air crash and he found the tail assembly dropping like a falling leaf, completely detached from the rest of the ship. Both doors from which Allen could escape were blocked but he lived to tell the tale. Lieutenant 'Buster' Peek, who had successfully ditched *Old Ironsides* in the sea on 22 June[16] and the rest of the crew, were killed. The husky, twenty-year-old blond-haired gunner with a sparse moustache, whose wife Ruth was living in Mishawaka, Indiana, was from South Bend, Indiana, and he had worked for Studebaker Corporation at West Bend where his father and brother were working on bomber engines. Allen recalled:

> We were flying along at 25,000 feet when there was a crash and a hell of a noise of metal ripping and tearing. I took a quick glance out the side window and saw another plane practically on top of us. Our ship started to fall and I started to get at my parachute, but before I could get it the ship started spinning and going into a dive. My ammunition was all over me and the force of the ship's fall held me down. We had fallen a good ways before I could get to my parachute and snap it on. I grabbed the release handle on the escape door and pulled it but it wouldn't work. I then opened the bulkhead door, which leads to the forward part of the ship. I intended to go up and bale out the waist, but as I opened the door I saw that I was all alone in the tail, which had been broken off completely from the rest of the

ship. I couldn't get out there because the sides were mashed up against the tail wheel.

I went back to my tail escape door and tried to open it again. I kicked and pushed and finally forced it open. All this time the tail was twisting and turning. I stuck my head out the door and saw that I was about 10,000 feet above the water. I hesitated for a minute because I was afraid to jump. I realized that I had to get out immediately, so I stuck my head and shoulders out and then my hips got stuck in the door and I couldn't move. I just kicked and wiggled until I fell free. After falling for about 500 feet, I opened my parachute. When it opened I saw that I was between 7,000 and 9,000 feet above the water. My one leg strap wasn't tight enough and the jerk of the chute when it opened nearly jerked my other leg off. The silk looked real nice floating above me. While I was floating down I saw an air-sea rescue boat heading for me, so I started spilling air out of my chute so I would come down clear to the boat and to shore. Wreckage from the two planes was falling all around me all the way down and bigger parts were burning on the sea below me. When I was about 30 feet above the water I inflated my Mae West. I hit the water quite hard and went under a ways, but my chute and life preserver brought me to the surface. I then freed myself from my chute because it was dragging me across the water and in the wrong direction. I kicked my flying boots off because they were dragging me down. I had a hell of a time too, because I was swallowing sea water and it tasted terrible, I started swimming toward shore but didn't make much headway because the water was a little rough.

A Spitfire and a couple Fortresses were circling around looking for us. I was in the water about five or ten minutes when the boat found me and it looked good as all hell to me because I was all played out and getting sick. They gave me some dry clothes and some hot soup and some brandy and then took me ashore and put me in the hospital. All I had wrong with me was some skinned places, bruises and some sprained muscles and I believe the Old Boy had his hand on my head that day.[17]

On Monday 6 September General Eaker sent 338 B-17s to the aircraft components factories at Stuttgart. Sixty-nine Liberators including the 392nd Bomb Group, recently arrived at Wendling, Norfolk, and equipped with the new B-24H and B-24J with power-operated nose gun turrets, flew a diversionary sweep over the North Sea. The Stuttgart raid was a complete 'snafu' from the start. Cloud interfered with assembly over England and prevented accurate bombing at the target. The B-17 formations came under sporadic attack shortly after crossing the enemy coast – an indication that the bulk of the fighter force was massing further inland for a concentrated strike. Thick cloud was also building up inland and the feeling among the B-17 crews was that the mission should be aborted. Brigadier General Robert B. Travis, who had assumed command of the 1st Wing from Brigadier General Williams, circled Stuttgart for approximately thirty minutes in a vain attempt to find the target. Claude Campbell flying in the 303rd formation behind Travis recalls:

> We flew around dodging flak, trying to find a hole in the overcast. Fighters were flying around as bewildered as we were. Eventually we dropped our bombs on God knows where [they hit a wheat field] and began to fight our way home.

The 388th was flying low Group to the 96th's lead in the 2nd Task Force. Their slot in the overall formation was known in military parlance as 'coffin corner'. Things began to go wrong shortly after the B-17s reached France. Heavy clouds surrounded Stuttgart, causing the bomber stream to break up as groups began seeking targets of opportunity in France and Germany. Approximately 150 fighters attacked the low groups and the low squadron of the 388th, the 563rd, was hit by flak after the IP (Initial Point) and finished off by fighters. *Shedowanna?*, flown by Lieutenant Earl S. Melville, was set on fire in the nose and one engine. Five of the crew managed to bale out near Strasbourg. The tail gunner was killed when the tail was blown off. Lieutenant James A. Roe Jr's *Silver Dollar* and Lieutenant Richard N. Cunningham's *In God We Trust*, which went down near Troyes, and Lieutenant Alfred Kramer's *Lone Wolf* were lost also. Cunningham's crew baled out and all except the pilot, who returned to England in late October, were captured. Flight Officer Myron A. Bowen's *Sky Shy* was badly hit by flak. The crew tried unsuccessfully to reach Switzerland and had to bale out near Ülm. The radioman was murdered by German civilians. *Wolf Pack*, flown by Lieutenant Edward A. Wick, had lost an engine on the way in and was then hit by flak on the bomb run. They left the formation and were attacked by fighters who blew off the right wing and the B-17 went into a spin. When *Wolf Pack* settled momentarily the crew baled out. Three men were killed. *Shack-Up*, Lieutenant Roy H. Mohr Jr's B-17, and another flown by Lieutenant Ray T. Wilken were shot down near Paris. There were no survivors on board

Wilken's Fortress, which had a fire in the nose from 20mm cannon. Mohr and three of his crew were killed. *Slightly Dangerous*, flown by 1st Lieutenant Demetrious Karnezis, was attacked by two 'Yellow Noses' at La Chapelle-Champigny, about sixty miles south-east of Paris. The plane caught fire and five of the crew were able to bale out. 1st Lieutenant William P. Beecham put *Impatient Virgin II* down in Switzerland. 1st Lieutenant Lewis M. Miller left the formation and crashed with the loss of seven crewmen. By the time Spitfires rendezvoused with the formation south of Bernay, six of the 563rd Squadron's aircraft had been shot down. Altogether, the 388th lost eleven of the twenty-one B-17s dispatched; the highest loss it had sustained on a raid since joining the Eighth in June 1943.

Many more Fortresses came off their targets with their bomb loads intact and 233 bombers released their bombs on targets of opportunity en route to the enemy coast. Ten B-17s in the 'Bloody Hundredth' attacked airfields in France for the loss of two Fortresses. One crash-landed and nine men were taken prisoner while *Raunchy*, piloted by Lieutenant Sam Turner, was knocked out of formation and headed for Switzerland, where it was demolished while ditching on Lake Constance. Joe Moloney, the ball turret gunner, had been killed, hit by a 20mm shell between the shoulder blades, but the remaining nine men in the crew survived despite some terrible injuries. By the time the B-17s were east of Paris red lights began to show on the fuel gauges and many crews began to wonder if they would reach England.

On the Stuttgart raid Second Lieutenant Chauncey H. Hicks, twenty-seven, son of Mr and Mrs Clarence Hicks of Chesapeake, was the bombardier in *Bomb-Boogie* in the 401st Squadron, 91st Bomb Group. Back home Chauncey attended high school in Chesapeake, graduated from Marshall College in Huntingdon and was well known as a toll collector on the Huntingdon Bridge. Overseas with the 8th Air Force, Chauncey was well liked for his skill as a bombardier, his infectious smile and his stability and sense of humour in the face of danger. Chauncey's combat career had a stormy beginning. His first daylight raid was over the German synthetic rubber plant at Hüls. His Fortress, *Old Ironsides*, sustained 150 enemy fighter attacks in a running battle lasting an hour and three quarters. On the way home the Fortress was forced to ditch in the North Sea with three engines out of commission, the tail wheel blown off, the landing gear dragging, the hydraulic system, and radio transmitter out, the top of the vertical tail shot away and the pilot's control severely damaged. *Old Ironsides* hit the water off the Belgian coast but the men were picked up by the efficient British Air-Sea-Rescue service within thirty minutes. During the battle a 20mm shell hit the nose gun Chauncey was firing.

> It knocked me clear back against the navigator, tore off my oxygen mask and inflated my Mae West life vest. 'Fragments peppered the side of my face and burst my eardrum. I was lying on the floor shaking like a leaf, but I looked out and saw more Focke Wulfs coming in. So I got back to my gun and started shooting better than ever because I knew they were out to get me. That's when I shot down my second FW.

They sent Chauncey to a rest home in southern England for a week. On his second raid he took part in the blitz on Hamburg late in July. The oxygen system was hit at 28,000 feet and the navigator lapsed into unconsciousness. Hicks took off his mask to revive the navigator and then passed out himself. When he regained consciousness he found that two of the B-17's engines were out of commission and that the top turret gunner had been shot in the arm. He administered first aid to the gunner and gave him a shot of morphine to deaden the pain.

Coming back across the North Sea the fuel gauge dropped to virtually zero and the men were throwing out guns and ammunition in an effort to lighten the ship. Chauncey thought he was going to be dunked in the water again. But the Fortress managed to reach England and land with only five minutes' supply of gasoline in its tanks.

Hicks was known as 'Tiger' at Bassingbourn and before a mission he would sit in the operations office and hum church hymns. He always carried a world atlas with him on raids 'to plan my escape in case I am shot down.'

Stuttgart was Chauncey's thirteenth raid and his Fortress did not return. *Bomb-Boogie* crashed at Laon in France after being attacked by enemy fighters. Chauncey Hicks and the five others were captured and taken into captivity.[18]

Four of Lieutenant Elwood D. Arp's crew evaded capture and the six others were captured and taken into captivity.

Forty-five B-17s altogether were lost, eighteen of them ditching in the sea. The 92nd, which lost three B-17s shot down over the continent, lost four more when they were forced to ditch in the Channel. Lieutenant Frederick T. Prasse ditched his aircraft only six miles off the French coast off Le Havre and the crew were picked up shortly afterward. Captain Blair Belongia, 1st Lieutenant John O. Booker and 2nd Lieutenant Robert O.

Carlson were also out of fuel and they were forced to ditch too. All three crews were rescued without incident. 2nd Lieutenant Basil M. Jones Jr crash-landed at Penhurst with slight injuries to three crew members.

At Bassingbourn there was no sign of two Fortresses. *Frisco Jennie* and *Connecticut Yankee* were 'gliding' across the English Channel, each on a single engine. *Frisco Jennie* was on her twenty-sixth raid; the *Connecticut Yankee* on its thirty-ninth. They both reached the English coast but neither would fly back to bomb the enemy again. The fuel tank from the *Yankee*'s last engine went dry as the B-17 hit the coast. The pilot, 2nd Lieutenant William G. Pegram, of Guilford College, North Carolina, ordered the nine members of his crew to bale out near Winchelsea while the bombers still had sufficient altitude and then he made a 'dead stick' belly landing in a swamp at pit level with the wheels up and all four engines out. 'It was a smooth landing – not even a jar,' Pegram said. 'The muddy swamp was just like grease.' The left waist gunner, Sergeant Frederick E. Hutchinson of Oakland, California, parachuted into a field where he was accosted by two British soldiers who demanded identification. When Staff Sergeant Hans W. Wobst, of Southampton, Long Island, New York hit the ground he was approached by Home Guardsmen, farmers with pitchforks and six women – one of whom had a first aid kit. Second Lieutenant Robert S. Cosgrove, of Dubuque, Iowa, the navigator, had to rip the canvas cover off his parachute to get it open. When he was twenty feet above the tree tops his chute collapsed and he dropped through the trees, but he was not seriously injured. Tech Sergeant Vernon C. Larson, top turret gunner, who was from Los Angeles commented that 'England is hard, but nice'.[19]

Frisco Jennie was ditched in the sea rather than crashing on land with the crew aboard. Second Lieutenant William R. Cox, pilot from Roswell, New Mexico, made a smooth landing on the water just 200 yards off shore. 'The landing was easier than we expected' said 2nd Lieutenant William R. James of Miami, Florida, the co pilot. 'There was no crash and thee ship floated for about an hour.' Half of the crew climbed into a rubber life raft and the other half remained in the water, hanging onto the dinghy. They kicked their way to within about 100 yards of the shore and were picked up by a coast guard boat after an hour.

The 388th Bomb Group were flying low Group to the 96th's lead in the 2nd Task Force. In military parlance their slot in the overall formation was known as 'coffin corner'. Things began to go wrong shortly after the B-17s reached France. Heavy clouds surrounded Stuttgart, causing the bomber stream to break up as groups began seeking targets of opportunity in France and Germany. Approximately 150 fighters attacked the low groups and the low squadron of the 388th, the 563rd, was hit by flak after the IP (Initial Point) and finished off by fighters. *Shedowanna?*, flown by Lieutenant Earl S. Melville, was set on fire in the nose and one engine. Five of the crew managed to bale out near Strasbourg. The tail gunner was killed when the tail was blown off. Lieutenant James A. Roe Jr's *Silver Dollar* and Lieutenant Richard N. Cunningham's *In God We Trust*, which went down near Troyes, and Lieutenant Alfred Kramer's *Lone Wolf* were lost also. Cunningham's crew baled out and all except the pilot, who returned to England in late October, were captured. Flight Officer Myron A. Bowen's *Sky Shy* was badly hit by flak. The crew tried unsuccessfully to reach Switzerland and had to bale out near Ülm. The radioman was murdered by German civilians. *Wolf Pack*, flown by Lieutenant Edward A. Wick, had lost an engine on the way in and was then hit by flak on the bomb run. They left the formation and were attacked by fighters who blew off the right wing and the B-17 went into a spin. When *Wolf Pack* settled momentarily the crew baled out. Three men were killed. *Shack-Up*, Lieutenant Roy H. Mohr Jr's B-17, and another flown by Lieutenant Ray T. Wilken were shot down near Paris. There were no survivors on board Wilken's Fortress, which had a fire in the nose from 20mm cannon. Mohr and three of his crew were killed. *Slightly Dangerous*, flown by 1st Lieutenant Demetrious Karnezis, was attacked by two 'Yellow Noses' at La Chapelle-Champigny, about sixty miles south-east of Paris. The plane caught fire and five of the crew were able to bale out. 1st Lieutenant William P. Beecham put *Impatient Virgin II* down in Switzerland. 1st Lieutenant Lewis M. Miller left the formation and crashed with the loss of seven crewmen. By the time Spitfires rendezvoused with the formation south of Bernay, six of the 563rd Squadron's aircraft had been shot down. Altogether, the 388th lost eleven of the twenty-one B-17s dispatched; the highest loss it had sustained on a raid since joining the 8th in June 1943.

Lieutenant Belford J. 'BJ' Keirsted's crew and twenty-eight others had been assigned to a replacement pool and after five days they were rushed to Knettishall, to the depleted 563rd Squadron. Tech Sergeant Larry 'Goldie' Goldstein, the twenty-one-year-old radio-operator, had joined the crew after volunteering for flying status in Salt Lake City at a replacement depot. He was hustled off to aerial gunnery school even before he had a chance to rethink his decision but 'Goldie' and his GI friends were impressed with the glamour of flying and all that went with it, the silver wings of a gunner, the promotions and the flight pay. But all that was about to change, as 'Goldie' recalls:

We were with a group of thirty that trained in the States. Of the thirty crews, only about five survived intact to finish twenty-five. We went overseas as a crew of ten, on the *Queen Mary*. I wondered when I would see New York again. 'So long America – see you soon' I said. We were bunked in stacked beds three high in very cramped quarters. The ship was divided into three sections, red, white and blue. All personnel were to stay in their assigned area. There were two meals a day, breakfast and dinner. The meals were very bad and most men chose to miss them and survived on Hershey bars and oranges. Every day a life boat drill was held. Each man was issued a life jacket. It added a very ominous tone to the trip. Fortunately the trip across the Atlantic was completed in five days. The night we arrived at Knettishall it was rainy, dark and cold; a typical English night. When we entered our Quonset hut, which held six crews of six enlisted men apiece, there were six men lying around on their bunks. The other thirty beds were vacant with their mattresses all rolled up. The six men were all from Thibodeau's crew who flew a B-17 called *Pegasus*. When we asked 'Why the empty beds?' we were told they were left by the men who had gone down recently. This was rather discouraging.

Our pilot was a strong quiet man from Uniontown, Pennsylvania, a tough coal town. 'BJ' had a dark, brooding look about him. He and his sister Dorothy had toured the country before the war as the ballroom dance team of 'Jan and Janis' (Belford and Dorothy apparently lacked pizzazz). At our first meeting 'BJ' asked us to work hard, become proficient at our jobs and possibly some day one of us might be responsible for the rest of the crew's survival. He along with our co-pilot 'Ace' Conklin prodded us to achieve perfection and at the same time were also working hard to sharpen their skills. Cliff Conklin was a Jock from New Paltz, New York State. He had been a business student. When Conklin was assigned to Keirsted's crew he was crestfallen. He thought, 'I don't want to be with this crew – we've got a ballroom dancer for a pilot!' but Keirsted proved he had more on the ball than a set of twinkletoes. Quiet, reserved, he exuded a calm authority that was universally respected and admired. When we met our first ground crew chief and our own plane was assigned to us, 'BJ' asked him how many crews he had. He said 'you are my third, the other two went down'. BJ's' answer to him was, 'We will make it, you can mark it down.' We were not as sure as he was, but his self-confidence rubbed off on us.

Beside the pilots, our crew was composed of Kent 'Cap' Keith the bombardier, a sheep rancher from near Ekalaka, Montana. Phil Brejensky, navigator, was also Jewish and from Brooklyn too. In training Kent Keith had given him the nickname 'Bloodhound', joking that there was a dog on his Montana ranch that could find his way home better than Brejensky. Jack Kings, waist gunner, from Huntington, West Virginia had never met anyone Jewish before. As a kid he fished for food. It was something to eat besides rice and beans. In the depths of the Great Depression his family was too poor to afford new shoes so they stuffed cardboard soles in the old ones.

'We kind of came up the hard way' he recalled. Later, in combat his attitude was, 'If you got hit, you were hit. If you didn't, you made it. I could never see any point worrying about it.' E. V. 'Pete' Lewelling the other waist gunner was a good ol' boy from Zolfo Springs, Florida. The tail gunner, Bob Miller, was a lunk from Chicago, Illinois and a loner. Howard 'Howie' Palmer, engineer, was from New Hampshire. He also was an ex-student and hailed from Boston. The ball turret gunner, Tech Sergeant Willie Suggs, came from South Carolina.

We soon fell into routine flying practice, practice and more practice. It seems that the 388th command demanded precision tight formation flying and we flew on many days. Tight formation flying brought more guns to bear and increased our overall protection. Enemy fighters seldom hit good formation flying outfits.

On 13 September VIII Bomber Command was officially divided into three bombardment divisions.[20] Colonel Leon Johnson moved from the 'Flying Eightballs' to command the 14th Combat Wing and Lieutenant Colonel James L. Posey, was promoted to command the 'Eightballs'. The changes did not stop there. At Chelveston, the 305th lost its 422nd Squadron, which became a night leaflet squadron, dropping propaganda literature over Germany. Ten months earlier the squadron had been earmarked for such a task, but daylight operations had continued to take precedence over night operations. The 422nd was not the only outfit to begin practising night missions. During the month the 94th practised taking off in squadrons and assembling as a group at night. The reason became apparent on 16 September when the heavies returned to the French Atlantic coast in what was then the longest trip planned by VIII Bomber Command. The 1st Bomb Division was assigned the port installations at Nantes while the longer range B-17s of the 3rd Bomb Division flew further south to bomb an aircraft plant at Bordeaux, at the mouth of the Gironde.

This involved a 1,600-mile round trip lasting eleven hours and meant that their return would be made in darkness. A third, smaller, formation would bomb Cognac airfield and act as a diversionary thrust for the two larger formations.

Claude Campbell in the 303rd went to Nantes.

It was our roughest raid yet. I never expected to get our ship back to England. I was leading the top squadron in our group that led the wing. FW 190s hit us hard after our P-47 escort left us but we evaded them. However, we encountered accurate flak over the target and the oil line to our number three engine was cut. We couldn't feather the propeller and the engine began to vibrate terrifically. It was so intense the bulbs in the instrument panel broke loose. Finally, the pistons seized and the propeller crankshaft broke and the prop' began to windmill at very high RPMs. We could not maintain more than 150mph without causing excessive vibration. I expected the prop' to come off at any minute and either cut me in two or wreck the plane.

The co-pilot told Howard Hernan, the top turret gunner, to look around for a good place to crash land.

I took a look and if anywhere would be good it was one of the many wheat fields. But I wasn't on my twenty-fourth mission about to make a crash-landing. I was for trying to fight it back home. I told the pilots it didn't look good. With that Campbell said he was going to try and get us home. He put the nose down and dived for the deck from 28,000 feet. But the rest of the squadron stayed with us because they didn't know we had an engine out. Ordinarily, it was a, 'no-no' as they were supposed to go back with the rest of the group. It was all that saved us.

Campbell continues:

Over the Bay of Biscay six Me 110s jumped us as we skirted Brest and made one pass at the formation, missing me but hitting my right wingman, Lieutenant Manning, and cutting his rudder cable in two. The next pass got my left wingman, Lieutenant Baker, cutting his oil lines but neither of the two ships was knocked down. By this time I had reached cloud cover which I took advantage of. One Fort, which was straggling along on our left, was knocked down by the Me 110s when they made another pass at us, which we avoided. We knocked down two of the Me 110s on their final pass and then shook the rest off in the clouds. We flew for over three-quarters of an hour with the prop' windmilling. Miraculously, the prop' stayed on and we landed at an RAF base at Exeter. Never did I welcome terra firma more. We had lost no planes from our group but the day's operation cost us thirteen bombers and bombing results were poor.

The third formation of B-17s, led by the 94th, visited Cognac airfield. However, only twenty-one bombers from the Rougham Group managed to find and hit the target because of thick cloud. The formation made its way back to England in gathering darkness but the 94th put down without difficulty thanks to its night practice mission a few days before. Groups in the force that attacked Bordeaux were not so fortunate. Just off the south-west coast of England the B-17s encountered heavy rain squalls and this and the impending darkness dispersed the formation. The storm front knocked radio altimeters about 1,000 feet out of calibration and many pilots got into difficulties. One B-17 ditched in the sea off the Northumberland coast after thirteen hours of flight, culminating in a vain search for an airfield. *Ascend Charlie* in the 390th suffered a similar fate when it crashed at Abergavenny, Wales. All of Lieutenant Herbert I. Turner's crew were killed.

In the 388th *Sandra Kay*, flown by 1st Lieutenant H. O. Cox, Jr, crashed just south of RAF Shobden and all ten crew members were killed. Second Lieutenant Henry J. Nagorka ditched *Old Ironsides* in the sea just north of The Wash. The two waist gunners drowned and the tail gunner lost a leg. *Gremlin Gus* flown by Lieutenant Jarrend crashed into the side of a hill at North Moulton, killing Ed Baliff, the cameraman, and seriously injuring the navigator and bombardier. Three others in the crew were slightly injured. The luckiest man on board must have been James F. Jones, the tail gunner. Shortly before *Gremlin Gus* crashed, it touched a hilltop and Jones was thrown violently against the tail gunner's door, which gave way, throwing him out into space as he pulled the ripcord. He spun through the air as his parachute released; the billowing silk helping to cushion his body as he hit the ground at around 200mph. Jones was knocked unconscious and he rolled almost 100 yards before stopping. About two hours later he remembered awaking and seeing a red flare in the sky. Incredibly, his only injuries consisted of a badly sprained leg and several bruises and contusions. When he arrived back at Knettishall, fellow group members listened to his story in utter amazement.

On 15 September a few heavy bombers flew a night mission with the RAF against the Montluçon Dunlop tyre factory. During the day almost 140 bombers attacked the Renault works and a ball-bearing plant at Paris, while a comparable force attacked airfields at Chartres and Romilly-sur-

Seine. Crews could have been forgiven for thinking they were now engaged on nocturnal missions because their return was made in darkness. Staff Sergeant John W. Butler from Wayland, Massachusetts, a gunner in *Tarfu* in the 'Travelling Circus' was on only his third mission. He recalls:

> We hit our target, which was the airfield at St André, pretty damn good. We really were on the beam. On the way back it was pretty dark and some fool started firing at a flak burst. Then someone mistook a B-24 for a bandit and set his No. 2 engine on fire. They all started to fire at the poor devil. Four 'chutes got out. I really sweated it out as tracers were going all over Hell. It was also the first night landing in the ETO. We landed back at Hardwick at 2125 hours. There was an air raid on when we arrived back over England and the sky was really lit up with searchlights.[21]

Next day the long-range B-17s of the 3rd Bomb Division flew a 1,600-mile; 11-hour round trip to Bordeaux to bomb an aircraft plant and their return was also made in darkness. Before this mission crews had, however, practised taking off in squadrons and assembling as a group at night. Just off the south-west coast of England the B-17s encountered heavy rainsqualls and these, plus the impending darkness, dispersed the formation. The storm front knocked radio altimeters about 1,000 feet out of calibration and many pilots got into difficulties. Three B-17s ditched in the North Sea and two others crashed, killing all ten crew in one Fortress and one crewmember in the other. The 1st Bomb Division encountered heavy fighter opposition on its mission to the port installations at Nantes, while most of the twenty-one B-17s in a diversionary force, which headed for Cognac airfield, failed to bomb because of thick cloud over the target. In all, the 8th lost thirteen bombers on the day's raids.

The 'Flying Eightballs', the 'Travelling Circus' and the 'Sky Scorpions' were ordered to North Africa again for a short time in mid-September, when the Salerno landings appeared to be in jeopardy. Meanwhile, on the morning of 24 September crews were alerted for a mission to Stuttgart again but adverse weather forced its cancellation. 'Pappy' Colby recalls:

> At 1130 they decided to have a wing formation practice mission following a Pathfinder aircraft and bombing a simulated target in the North Sea.

Bomb loads were hastily changed and machine-guns re-installed. The B-17s completed assembly without incident but over the North Sea about fifteen German fighters bounced them. Colby continues:

Of course we had no fighter cover. They shot down one ship in the group behind me. As it glided down, one 'chute came out and then it blew up. Seven Bf 109s came on through and one started an attack on us, as I was the last airplane. Luckily, our tail gunner had gotten his twin fifties installed and he fired a long burst and the fighter turned away.

In the 'Bloody Hundredth' formation, *Damifino II* came in for some particularly heavy attacks by fighters using the sun to excellent advantage. They raked the fuselage and a 20mm shell started a fire in the oil tank behind the No. 3 engine. Lieutenant John G. Gossage, the pilot, held the aircraft steady while all the crew baled out. Theodore J. Don, the bombardier, baled out at 1,000 feet and hit the sea almost at the instant his 'chute deployed. He was later rescued by a flotilla of MTBs en route to the Dutch coast but the co-pilot and the navigator were dead when they were picked up. The two waist gunners and the ball turret gunner were never found. The bomber hit the sea nose down and quickly began to sink. Gossage was trapped but managed to pull himself free and float safely to the surface.

The H2S radar trials carried out on 23 September proved so impressive that General Eaker instructed that similarly equipped Fortresses should accompany the force of 305 bombers to Emden on 27 September. This small port was handling about 500,000 tons of shipping a month as a result of damage inflicted on Hamburg. Emden was also chosen because of its proximity to water, which would show up reasonably well on the cathode ray tubes. In all, 244 bombers hit the target and the Fortresses, which bombed with the aid of H2S-equipped B-17s, and did remarkably well. One of the three combat wings in the 3rd Division managed to bomb visually after exploiting a gap in the clouds but subsequent photographic reconnaissance proved that only the H2S-assisted formations had achieved a fair concentration of bombs on Emden. Other bomb patterns ranged as far as five miles away from the city. Back at Snetterton Heath ordnance experts studied one of the largest pieces of flak yet known to have struck an American bomber at operational altitude – a 12lb chunk of steel eight inches wide and almost three feet long. The flak fragment imbedded itself in the upper side of the B-17 *Skin and Bones*' left wing just as the bomber, piloted by 1st Lieutenant Franklin Berry of Poughkeepsie, New York, left the target area over Emden. Ordnance men said that from a preliminary examination of the flak it probably came from a shell or rocket weighing at least 125lb.

Orlo Natvig, a radio operator in the 91st, was captured on 27 September when his B-17, *Local Girl*, was shot down over Holland after dropping its bombs on Emden. *Local Girl* was attacked by Bf 109s that made their attacks from below because the ball turret was out of action, the gunner having passed out through lack of oxygen. The No. 2 engine was set on fire and a shell exploded in the radio compartment. Splinters missed Natvig by inches. The intercom was knocked out and most of the crew began evacuating the aircraft. 2nd Lieutenant William G. Pegram, the pilot, remained true to his word that in the event of an emergency he would remain at the controls to allow the rest of the crew to bale out. (The brave pilot was later found dead among the wreckage of the bomber.) Eight men baled out of the doomed bomber over the coast of Eems. For some it was a close shave, as Natvig recalls:

Staff Sergeant Hutchinson, the waist gunner, and I put a parachute on the ball turret gunner and pushed him through the waist door hatch, pulling his ripcord as he went. I pulled at the coveralls of Melvin Peters, the other waist gunner, to get him to go with us but he made no effort to follow us and we did not have time to force him, as he was still hanging on to his waist gun. (Peters went down with *Local Girl*, firing his gun to the end.) Larson the engineer and Cosgrove the navigator, drowned when the cords of their parachutes became entangled in the *botschuttings* or 'flounder fences' – a device of twigs and branches to catch fish – and in their heavy clothing they were powerless. Norman Eatinger the bombardier was more fortunate. He was rescued by a Dutch fisherman who at that moment was fishing on the Dollart and rushed to the scene.

I landed on a *huielder* behind a dyke about 200 yards outside the village of Ouderdom. I had missed landing in the water by only 100 feet. I noticed a group of people coming towards me. I got out of my parachute, gathered it together and walked over to meet them. One of the group was a policeman so I raised my arms to show I had no weapons. I handed over my parachute to the civilians and gave away my escape and emergency ration kits. One of the Dutch people made a wedding dress from my parachute and another used part of it for a christening set. I asked a young Dutch lad about half my age if there was any chance of escape. He said the area was heavily defended and the Germans would arrive shortly. I was taken to the cafe of Jan van der Laan and taken prisoner by the Germans who lost no time in getting to the scene. It was quite a shock to have a fully fledged German officer walk up to me brandishing a .38 pistol and cocking it before he reached me. He stuck it in my stomach and my blood turned to water.[22]

Notes

1. *Luck Is No Lady, First of the Many* (1944). Born John Reagan McCrary in 1910 in Calvert, Texas, the son of a cotton farmer hurt by the Depression later attended Phillips Exeter Academy and Yale where he was a member of Skull and Bones. He started in journalism as a copy boy at the *New York World-Telegram*. He left to join the *Daily Mirror*, later becoming its chief editorial writer. After divorcing his first wife in 1939, McCrary began writing the column '*Only Human*' and in 1941 met Jinx Falkenburg. When he interviewed her, she was starring in Broadway tuner *Hold Onto Your Hats* with Al Jolson. McCrary joined the AAC in WWII and became a photographer and PR officer. In 1945 he was one of the first Americans to visit Hiroshima after the atomic bomb was dropped. He advised journalists not to write about what they had seen because he did not think Americans could stand to know 'what we've done here'. After John Hersey published his account in the *New Yorker*, McCrary said, 'I covered it up and John Hersey uncovered it. That's the difference between a PR man and a reporter.' After the war McCrary edited the American *Mercury* magazine. He soon renewed his friendship with Jinx Falkenburg, who had become a star under contract at MGM and was one of the nation's highest-paid models. They were married in June 1945. Although they were separated years later, they never divorced. McCrary and his wife had two radio talk shows, *Hi Jinx* and *Meet Tex and Jinx* and a TV show, sometimes broadcasting from Gotham's Waldorf-Astoria Hotel where they could nab celebs, as they stopped to pick up their room keys. McCrary died aged ninety-two in New York.

2. The *Bolevich* was shot down en route to Schweinfurt and all of Merchant's crew were taken prisoner. See *The Schweinfurt-Regensburg Mission* by Martin Middlebrook (Penguin 1983).

3. Of all the bombardment groups in WWII perhaps the 100th BG is the best known. In the less than two years the 100th was in action in Europe, the 'Bloody Hundredth' lost 229 Fortresses – 177 MIA and 52 from 'other operational losses'. It is the third highest total among 8th AF units: More precisely, the 100th had the highest loss rate among its sister groups for the twenty-two months it was operational. When it left England in 1945 the 'Bloody Hundredth' had become perhaps the most famous, albeit 'jinxed' BG in the 8th.

4. *Eighth Air Force: The American Bomber Crews in Britain* by Donald L. Miller (Aurum 2007). Miller also states that when Colonel Curtis E. LeMay visited Thorpe Abbotts for an inspection, a rowdy corporal sped by him in a truck pulling a bomb trailer, nearly hitting him. Minutes later, a jeep driven by a crew chief slammed into the side of the Colonel's command car. LeMay found

the men's quarters in wild disarray, with beds unmade, empty rum bottles littering the floor and laundry piled in rank-smelling heaps. When he asked to see Gale Cleven, having heard that he and John Egan were the source of the group's 'raunchy discipline; a sergeant told him that the squadron leader was nowhere to be found.'

5. On 25 February 1944 Colonel 'Chick' Harding led the Third Division on the raid on Regensburg. He was suffering from jaundice and gall stones but had 'simply refused' to report to the medics. By early March preparations were being put in hand to send him back to the United States for an operation. Meanwhile, Colonel John Bennett assumed temporary command at Thorpe Abbotts. On 15 March Harding, who had been acting CO of the 13th Combat Wing, flew back to the USA but before he left he did 'a masterly job of buzzing headquarters – firing flares like one of the boys completing his missions'. *Century Bombers; The Story of the Bloody Hundredth* by Richard Le Strange.

6. The ball turret gunner evaded also (7 PoW).

7. British-born Anne Brusselsman, a thirty-nine-year-old mother of two, risked her own life, as well as the lives of her husband and two young children and an estimated 130 Allied airmen eventually found their way to freedom because of her efforts. Hank never forgot the kindness and sacrifices made by Anne Brusselsmans and her family and stayed in close contact throughout his life. He enjoyed a long career in the USAF and retired at the rank of Lt Colonel in 1965. He and Regina raised twin daughters, Roberta and Regina. Hank died at the age of seventy-eight in 1999. Submitted by Dr Vivian Rogers-Price Research Center Director, Mighty Eighth Air Force Museum.

8. The 390th had placed 58 per cent of its bombs within 1,000 feet of the MPI and 94 per cent with 2,000 feet. The last two groups over the target, the 95th and 100th, added their incendiary clusters to the conflagration, which was now marked by a rectangular pillar of smoke towering to 10,000 feet.

9. All ten men were taken prisoner.

10. *The Mighty Men of the 381st, Heroes All: A Chaplain's Inside Story of the men of the 381st Bomb Group* by James Good Brown (Salt Lake City: Publishers Press 1994).

11. James Judy and the crew of *The Old Stand By* were shot down on 9 October 1943 on the mission to Anklam. Judy and Earl Cherry and seven others survived to be taken into captivity.

12. All ten crew survived to be taken prisoner.

13. Harry Lay joined the 84th Fighter Squadron, 78th Fighter Group at Duxford. After losing his original owner, 'Major', an Alsatian dog, eventually took up with the Captain. The mornings of his missions, 'Major' and Harry would walk together out to the P-47. On the morning of 17 July 1944 they changed their routine and rode together in a Jeep out to his P-47. By 1018 hours, Lay

was strafing a German troop train near Liffel-le-Grand, France. His P-47 was quickly crippled by AA fire and he had to take to his parachute, which dropped him safely into a field and he was seen to run into some woods to the east. Troops from the train swarmed after him as the circling P-47s held them back with their wing-guns. Inevitably the Thunderbolts ran out of ammo and were forced to leave Captain Lay to the mercy of the avenging troops. Harry Lay's exact fate was never determined. At the end of the war the father of 'Major's first master came to England and took the dog back to America with him. *Eagles of Duxford: The 78th Fighter Group in World War II* by Garry L. Fry (Phalanx Publishing Co Ltd 1991)

14. *Patches*, flown by Douglas Mutschler who was from Goodrich, North Dakota, came under attack by a FW 190 piloted by Adolf Glunz. Two of *Patches'* engines were set on fire and while the crew were baling out, the B-17 exploded killing Mutschler and two of his crew.

15. Adapted from *Hartford Is Heaven in First of the Many* by Tex McCrary who talked to the survivors a few nights later in London.

16. See *Clash of Eagles* by Martin W. Bowman (Pen & Sword 2006).

17. *Eager Beaver* had collided with B-17 41-24523 *Snooks* in the 323rd Bomb Squadron flown by Lieutenant Richard C. Rodman. Allen was the only survivor from the two B-17s; only two bodies were pulled from the sea.

18. Chauncey Hicks escaped from the continent and rejoined his Squadron on 29 March 1944.

19. Lieutenant Pegram and crew and *Local Girl* were lost on 27 September when they were shot down by Bf 109s over Holland on the raid on Emden. Pegram remained at the controls to allow the rest of the crew time to bale out and he was found dead in the wreckage of the aircraft. Eight men baled out of the doomed Fortress. Melvin Peters, one of the waist gunners, went down with *Local Girl*, firing his gun to the end. See *Home By Christmas?* by Martin W. Bowman (PSL 1987).

20. The nine groups in the 1st Bomb Wing formed the 1st Bomb Division, commanded by General Travis and the six B-17 groups forming the 4th BW were renamed the 3rd BD, under Colonel Curtis E. LeMay. All four 202nd Combat Bomb Wing (Provisional) Liberator groups became the 2nd Bomb Division, under the command of General James Hodges, with its HQ at Ketteringham Hall.

21. *Tarfu* and Lt Andrew M. Reynolds' crew FTR on 4 January 1944. Six men were KIA and three survived to be taken prisoner.

22. Natvig and five others were transported to *Dulag Luft* at Frankfurt, stopping off at a German fighter base at Jevers.

CHAPTER 3

Night and Day

The raid went off like a military drill. It's not often you come back from a mission in which everything went off to perfection. I was particularly impressed by the discipline of our men. Our bombs went down together over the target. It was a good show and I was very pleased with it.

Brigadier General Robert B. Travis speaking to reporters after the Emden mission, Monday 2 October

At Great Ashfield Lieutenant Robert 'Tex' Taylor's B-17 crew in the 385th Bomb Group waited impatiently to fly the first of their twenty-five missions. In early September the crew had left Grand Island, Nebraska, and flown the northern route to England via Bangor, Maine, to start the first leg of the journey to Goose Bay Labrador. Next day they were over the ocean again. They saw a large convoy and several icebergs before landfall in Greenland. The next hop was to Iceland and they ran into bad weather before they landed. Lieutenant Joel Punches, navigator, recalled:

It was fall at home, but winter in Iceland. The weather kept us grounded and we were forced to lay over a day. Some of us started to hike down to a fishing village along the cold blue sea, but we 'aborted' that chilly walk. Iceland was a cold, windy and barren place full of boulders. Someone later said that Icelanders sided with the Germans, so it was probably a good thing we turned back. Next day the weather eased up, but we weren't cleared for take-off until noon, several hours later we landed safely at Prestwick, Scotland. We had flown the northern route across the North Atlantic in about a week. Our next 400-mile trip was in a carriage of a small English train to temporary quarters and a training site for new arrivals north of London. The classrooms were cold Quonset huts. We had five days of survival classes on about everything from ditching a plane to how to escape if shot down over enemy territory. In our free time we learned that English beer (bitters) was really bitter, Nazi 'buzz bombs' could hit any time and there were four girls for every guy at the local dances. English blackouts were strictly enforced because German bombing raids were a constant threat. One night, they hit an airfield about ten miles north of us. We heard the explosions and flashes of the exploding bombs lit up the night. Two weeks later we finished the training classes and were assigned to the 385th Bomb Group. We packed our bags, boarded army trucks and moved out to our combat base.

Now, we thought we were ready to take a bomber into combat, but we were wrong. New aircrews were needed, but not until they were ready. Group commanders, mission leaders and every bomb crewman wanted to be sure the 'replacements' were ready to fly in a combat formation. Nobody wanted a bunch of 'greenhorns' flying close formation with them on a mission. Mid-air collisions were too frequent and too deadly! Therefore, new crews spent the next nine days in classes on the ground and in the air over England. It was great to get aboard a B-17 and back into the air. Ground instructors and those on the training flights made sure every man knew what to expect on long high altitude missions.

Our training did not keep us isolated from the realities of war. I suppose the same type of events were happening at our other forty two heavy bomber bases in England, but it did seem like our base was extremely active. A loaded B-17 with 23,000 gallons of gas caught fire in the flight line and exploded killing a fireman and blowing the engines two blocks away. A plane in the landing pattern ran out of gas and crashed with no survivors. A gunner on the flight line accidently fired his 50 calibre machine gun and killed a ground crew mechanic. One night an RAF plane on fire, spun and crashed near the base. Our 'final exam': a simulated mission of all three squadrons (fifty planes) out over the North Sea was a practice mission, so none of the bombers had machine guns. The lead navigator took us out too far and we ended up about twenty miles from the Dutch coast and a German airbase (Schiphol). We turned tail and ran for home, but three Me 109 fighters hit the rear squadron and shot down two B-17s before anyone knew they were there. One bomber exploded and the other managed to 'ditch' in the North Sea. We lost two bombers and twenty men. Those fighters could have shot down everyone our unarmed planes! Somebody should be court-martialled for that fiasco!

Finally, on 28 September we went on our first mission, to Rheims. We flew 130 miles into France to bomb an airbase with an escort of P-47 fighters for protection. We had some flak on the way in, but could not drop our bombs because of the overcast. We saw ten Me 110 fighters on the way home but they did not attack. We dropped our bombs in the English Channel and were cruising along at about 7,000 feet about ten miles from home and safety when there was a mid-air collision! A pilot in a bomber off our left wing lost control. He came up and crashed into the plane ahead. His propellers cut off that plane's tail; it flipped and went down. Then a wing came off his plane and he crashed. Just then, our No. 2 engine caught fire. We put it out and made a good landing with three engines. Two bombers and crews were lost due to carelessness; only twenty-four missions to go!

H2S sets seemed to provide the answer to the 8th's problems and Eaker was anxious to use them again as soon as possible but a period of bad weather gave the technicians time to iron out some of the teething troubles before the bombers were dispatched to Emden again on Monday 2 October with two H2S-equipped aircraft in the 482nd Bomb Group. Brigadier General Robert B. Travis led the mission in *Little America*. This time the H2S sets worked perfectly, although inexperience resulted in one Pathfinder aircraft releasing its bombs too early and many B-17s dropped their loads short of the target. Winds also carried away smoke markers and spoilt the aim of the following formations.

Despite a strong P-47 escort the *Luftwaffe* was again up in force. *The Eightball*, piloted by Lieutenant Bill Cabral, in the 390th lost its No. 3 engine to flak and began trailing smoke. Cabral lost altitude and made a solo run on the docks at Emden. When he turned for home the bomber was still alone and therefore an easy target for preying *Luftwaffe* fighters. Lieutenant Richard H. Perry, the co-pilot, recalls:

It looked like the whole *Luftwaffe* was waiting for us at the German coast. I started calling them and our boys went to work at the guns.

Soon *The Eightball* had twenty fighters on its tail and Cabral was forced to dive as fast as he dared into cloud cover at 16,000 feet below. A fighter dived in at 12 o'clock and the whole bomber shuddered with the recoil as Lloyd J. Wamble opened fire from his top turret. Wamble hit the fighter in the fuel tanks and it exploded, showering the sky with debris and smoke. For the next twenty minutes *The Eightball* came in for repeated enemy attacks and two more fighters were shot down. Finally, *The Eightball* entered cloud cover at 3000 feet and Cabral asked the crew over the intercom if everyone was all right. Dean C. Ferris, bombardier, replied that he was but thought he had better mention that the No. 4 engine was on fire. Orange flames covered the wing and threatened to ignite the fuel tanks. By now *The Eightball* was over Holland and Cabral asked the crew if they wanted to bale out or keep going. All wanted to keep going.

Cabral steered the ailing bomber around the flak at Rotterdam and headed out across the North Sea towards England. *The Eightball* lost altitude rapidly and soon the badly damaged bomber was so low over the sea that salt spray entered the waist windows and splashed the gunners. The engine fire threatened to engulf the No. 3 engine and Cabral ordered the crew to take up their ditching positions. He was about to ditch, when in the distance he saw a large rolling wave and decided to fly through it, gambling that it would extinguish the raging fire. He took the B-17 in as low as he dared and the wave washed over the wing. Cabral and Perry threw the throttles forward and lifted *The Eightball* clear of the water. The fire was out! Cabral cancelled the SOS to Air-Sea Rescue (ASR) and flew on to the coast of England, where he brought *The Eightball* in for a smooth landing at an emergency base. As the aircraft hit the runway, the propeller of the No. 4 engine spun off and rolled some distance down the runway.

General Travis was pleased with the results. Apart from the bombing, losses had been negligible during this and previous raids on Emden. This was due mainly because the raids were carried out within the range of P-47s fitted with larger-capacity drop tanks. Also, the *Luftwaffe's* single-engined fighter pilots, ill trained for blind flying on instruments, had difficulty in making interceptions through overcast conditions.[1]

In the late afternoon of 3 October Lieutenant Thomas S. Seay's crew in the 422nd Squadron, 305th Bomb Group, was alerted to take part in a raid that night. His squadron had already done a few trips at night. The reason for the switch had been the heavy losses on the Schweinfurt mission and the need to conserve the crews while the whole strategy was re-assessed. They were assigned ship 42-3091 as it had 'Tokyo Tanks' (long-range fuel tanks) and their own *Sam's Little Helper* did not. Sergeant Bernard Resnicoff recalls:

> Our regular bombardier who was on pass, had been recalled for the mission but did not make it in time for the briefing at 1600 hours. Lieutenant Pierce was assigned in his place. Our regular ball turret gunner, S/Sgt Abbott, had a cold and was replaced by S/Sgt McCoy. I could have been grounded with a bad back that I had hurt on the

Munich raid two days before but as my crew was a few missions ahead of me, I said nothing. After this mission, we were due for some R & R, to which we were all looking forward. The target was to be Frankfurt, which the AAF had bombed that afternoon. The RAF officer briefed us on the Bomber Command times on target. We were to fly above them and bomb on their target indicators. Our load was 6 × 500lb HE, one photoflash for the camera shot and over a quarter of a million propaganda leaflets. There would be a diversionary attack near Frankfurt, which would hopefully draw off some of the night fighters. Our regular bombardier, Lieutenant Harkavy, arrived half way through the briefing. Our S-2 finished off with the usual weather, radio information and time check. We were scheduled to start engines at 1930 and take-off was at 2000. It was decided to go with Lieutenant Pierce as bombardier. We had no time to go to the mess hall for a meal and had to make do with a crummy sandwich, not exactly the best meal before a mission. We watched the planes from the day's mission land and then got on board the truck and went out to a tent beside '091'. After the crew did all their pre-flight checks, we sat around waiting to start engines and talked of what we would do on our leave. Lieutenant Troph, the co-pilot, handed us our escape kit, money, a Milky Way and a pack of gum.

Just as we were due to start engines, Lieutenant Seay decided to visit the toilet by the tent. It didn't take long but it was a delay we didn't need. I sat down on an empty ammo box while they started the engines. No. 1 started OK but No. 2 coughed and died. The ground crew swarmed all over it and we tried again. Two more attempts and then we were told to grab our gear and get over to '056' the stand-by ship. We piled on a jeep nearby and all you could see was ten men who seemed to be riding on something. They were still working on a generator on No. 1 engine but the crew chief said it would be fixed momentarily. I had a mad dash back to '091' for my oxygen mask and when I got back, I found that the 'stand-by' crew had not cleaned the guns. Ground crew offered to help but would only have got in the way. I wanted to do my own anyway as I recall that one armament had put in a gun for Williams, our left waist gunner, and when he went to charge it, he found the breech block had been put in backwards. We were set to go when we were told that the generator could not be fixed and that our original machine was now fixed, so once more, we scampered back to '091'. Tempers were getting short and everyone felt that the mission was 'jinxed'.

All four engines started, given a fast warm-up and we were on our way, thirty minutes late. At the end of the runway, we got the green light. Full power, brakes off and we rolled down the runway with the lights flashing past. A couple of gentle bounces and were in the air. At 1000 feet, we circled the field and set course over the tower, climbing out on course. I checked William's mask, he had just turned eighteen, and he checked mine. Lieutenant Troph called for check-in. Burney in the tail checked in first, then Williams and myself; McCoy in the ball, Cox in the radio room and finally Browser in the top turret. Williams and I charged our guns twice, making sure we had a round in the chamber.

We passed over London and could see the searchlights although the city was blacked out. There were intruder planes in the area but we saw none. We crossed the coast at Beachy Head and headed for France. We were at 10,000 feet and had a partial moon. We crossed France between Calais and Dunkirk and Williams and I got to our feet in readiness. Troph had us check in every fifteen minutes making sure we had not fallen asleep.

As we crossed into Germany Seay told the bombardier that we couldn't make 30,000 feet and to set the sight for 27,000 feet. After the turning point, Seay said, 'set the sight for 25,000 feet'. As we hit the IP the best the ship would do was 24,500 feet. Pierce opened the bomb doors and had Cox check that they had opened. This was 2230. Sarrat called the pilot and told him as soon as 'bombs away', turn left 90° and head north. I could see the target by slightly leaning out of the window. Different coloured target indicators were going down and I could see the fires and the lights in the city. The ship lurched slightly upwards and Pierce called 'Bombs away'. This was confirmed by Cox in the radio room. One box of pamphlets didn't fall, which meant someone had to go into the bomb bay and manually release them. Thirty seconds later the searchlights picked us up. I had seen a beam come from '12 o'clock' and sweep towards us over the right wing and stabilizer and pass on. It swept back over us a couple of times and then stopped. Immediately, the rest of the beams joined it and we were 'coned'.

Seay called and had the bomb doors closed. Seay started evasive action and Williams and I were thrown around. Williams let go of his gun and put both hands above his head to hold on to the armour plating to prevent his head from hitting it. I had put my left hand above my head and held on to the gun with my right hand. It was bright enough in the plane to have read a book. Standing and floating half the time, I bent my knees to absorb shock as we pulled up from a dive and when we started a dive, my arm kept me from hitting the roof.

Suddenly, it became inky black. The lights had gone out. Seay levelled off and I put my chute on the floor in front of me and put my foot on it to keep it from being thrown around. Standing up, I slipped off the 'safety'. I glanced at Williams and he was still holding on to the roof as if the ship was still doing evasive action. I grabbed his sleeve and pulled but he wouldn't let go. I was expecting an attack by fighters. I had been told when the lights left, to expect them. I pulled him again but having been knocked around must have dazed him.

Then it happened. Fighter in the 6 o'clock (tail) position. Tracers and incendiaries in twin paths flicked under the right stabilizer and wing. I could hear the tail guns firing and then the ball turret opened up. Bowser in the top turret called Seay to say that there was a small finger of flame between No. 3 and 4 engines. Seay dove the ship until the co-pilot and top turret said it had disappeared.

I couldn't see our attacker but by following the tracers, I saw where they had come from and eventually saw him. He passed out of range but the ball turret was still firing at him. As he came in from under the stabilizer, I let go with my gun. I had a nice belly shot at him then. I blinked and he was gone. It was a Me 109.

A gun started firing and Cox yelled, 'Who in hell is firing?'

I couldn't see the attacker but some of his tracers were going past underneath my window. I didn't know it at the time but we had been hit below the cockpit where the oxygen bottles were. Sarrat grabbed a fire extinguisher and fought the fire. It swept up into the pilots' compartment and Dowser got out of his turret and fought the flames there. The attacker was at the 6 o'clock position and the tail and ball were firing again, but I couldn't see a damned thing. The whole fuselage from the rear part of the radio room to the tail was raked by 20mm cannon fire. It sounded as if someone had tossed a handful of gravel on a tin roof. I saw sparks as the 20mms hit the metal and disintegrated in all directions near me. I felt a twinge, but no hurt in my right arm. I glanced at it and looked around at Williams. He was just standing there with a shocked expression on his face as if he couldn't believe what had just happened. A huge red splotch was forming across the stomach of his overalls. I can imagine what thoughts shot through his mind in that split second – Home, Mother, Father, Sister and Girls. What would they say? Who would tell them? He didn't fall down, but just stood there. I took it for granted he was just scratched.

I still couldn't see the fighter and I heard Troph ask if anyone was hit. I tried to reply that Williams was. The tail and ball were still firing and I turned as Williams slid down against me, to the floor. I tried to help him but the firing stopped and the whole ship began bucking and floundering in the air. I was thrown across him and was wondering if this was it and what had happened. (Burney later told me that a FW 190 had attacked from 6 o'clock low and he had shot its tail off.) It had come up underneath and sideswiped us just beneath the radio room.

Then I heard Troph yell, 'The whole right wing is on fire! Better get out before she blows up'.

Pierce asked casually, 'Do you want the bomb doors open?'

Cox replied, 'Roger, that's the only way I can get out'.

When I fell, my oxygen mask and throat mike had torn loose. Disregarding them, I scrambled around trying to find my 'chute. I tried to hook both hooks on at the same time standing up, but only got one strapped on and let it hang lopsided. The glare from the fire threw an eerie light into the waist. The whole ship was a mass of flames, shooting back as far as the stabilizer. I stumbled over Williams as I headed for the waist door. I realized that I should help him and I looked for his 'chute. I couldn't find it as I floundered around the reeling ship. I was beginning to feel weak and dizzy from lack of oxygen. My mind seemed hazy but I remember opening the door handle as instructed and giving the 'release' a hard jerk. I gave the door a kick and it disappeared in front of me. I was panting now and as I took one last look at Williams, it seemed to me as if his face, reflected in the red glare, was looking right at me and pleading, 'Please don't leave me!' I'll never forget that. I ignored my thoughts and finally got the other hook snapped on. I fell forward in a half dive out the door with my hands folded over the chute to protect it from the flames.[2]

On 4 October 361 bombers were dispatched to industrial areas of Frankfurt, Wiesbaden and Saarlaütern and marshalling yards at Sarreguemines and Saarbrücken. At Bury St Edmunds (Rougham) the target for the 94th was a synthetic rubber plant at Hanau just east of Frankfurt. Staff Sergeant Vance Van Hooser, Bill Winneshiek's gunner and assistant engineer, recalled:

> When the alert for the Hanau mission was called, the officers were in London but made it back in plenty of time. Dick Martin, the engineer, had completed his missions. We were assigned *Double Trouble*, the oldest 410th Fortress of the line since ours was crippled.

When Vance approached his aircraft that morning, he told the crew chief, 'Your ship won't make it back today. I have a feeling that my time has come.' The crew chief responded by saying, 'Van you're just tired; you'll be back.'

'No. I have known since I was a kid that I would be killed or crippled in battle and this is it' Van replied. He started not to go but loyalty to the crew overruled his fears. Staff Sergeant Emery Hutchings, another friend of Vance, fell off the back of a truck skinning his hands badly and had to be replaced. Vance went on:

> The skipper briefed us and was so nervous that he didn't do well. We learned later that he had just become the father of a new baby girl. I couldn't have gone at all under such pressure. So, with a new co-pilot, ball turret gunner and engineer, we took off and joined the formation in a top position in the diamond.

But without PFF (Pathfinder Force), cloud ruled out accurate bombing at all primary targets. Twelve B-17s were shot down and losses would have been higher had it not been for the strong P-47 escort and a diversion mission flown over the North Sea by thirty B-24Hs of the 392nd, together with six Liberators in the 'Flying Eightballs' and the 'Travelling Circus'. (These two Groups and the 'Sky Scorpions', newly returned from North Africa, were still licking their wounds, the 44th having lost sixteen B-24s shot down or written off in crash-landings three days before on a mission to Wiener Neustadt.) They certainly flushed the fighters, for over the North Sea thirty Bf 109s and FW 190s jumped them.

Captain Myron H. Keilman the 579th Squadron Operations Officer whose brother Paul, a bombardier in the 'Flying Eightballs', had been killed when his B-24 had been rammed by a FW 190 over the North Sea on 27 January[3] was flying deputy group lead.

He recounts:

> The rate of closure was so fast that I hardly had a chance to spot them before I saw their guns blinking fire. They dove below our formation

and circled for another pass. Then there was a second wave of five or six of them and another – and another. I lost track of how many. I am sure that they were surprised at having our new nose turrets returning their fire but it didn't seem to deter them. Each B-24H had four turrets of twin .50 calibre guns plus a flexible .50 at each waist window. Sitting there, I was dismayed for something useful to do. After the third attack or so I couldn't sit there any longer, so I slapped the airplane commander on the arm and hastily took over flying the airplane. That lasted only a few minutes because he couldn't stand watching those fighters either. This exchange continued for the duration of the battle. Besides the 13mm and 20mm guns of the '109s and FW 190s there were occasional large single flashes of fire from their 210mm rockets. Each packed the wallop of a large anti-aircraft artillery shell and could readily blow up a B-24. We were lucky, though. Because they were time-fused, the time and distance of launching the rockets was very critical for them to explode among the airplanes of our formation. With closing speeds of 700mph or more this wasn't easy. The use of head-on attacks was relatively ineffective but it was real scary.

A German fighter failed to pull out in time and it rammed *The Drip* , one of the lead aeroplanes in the High Squadron, flown by Lieutenant James A. Feurstacke. All ten crew and the 579th Squadron CO, Major Donald A. Appert, who was on board, were killed.[4] Myron Keilman was promoted to squadron commander that evening.

Eight B-17s failed to return from the mission to Frankfurt and others, like *Buccaneer* in the 91st Bomb Group, only just made it home. Lieutenant Charles S. Hudson, the twenty-eight-year-old bombardier, fresh from the States, who was flying only his second mission, sounded like a good man to ride with. The rugged, ruddy-faced Irishman used to be a 'roughneck' in the oilfields around Kern County, California, and fought sixty-three bouts as an amateur welterweight. Nearing the target there was a panic-stricken cry on the gravel-voiced interphone. It was the radio gunner: 'Sir! The two waist gunners are lying on the floor back here. They're dying I tell you; they're dying!'

Charlie Hudson slipped out of his cumbersome armoured flak suit, put on a portable 'walk-around' oxygen mask and started back to the waist. On the way he grabbed two more walk-around bottles from the cockpit and radio room. The one waist gunner, Jim, was lying on his back, unconscious. He was a hideous blue and frost covered his face and was clinging to his eyebrows. The other gunner, Harry, though conscious, was sitting in a starey-eyed stupor, unable to move. He had vomited all over the floor. Charlie slapped the frost off Jim's face, pinched his cheeks and put one of the temporary oxygen masks on each of the sergeants' faces. He tried the two guns and found both were frozen out of commission, so he closed the waist windows to cut out some of the freezing gale that was whipping through the Fortress. As he closed the right window, he noticed that they must be approaching Frankfurt. Hastily he propped the unconscious Jim up between two ammunition boxes so that his regular mask, now hooked into an undamaged oxygen line, would reach his face. At their altitude every slap was sheer labour and though he was exhausted, Charlie struggled the length of the bomber in time to work over his instruments in the nose and get his bombs away. Then he wormed his way back to the waist. Jim had fallen off to one side, pulling his oxygen mask partly off. Harry seemed to be perking up a bit but still seemed drowsy and stupid, unable to help Charlie as he rubbed Jim's arms, legs and face in an effort to restore circulation. A few minutes later Charlie was back in the nose manning his gun.

Back at Bassingbourn the *Buccaneer* fired two red flares as it came in for a landing and an ambulance sped to meet the taxiing Fortress. Charlie Hudson sighed 'I'm the tiredest I've ever been in my life' and headed for his bunk. A couple of days later Jim and Harry were none the worse for their experiences, though at least one of them owed his life to Charlie Hudson.

At Bury St Edmunds meanwhile, there was no word from *Double Trouble*. Staff Sergeant Vance Van Hooser recalled:

> The weather had closed in before we reached the target requiring that we split up into two groups. We bombed the aerodrome at St-Dizier in France. Soon Focke Wulfs – 'Goering's pets' or 'yellow noses' – hit us with 20 millimetre fire through the No. 3 oil cooler. The co-pilot feathered the engine promptly. The fighter attacks increased as we fell behind so the co-pilot restarted number three engine. This didn't work and since we had lost our oil the engine wouldn't feather again. It was impossible to keep up so the skipper said, 'Hang on; we are heading for the deck.' By now I realized our time had come and I had a deep desire to take as many enemy aircraft with me as possible so I fired continuously.

As Winneshiek did a wingover to the left and headed down, Van Hooser was lifted into mid-air and recalled feeling his head hit the windstream outside the waist gun window. With all of his physical strength and his

Mae West and parachute harness hooked over his guns he was able to recover. 'I immediately snapped on my parachute,' he said. The windmilling prop limited their desired dive speed. The aircraft was shaking badly and the high pitched scream was Van's last recollection for a time.

The next thing Van remembered was a voice saying, 'Here he is.' He regained consciousness enough to realize that he was too close to the ball turret for safety. Staff Sergeant Jim May was squatting on the floor on the catwalk with his hands over his eyes. Van managed to kick May and signalled for help. Van tried to stand but fell to the floor dazed and wondering what had happened. May placed a duffel bag under his head so the oxygen hose would reach as Van vomited. Vance Van Hooser had been hit in the head by 20-millimetre fragments and was badly wounded. Van's next recollection was of the navigator Lieutenant George Dowling saying 'We are going to ditch; throw out everything.' Dowling helped Van to the radio compartment where they removed his 'chute. Shortly thereafter *Double Trouble* touched down but instead of a splash there was a scraping sound. Van heard someone say: 'Help Van out' but in the confusion no one came. Shortly Van recognized Winneshiek's voice saying: 'Van, the plane's on fire. Can you walk?'

With some help, he crawled a safe distance. Thinking he was still in Germany, Van told the crew to leave him so as to avoid capture. Bill Winneshiek had trouble explaining that they had landed in England near Margate and a hospital. By the time the ambulance arrived, Van was sick, could see and was in great pain. A nurse cleaned his wound as Van lost consciousness. He awoke later, unaware of how much time had passed and experiencing terrible pain and mental disturbance. Van Hooser was in a serious condition for several days and in addition to being in great pain, much of the time was in the twilight of consciousness. His heart was broken over the fact that he probably would not be able to complete his twenty-five missions, which was the prescribed tour. His crew carried on and they can truly say that Vance Van Hooser contributed more than his share to the cause.[5]

On 7 October there was heavy rain and the mission was scrubbed one minute after the start of the briefings. Then the sun came out and the skies cleared. At Thorpe Abbotts two Pfcs in the Gas and Oil Supply Section took advantage of the break in the weather and planted a Christmas tree in front of their office. For many combat crews Christmas had indeed arrived early for it meant that they had another twenty-four hours to live. Then they had been alerted early that evening for Bremen again. But the mission was scrubbed again. There was a Red Alert at about 2230 hours when enemy planes bombed Bungay and Norwich. Personnel at Thorpe Abbotts saw ack-ack and a dozen aircraft were reported shot down within a few miles of the airfield, several in flames. An early radio report announced that 175 enemy aircraft were over England. At 0500 hours the 'Bloody Hundredth' was alerted again, this time to be briefed to lead the 13th Wing to Bremen with take-off set for 1145 hours. More than 350 bombers in the 1st and 3rd Bomb Divisions would attack the port at Bremen and Vegesack. The area was noted for its flak defences and much of north-western Germany's fighter strength was concentrated nearby so several attempts were made to reduce the effectiveness of the *Jagdgruppen*. In order to split the enemy fighter force, the 1st Division would approach the target from Holland while the 3rd Division crossed the North Sea and approached the target from the north-west. Fifty-five B-24s in the 2nd Bomb Division, living up to their nickname, the '2nd Bomb Diversion' would fly a long, curving route over the North Sea to Vegesack. Bremen was the sort of raid that caused men to become religious or made them seek solace in their chosen faith. Others knew deep down that the time had come to catch up on correspondence and put their affairs in order. At Thorpe Abbotts heavy losses had become all too familiar and premonitions were more pronounced. Men like Richard 'Dick' Agor, a gunner in Frank Meadows' crew, had long since reached the point where they knew that they were all living on borrowed time even though he had flown barely half a dozen missions. In letters home he had never once mentioned war. He could not say that he was the ball turret gunner on *Phartzac* but in a recent letter to his favourite uncle he confided that he had prayed about coming home that day. Sharing premonitions the others felt, he had ordered roses to be sent to his mother for Christmas.

One week after the bombing of Pearl Harbor, Harry H. Crosby left the Master of Arts programme in writing at the University of Iowa and joined the Air Corps, leaving behind a girl in Iowa City he had fallen in love with but who had shown little long-term interest in him. A few weeks later, Crosby washed out as a pilot and was sent away to re-train as a navigator. When he was awarded his gold bars and wings he was assigned to the 'Hundredth' and the first time he saw a Fortress land, it crashed killing everyone on board.[6] Lieutenant Crosby, who married the girl he had been chasing after she had written to him expressing a renewed interest, was now a lead navigator, Captain Everett E. 'Ev' Blakely, a lead crew pilot, and Lieutenant James R. Douglass, lead bombardier, had received two days of pre-briefing during secret trips to Elveden Hall and so they knew what was planned. Crosby recalled that the general idea was that, 'many hundreds of planes of heavy bombardment were out to "Hamburg" Bremen'.

Crosby continued:

> The unusual thing on this trip was that we were to lead the 3rd Combat Wing. This meant additional strain and responsibility on the part of our crew was a load to which we were more accustomed after having been in this position a few times previously. Major John B. Kidd, who had done such a creditable job leading the 'Hundredth' on the important Regensburg raid, was the command pilot sharing the piloting duties [aboard the lead aircraft, *Just a Snappin'*] with Captain Everett E. Blakely, now commander of the 418th Squadron. Our co-pilot, Lieutenant Charles A. Via, would ride in the position of tail gunner serving the vital function of formation control officer. S/Sgt Lyle F. Nord would act as radio gunner and assistant to T/Sgt Edmond C. Forkner. We'd always known we had a good crew. Way back in 1942 when the 'Hundredth' was first formed, the first crew, which served as the nucleus of the group, was Lieutenant Blakely's crew. It had been formed from selected material from three first phase schools. This condition caused the crew to suffer from the stigma of being called the 'model crew'. They held several engineering records such as flight for endurance and maximum performance, which lasted for seventeen hours, which drew them commendations from a general in the 2nd Air Force. I personally was a recent addition to the crew, necessitated when their regular navigator was made group navigator. But with all of this aside, from being regular guys and devoted to duty and good at it, our gunners waited till this day to not only prove themselves but also to illustrate just how vitally important it was that all crew members must be tops at their jobs when the time came.

Major Gale W. 'Bucky' Cleven who was from Odessa, Texas, and was 350th Squadron CO, decided to fly the mission in the right-hand seat of *Our Baby* with Captain Bernard A. 'Benny' DeMarco's crew, which would be deputy lead. Squadron commanders were required to fly ten missions but Cleven was on his twentieth and he had never bothered to call for his DSC awarded him for gallantry on the 17 August raid on Regensburg. Just before take-off the co-pilot, Flight Officer James 'Skip' Thayer, had been

Professor James Dobie, who came from Texas and took up residence at Emmanuel College, Cambridge, talking to one of the crew of a B-17F 42-30793 in the 388th Bomb Group named *Tom Paine*, after the author of *The Rights of Man*, during a visit to Knettishall. In October 1943 a group of American officers at Knettishall donated a plaque in memory of Tom Paine, one of the most distinguished (if controversial) sons of Thetford, who on going to Pennsylvania in 1774, immediately began campaigning for freedom for the slaves. He was credited with being the first man to use the term 'United States of America'. *Tom Paine* carried his quotation 'Tyranny, like hell is not easily conquered'. The B-17 landed at Beccles with four wounded and injured men on board on 11 April 1944 and the aircraft was subsequently salvaged. *(USAF)*

Coffee break. *(USAF)*

An English lad waits patiently at the main gate at Deenthorpe. *(USAF)*

'Pubbing'. *(USAF)*

American servicemen having tea with their English hosts. *(USAF)*

Girls (beleived to be from a visitng USO troupe) at Horsham St. Faith (Norwich)
watching mechanics at work on a B-24. *(USAF)*

B-17F 42-29591 *The Shamrock Special* in the 401st Bomb Squadron, 91st Bomb Group, which crashed on 9 July 1943 and was repaired by 2 SAD using the tail assembly off another Fortress. The aircraft was finally scrapped, at Kingman, Arizona, in November 1945. *(USAF)*

B-17F 42-29688 *Kayo* in the 305th Bomb Group piloted by Lt Ron Barstow, which returned to Chelveston from the Villacoublay raid on 24 August 1943 with wounded on board. Sgt James Frazier, the tail gunner, is on the stretcher, and Flight Surgeon Karl Bergener is on the left side of the stretcher. Walking wounded Sgt 'Joe' Kocher and Owen Hansen are already in the ambulance. (*via Bill Donald*)

B-17F 42-3299 in the 390th Bomb Group, which pancaked at Framlingham on 12 August 1943. The aircraft was repaired and in March 1944 was transferred to the 457th Bomb Group and in turn, the 306th Bomb Group, when it was named *Fightin' Carbarn Hammerslaw*. It FTR with 2nd Lt Charles F. Manning and crew on 5 December 1944. All nine crew were killed. *(USAF)*

B-17F 41-24527 *The Great Speckled Bird* in the 91st Bomb Group, which FTR with Lt William S. Munger and crew on the mission to Schweinfurt on 17 August. All ten crew were taken prisoner. *(USAF)*

The crew of *Our Gang* in the 324th Bomb Squadron, 91st Bomb Group, at Bassingbourn. 2nd from left is Sergeant Jake Levine of East Nassau, Long Island, who was the top turret gunner. B-17F30-BO 42-5069 *Our Gang* was lost with Lt William H. Wheeler's crew on the 17 August 1943 mission to Schweinfurt. *(USAF)*

B-17F-30-VE 42-5867 *Alice From Dallas* in the 350th Bomb Squadron was lost with Lt Roy F. Claytor's crew on the mission to Regensburg on 17 August 1943. Claytor, who was leading the second element of the low squadron, was shot down by flak bursts at 1020 hours while over eastern Belgium. The B-17 erupted in flames. Eight men baled out safely but Edward Musante's - the right waist gunner – parachute fouled the horizontal stabilizer and he was killed when the aircraft exploded. The ball turret gunner was also killed after failing to get clear in time. For most of the crew it was only their tenth mission. *(via Michael P. Faley)*

Pursued by a FW 190, a Fortress believed one of five lost by the 384th Bomb Group begins its descent to earth 20,000 feet below during the Schweinfurt mission, on 17 August 1943. (USAAF)

The Messerschmitt factory at Regensburg under a cloud of smoke, midday on 17 August 1943, photographed from a Fortress of the 385th Bomb Group as it began the long flight to North Africa.

Strike photo of Regensburg on 17 August 1943 just after the 390th Bomb Group had passed over the target. *(USAF)*

Left: A photo taken from Charley Sackerson's *Wham Bam* in the 305th Bomb Group of a disintegrating Bf 110 fighter going down over Schweinfurt on 17 August 1943. The Messerschmitt was blown apart when two P-47s of the 56th Fighter Group fired at it simultaneously. *(via Michael Gibson)*

B-17s in the 100th Bomb Group crossing the Alps on the mission to Regensburg. *(USAF)*

B-17F-100-BO 42-30372 *Fertile Myrtle III* and B-17F-85-BO 42-30130 in the 96th Bomb Group crossing the Alps after bombing Regensburg on 17 August 1943. Brigadier General Curtis E. LeMay who in July 1943 had been promoted 4th Wing CO led the raid in Captain Tom Kenny's B-17F-100-BO 42-30366, *Fertile Myrtle III*, in the 338th Bomb Squadron in the leading 96th Bomb Group. After the target the surviving 128 B-17s, some flying on three engines and many trailing smoke, were attacked by a few fighters on the way to the Alps. LeMay circled his formation over Lake Garda to try to give the cripples a chance to rejoin them. Although the Snetterton Heath group did not lose a single B-17 the 4th Wing lost twenty-four aircraft, while sixty Fortresses that made it to North Africa had to he left behind for repairs. *Fertile Myrtle III* was badly shot up over Bremen on 16 December 1943 and crashed at Taverham near Norwich after being abandoned by Kenney's crew. *(via Geoff Ward)*

B-17F-85-BO 42-30066 *Mugwump* in the 418th Bomb Squadron, 100th Bomb Group, seen here with Lt Walter Moreno and his crew. *Mugwump* was flown on the Regensburg mission on 17 August 1943 by Charles Cruickshank and crew with Major John Egan in the co-pilot's seat. It survived the flight but landed in North Africa so badly damaged that it was abandoned but eventually it was repaired and returned to England where it was re-assigned to the 96th Bomb Group at Snetterton Heath and re-named *Rum Boogie II*. Early in 1944 it was transferred to the 803rd (Provisional) Group at RAF Oulton, Norfolk, where it was fitted out with *Mandrel* and *Carpet* jamming equipment for use as a RCM aircraft. In July 1944 42-30066 was re-assigned to Project *Aphrodite*. Filled with Torpex HE it was flown from Fersfield, Norfolk, on 30 October 1944 headed for the U-boat pens at Heligoland where it was aimed after 1st Lt Barnes and his co-pilot, 1st Lt McCauley, had baled out and a mother aircraft guided it towards its target by radio control. The plane and a second B-17 missed the target and both aircraft were destroyed, one being hit by flak before the target and the other crashed and exploded in Sweden. (*TAMM*)

Lt Robert Wolff's B-17F-100-BO 42-30061 *Wolf Pack* (centre) in the 418th Bomb Squadron and three other 100th Bomb Group B-17Fs head for North Africa after the 17 August raid on Regensburg. Note the damage to Wolf's aircraft, which received 20mm cannon fire to the tail fin and a life raft released, which hit the left tailplane. The top aircraft is B-17F-30-VE 42-5861 *Laden Maiden* flown by Lt Owen D. 'Cowboy' Roane in the 349th Bomb Squadron. Below this is B-17F-40-VE 42-5957 *Horny*. These three B-17Fs managed to reach North Africa; nine other 100th Bomb Group Fortresses did not. *Laden Maiden* FTR from a raid on 30 December 1943 with Lt Marvin Leininger's crew; only the bombardier and navigator survived and these evaded capture successfully. The rest of the crew were KIA. *Horny* was salvaged on 9 May 1944. *Wolf Pack* returned to the ZOl on 12 July 1944 for War Bond publicity tours or for training duty before being declared surplus on 17 April 1945. (*TAMM*)

Back on the ground in North Africa Fredric White (front row second left) the bombardier in Lt Robert Wolf's (smiling second from right) crew re-enacts their attack on Regensburg on 17 August 1943. (*TAMM*)

B-17F-60-BO 42-29557 *Yankee Gal* in the 366th Bomb Squadron, 305th Bomb Group, at Chelveston on 22 August 1943. Note the extra pair of .50 calibre guns for frontal defence. This aircraft was transferred to the 384th Bomb Group at Grafton Underwood. On 10 October 1943 2nd Lt William E. Kopf crash-landed at RAF Desford where *Yankee Gal* hit a hangar and the Fortress had to be salvaged. *(via Bill Donald)*

B-17F-55-BO 41-29508 *Southern Comfort Jr* in the 364th Bomb Squadron, 305th Bomb Group, which caught fire at Chelveston on 26 August 1943 during run up after an engine change and was towed out of harm's way shortly after this picture, was taken. The bomb load exploded and blew the Fortress to oblivion. *(via Bill Donald)*

B-17F 42-29944 *Buzzing Bronco* in the 303rd Bomb Group, which crash-landed at RAF West Malling on 6 September 1943. (USAF)

B-17F 42-29896 *Tondelayo* in the 379th Bomb Group, which went MIA on 6 September 1943 when 2nd Lt John E. Fawkes Jr ditched in the North Sea. All ten crew were rescued. (USAF)

The wing of B-17F 42-3290 *Raunchy Wolf* in the 551st Bomb Squadron, 385th Bomb Group, provides shade from the fierce African sun. Aircrew had to perform maintenance before the flight back to England, attacking a target in France en route. On 26 September 1943 this B-17F was lost in a collision over Bulphan in south-east Essex while returning from a mission. Only one gunner survived of the twenty aircrew involved. *(USAF)*

Activity on the hardstand at Ridgewell on 26 September 1943 as bombs are ready for loading aboard a 381st Bomb Group B-17F. *(USAF)*

One significant outcome of the XB-40 gunship was the adoption of the chin turret on B-17G models and also Douglas-built F models from -70-DL on. At Boeing it was intended to fit chin turrets to B-17F-135-BO, but this block was re-designated B-17G-1-BO and no Boeing-built Fs received chin turrets on the production line – although many Fs acquired them at modification centres in the US and in the ETO. B-17F-75-DL 42-3522 *Gremlin's Delite* in the 533rd Bomb Squadron, 381st Bomb Group, was one such late model 'F' with a chin turret. This aircraft, which at first was assigned to the 96th Bomb Group on 27 September 1943, finished its days at Walnut Ridge, Arkansas in 1946. *(USAF)*

B-17F 42-30172 *Darlin' Dolly* in the 335th Bomb Squadron, 95th Bomb Group, salvoes ten 500lb GP M-43s over Emden on 2 October 1943. The ball turret guns are facing forward as the gunner on Lt K. S. Knowlton's crew checks that all bombs have released – standard operating procedure when not under attack. Sticking bomb shackles were not uncommon in severe icing conditions. *Darlin' Dolly* was eventually modified to carry 20,000lb of explosives as a radio-controlled flying bomb. It was launched at Oldenburg on 1 January 1945, the last operation of the *Aphrodite Project*. *(USAF)*

B-17F 42-5888 *Elusive Elcy* in the 94th Bomb Group, which went MIA with Lt Harley G. Roberts' crew on 27 September 1943. Ten crew died and one man survived.

instructed to proceed to London to receive his commission as a second lieutenant. After chatting to Cleven he was given a choice – 'fly or go get the commission.' Thayer decided to fly the mission. 'He'd get the commission tomorrow.'[7]

Captain Thomas E. Murphy, who had flown the Regensburg mission with Colonel Lay, was flying *Piccadilly Lily* on what was his twenty-fourth mission with Captain Alvin L. Barker, the 351st Squadron Operations officer, taking co-pilot 2nd Lieutenant Marshall F. Lee's seat. Lee would go along as ball turret man to observe the formation. Murphy's radioman and right waist gunner had completed their tours four days earlier. T/Sgt Derrell C. Piel, whose regular crew had failed to return from the mission on 3 September to Paris and S/Sgt Elder D. Dickerson, whose regular crew had completed their tour on 16 September, were drafted in as their replacements.

For some reason *Our Baby*, the deputy lead ship, reached the end of the Thorpe Abbotts' runway at 1143 hours for take-off first and once in the air, *Just a Snappin'* would have to manoeuvre a little to retake the lead spot. At thirty-second intervals the rest of the High Squadron followed. *Heaven Can Wait* followed *Our Baby* down the runway and *Squawkin Hawk*, a scheduled spare aircraft, was the last to get airborne. Lieutenant Harry H. Crosby continues:

> Briefing, take-off and assembly of the group were as usual except that the group formed in the record time of 18 minutes. The group climbed to 9,000 feet and passed over Buncher 8 at Framlingham, about 40 seconds behind the briefed time of 1246. However, the 'Hundredth' in the lead position was joined by the 390th and the 95th without difficulty. The 13th Combat Wing passed over Spalding in excellent defensive formation at the exact time as briefed, 1312. By essing slightly, our combat wing fell into position as the third combat wing as scheduled. At 1329 the Wing, in unquestionably the best formation flown during my experience, passed over the English coast nine miles north of Splasher Beacon 4. The course flown was nearly as briefed but a few minutes were lost due to slight discrepancies in turns and metro data. The journey over water was made unnecessarily hazardous due to the fact that planes, which aborted instead of clearing the formation, persisted in attempting to fly through our combat wing formation. On one occasion an entire six-ship squadron in good formation flew between the 'Hundredth' and 390th Groups. Six minutes later a flight in equally good formation threaded itself through our formation. Two minutes later a single

ship with what appeared to be a 'T' marking on the tail repeated the process.

Our combat wing started the turn onto land near the island of Borkum. At this time we had twenty-one ships in our group formation and our other two groups were in total or nearly complete strength. We crossed the coast at 1456 on course. Although a slight haze and a two-tenths undercast of low stratus were present, it was possible to determine our exact position by pilotage (visually). Reception on Gee failed upon crossing the coast due partially to jamming and lack of strength on transmission of the 'A' marker.[8] We approached Groningen on course and turned toward the IP [Initial Point] two miles to the left of course in an effort to clear the combat wing ahead of us. On the approach to the IP it was observed that Emden, apparently remembering the two previous trips (27 September, 2 October) of the 8th Air Force to that area, had sent up a dense smoke screen. Also it was noted by several members of the crew that FW 190s, instead of devoting all their efforts on the Fortresses, in a few cases turned on our escort, long-range P-47s, and engaged them in combat. The escort apparently was ahead of us defending the lead combat wing of the air division. The IP was reached at 1521.[9]

2nd Lieutenant Frank P. McGlinchey, bombardier in 1st Lieutenant William H. 'Bill' MacDonald's crew in *Salvo Sal* in the 'Hundredth' formation, recalls:

The P-47s had given us good support and things seemed rather quiet as we winged our way towards the target. Minutes passed and soon we were over the IP. With bomb bays open we turned on the target. The groups in front of us were enveloped in a large black cloud as they passed over the target and dropped their payloads. It was the most intensive flak I had ever seen.

The German flak defences had already calculated the height and speed of the previous wing and had no need to alter those calculations as the 'Hundredth' sailed over the target at much the same height and speed. Captain 'Ev' Blakely and Major John Kidd in *Just a Snappin'* led the group through the ugly bursts of flak, so thick they formed one large oily cloud. 'Jack' Kidd had wanted to be a pilot since the time he saw Jimmy Doolittle win an air race over a grass field near his boyhood home of Winnetka, Illinois. He was smart, steady and cool under pressure.[10] Lieutenant Harry H. Crosby, one of Blakely's closest friends, continues:

By now much of the ground haze had cleared away. My calculations had been proving accurate in my dead reckoning. But all these opportunities to check my navigation were unnecessary. Everyone on the crew knew that the intense black cloud ahead of us marked the vicinity of our target, the town of Bremen. I have been exposed to flak before and hadn't been particularly perturbed by its presence. I remember that in all of those instances each little burst of *Flieger Abwehr Kanonen* was a distinct mean-looking little black ball. But now, over Bremen, each little ball had lost its individuality and the whole thing was blended into a huge angry cloud. Too late I realized that our combat wing had been briefed to fly at an altitude too similar to that of the previous wing, for we sailed right into the midst of that cloud. I could just visualize the gunners on the ground checking back on their computations and sending up volleys using the same data... At any rate, two minutes before we hit the target our plane was hit by the first burst of flak. Our ball turret operator, S/Sgt William F. McClelland, announced in a calm voice that his turret had been struck but not pierced, by a flak burst. From that time his turret operated in a jerky fashion.

Everett Blakely did not need maps or their dead reckoning to tell them they were getting close to the target nor to tell them that their arrival was expected.

We could look ahead and see an immense, black, smoke-cloud hiding most of the business area of Bremen. What was worse, we could see a tremendous carpet of flak coming up to greet us. Not a few individual shots and some small black balls but so much solid flak you could almost slice it like a cake...we figured about 300 anti-aircraft guns were firing at us...

A few minutes before bombs away Blakely saw a FW 190 collide with *Marie Helena* and he was left with a 'very sobering feeling in the pit of the stomach'.[11]

Harry Crosby again:

Thirty seconds before the bombs were dropped a burst of flak hit our nose compartment shattering the window to the right of the bombardier's head. One fragment struck the bombardier, James R. Douglass, in the left side. It tore through his clothing and ripped the cloth of his flak suit but did not touch his skin. Despite this distraction and I am certain that Douglass thought he had been injured by the expression on his face, he continued the manipulation of his bombsight and bombs were away at 1525. (Even accepting the fact that we had been hit by flak, annoyed by fighters and had been searching for a target obscured by the typical smoke screen, our own and PRU photographs showed that his bombs were dropped accurately and destructively.) A mere matter of seconds later our No. 4 engine was destroyed by flak. The control wires were shattered and the left elevator was ripped to shreds, plunging our plane into a sort of spinning dive, completely out of control. We were plunging down in a helpless, careening dive. Flames were blazing from our No. 4 engine. Our control surfaces were all cut and torn. (I might add, parenthetically, that the 95th reported later that we were seen to fall into a flat spin, on fire and that three parachutes were observed to open from our plane.) The normal reaction on the part of our pilots should have been to think of their own personal safety or in cases of extreme nobility of character perhaps they would have been thinking about the other members of the crew. But they did not, even in this crisis, forget for one minute that they were the leaders of a great formation. Their first thought was of the crews behind them. In unison, as we fell into our dive, the words came over the interphone to our tail gunner. 'Signal the deputy leader to take over.'

I can't help but think that as they fought for their lives they might have been excused for being too busy to think of their command but such was not the case. By this signalling the remainder of the formation was notified immediately that we had been hit and were aborting. This act would have prevented any planes being pulled even a few feet out of position into danger from the enemy aircraft buzzing about. (It was the misfortune of the 100th Bomb Group that the deputy leader was destroyed at this time and so many of the flight leaders likewise, that the group was left to do its best by tacking onto the 390th.) Back in the radio compartment our young radio operator knew what was going on. He knew he was in imminent danger of his life. But he also had a duty to do. Consequently he still remained at his position and radioed in to Wing HQ that, 'the target was bombed at 1525'.

For 3,000 feet Blakely and Kidd fought to get that plane under control. It was only because of the superior construction of our bomber and its perfect maintenance, plus the combination of two skilled pilots that we ever even recovered from that dive. If I were an expert on stress and strain analysis, or a mechanic, or even a pilot, I would dwell at length on the manner in which the plane was restored to normal flying attitude. As it is, the procedure defies my description but I am certain it was a very great accomplishment. Blakely's description was a simple comment, 'You can lose altitude awfully fast when one engine goes sour and your controls are chewed to ribbons.' We dropped for 3,000 feet before Major Kidd and I could regain control. Most of the crew not strapped to their seats were thrown to the floor, shaken severely – but at last the ground was once more back where it ought to be, instead of standing up on one ear. Once more we were in level flight and, at least temporarily, safe. At 19,000 feet we were able to look out the windows and were temporarily assured to note that the ground was now in the right place. A hurried consultation was held over the interphone to determine a plan for fighting our way back to England.

The following facts had to be considered: We had lost all communication back of the top turret, so it was impossible to determine the extent of injury and damage. Our control wires were fraying as far back as the top turret operator could see. At least two of the crew had reported being hit immediately after we left target. One engine was in such bad condition that bits and finally the entire cowling, was blasted off. We were losing altitude so rapidly probably because of the condition of the elevator that any but the shortest way back was beyond contemplation. So we headed across the face of Germany for home.

Our Baby, the deputy lead ship, had also started down[12] and *Marie Helena*, *Piccadilly Lily*, *War Eagle* and *Phartzac* followed in quick succession. Two of the bombs aboard *Phartzac* failed to release and these were hit by flak causing the plane to ignite and explode 'somewhere southeast of Bremen'. Bombardier William Hubbard, who baled out, watched the remains spiral down and crash on an autobahn. He believed that Meadows and his co-pilot, Lloyd Evans, had been killed by a flak burst. Navigator Frank Bush said, 'I'm getting the hell out of this plane' and baled out through the nose-hatch where his parachute caught fire and burned in mid-air. Waist gunner James Ward was lucky enough to get out alive with quite a few injuries. After baling out he remained unconscious for ten days. After his capture, William Hubbard was 'clapped in solitary and threatened with death unless he talked'. He refused and the Germans forced him to walk 100 miles to prison. The rest of the crew and Dick Agor were killed. He would not be home by Christmas but the ball turret gunner had long since known that. Of the 350th Squadron, only Blakely's ship and Bill MacDonald's *Salvo Sal* remained. Frank McGlinchey scanned the sky.

I looked for our two wingmen but saw no one. Our whole squadron of nine ships had been knocked out. (I learned later that only the lead ship made it back to England.) Although out of formation and heading back to England by ourselves (just after the bomb bay doors had closed our ship jumped as we received a very bad hit to the rear of No. 2 engine), we seemed to be doing all right until a flight of German fighters bounced us. Suddenly, the intercom was alive with reports of fighters bearing in from all directions. All of our guns, with the exception of the two nose guns, were knocked out in fifteen minutes. Our waist gunner, Douglas Agee, was killed by a direct hit from a fighter about two minutes after the attack started. All our left controls were shattered and we had to put out several fires. Our radio too was gone. One engine was running away and two more were just about to go. We were losing altitude rapidly and it was apparent we would not make it back to England. Suddenly, fire shot out from the rear of the undercarriage and beneath the wings. With the Zuider Zee directly in front of us, Bill MacDonald gave the order to bale out.[13]

Lieutenant Harry H. Crosby, aboard *Just a Snappin'*, continues:

As we ploughed across Germany with Blakely and Kidd carefully nursing the loss of each precious foot of altitude and flying at 120mph, we were subjected to the threat of innumerable attacks from enemy fighters. I will say that there were other straggling Fortresses who received a lot harsher treatment than we did. And I will venture a reason for this fact. Ahead of us a lone B-17 was limping along. A flight of three Messerschmitts was harassing it, darting in and out but not attacking. Finally all three swooped in and fired for a long time at the bomber. The bomber didn't go down but neither did any of the fighters. And those three small planes kept attacking that plane receiving no damage to themselves till finally the B-17 caught on fire. It was with a helpless feeling that we saw our last ally turnover, spin slightly and then burst into a huge ball of flame. Now the victorious Germans turned to us. And now comes the reason that we were able to return. From that point on there wasn't one single attack upon us that at least one enemy fighter wasn't destroyed. I believe that T/Sgt Monroe B. Thornton got the first one.

On this attack, which came slightly from the right, Thornton started firing when the fighter was about 800 yards away. At about 300 yards the effect of his firing began to show and the propeller fell off. Douglass and I both saw the pilot jump. Thornton got a couple of others too. One of them was an Me 110. It came at us high and from the right side. Another plane was flying with it in a stacked, slightly echeloned, position. Thorny said that it was firing at us before he was able to get his sights on either of them. The right engine of the fighter caught on fire and pieces flew off the left engine or wing. Our left waist gunner saw two occupant's bale out and both chutes open. His (Thornton's) third came very near to the Dutch border.

Douglass got a Ju 88 that flipped around a long time before it came in on us. It came in about 300 yards and ended up in a vertical bank with its belly towards us. I saw almost the whole tail assembly shatter off before it fell into a spin. Smoke was pouring from its rear as it went down. Three minutes later another Ju 88 came at us from 10 o'clock. I was positive that my shots were hitting the plane at its exposed belly but the plane did not go down. It made no more attacks. Back in the tail, waist and radio compartments, our gunners were paying a heavier price for their planes. About the time that we went over the target, Via had reported that he was hit. We didn't know whether he meant his compartment or himself. That hit was a serious flesh wound in his right leg. But this didn't stop his shooting. As nearly as we can tell from his and the waist gunner's reports he destroyed his first for that day soon after Thornton hit his No. 1.

Two Me 210s came in together after hovering for some time at 1,000 yards. Via picked out the second one and the left waist gunner and the radio gunner say it disintegrated in mid air. His second claim was the partner of one that our top turret gunner destroyed. Thornton saw it blow up nearly 500 yards out. Credit must be given to Via's shooting but when another fact is considered, his performance can be called truly heroic. In between his first and second planes, Via had had a projectile pass from the fat of his hip through his pelvis, severing his sciatic nerve, opening several blood vessels and passing on out his hip. Yet, even with this horrible injury, Via stuck to his position and didn't come out till we had crossed the enemy coast. S/Sgt Lyle F. Nord was pretty busy scratching flak fragments out of his face, head, neck and clothing but he still managed to bring down a fighter from a difficult position. Two Me 210s came in stacked up from about 600 yards out. Nord took one of them and our left waist gunner the other. The plane side-slipped to the right and then blew up. Pieces of the fighter splattered against our plane.

The waist gunners each got two but the price was infinitely great. S/Sgt Edward S. Yevich had a double compound fracture in his forearm and a deep gash in his leg. S/Sgt Lester W. Saunders fought a gallant fight against death but succumbed in a hospital bed one week after our return. Yevich had been seared across the back by flak fragments at the target so he had a grudge against the first fighter who approached from the left side. He got it going away and two members of the crew saw it explode in midair. Saunders, at the other waist window, had already knocked his first fighter down too. (It was a Me 210.) Almost immediately after Yevich's first went down, a 20mm shell tore through the left waist window into the pit of Saunders' stomach and hurled him back against the other side of the plane. I believe it was the same shell that hit Yevich's gun and ricocheted into his arm. Yet in this gravely wounded condition, both of these gunners actually retained their positions and each one of them knocked out another fighter.

After his first remark, we hadn't heard much from S/Sgt William F. McClelland. It wasn't till shortly before our crash-landing that I learned why. He had destroyed two aircraft with his damaged turret before he himself was hit. The first flak that hit him tore deep into his scalp. But he kept his position. Later another burst, or perhaps an exploding 20mm, scraped his face and made shreds of his oxygen mask, headset and clothing. Some place along the line he received an injection of flak in his leg. When the last volley rendered his turret useless – the door was blown clear off – he climbed out into the radio compartment. As we crossed the Dutch coast another burst of flak hit the flak suit on which he was lying and threw him into a bloody heap.

All this time the pilots had been pretty busy piloting and I was occupied with navigating. The terrain was distinctive so it wasn't hard staying on the course we had selected. I did try to use the Gee box and I am positive I would have had a fix at 8,000 feet over the German-Holland border but some sort of projectile came through the floor and shattered the cathode tube. The radio, along with most of the electrical equipment, was long since non-functional.

Meanwhile, the remnants of the 'Hundredth' formation flew on in disarray. Major Robert O. Good, the 390th leader, flying in *Six Nights in Telergma*, piloted by Captain Hiram C. Skogmo, had a ringside seat in the disaster. Seeing the 'Hundredth' being destroyed before his very eyes, Good radioed the other group commanders that he was taking the twenty aircraft in his group into the lead slot. The 390th made its bomb run over the centre of Bremen and then headed for the crippled 'Hundredth' formation ahead. A group above covered the 390th as it made its manoeuvre, which allowed the 'Hundredth' an opportunity to slide into position behind the 390th as it passed by. The survivors in the 'Hundredth' realized the plan and fell in tightly from the rear. Major Good then slowed the formation to give the stragglers a chance to form up. The manoeuvre prevented the loss of at least four more B-17s that might otherwise have been lost to fighters or flak. Good said later that it was a demonstration of the finest teamwork he had ever seen in the air.

Crosby again:

We crossed Germany and Holland on a line thirty miles north of Lingen, Ommen and Zwolle. We evaded all known flak areas and large towns. I remember a feeling of futility I experienced when explosions burst in and around our compartment. I was so certain that I was safe from flak area, yet here it was all around us. I yelled out over the interphone for someone to tell me where the flak was coming from. The bombardier told me that those explosions were 20mm shells. I didn't feel any better. I remember another instance when the bombardier turned around and looked at me. Two holes appeared on each side of the compartment and cotton batting sifted down as a bullet went between us. I don't remember his looking back at me again.

Finally at 1620 we hit the Zuider Zee. We realized our predicament was still acute but just the same that water looked good to all of us. To avoid known fighter fields we turned to a course of 340° to cross over the West Friesian Islands. I was uncomfortably aware that a few weeks ago enemy fighters at precisely that point attacked a big formation on a practice mission. I hadn't even considered the coastal batteries. At our usual altitude they didn't bother us at all but at 7,000 feet, flying at 120mph, even popguns would have been a menace. They threw everything at us. Whole acres of some sort of light guns flashed up at our ship. Tracers from machine guns laced all around us. In credit to their gunnery we can say that we were hit plenty. Our No. 3 engine, revolving feebly at least, now was non-existent. The whole situation was a series of cracking noises much like the closing of a book as volley after volley hit their target. Blakely and Major Kidd were risking everything in some last evasive action. One of them would see flak on one side and jerk the plane on one heading. The other would spot some on his side and back we would go. Their efforts were effective though, because we got through their last defence.

We had survived everything that the Germans could send up at us but there was still one thing to consider – gravity. Crossing the coast had cost plenty and we were now at 3,990 feet and sinking rapidly. Major Kidd asked for a heading to the closest part of England and I gave it to him. My ETA ran out and then some. As I checked back over my figures I glanced at my airspeed indicator and thought it looked suspiciously immobile. I rapped on it with my fist and the needle dropped to zero. It was then that I learned from a consultation with the pilot that we were making only 120mph instead of 150, as I had believed. I hurriedly redid my calculations and gave a correction in our heading. Bull knew we were a long way from home.

Ditching seemed the next answer. Douglass went back to make the preparations. Two minutes later he was back with the news that we couldn't ditch, that our crew members were in too bad a condition to endure the movements ditching would cause. Moreover, our dinghy compartment was in shreds and at least one of them was in ribbons. That was the first that we in the front had learned of the severity of the situations back in the rear of the plane. Our next thought was to lighten the load of the plane. We threw everything away. Our guns went first and all the ammunition with them. I threw away my flying equipment, my Gee box, radio, anything with even an ounce of weight. Now comes an amazing fact: although our airspeed still remained at 115–120mph, a very small number of miles above the stalling speed of our plane, Blakely not only managed to keep the plane level but actually gained 300 feet of altitude.

England seemed so far away. The ship was listing in such an attitude that our floating aperiodic compasses stuck on the side. I figured the sun should hit the Plexiglas front of the plane and called the pilot to correct him every time he went someplace else. By now our gas problem was serious. The very first airfield sighted, at Ludham, seemed large enough and occupied so we prepared for a crash-landing. Most of us ganged up in the radio compartment. Saunders walked unaided to the radio compartment and smiled at us as we bustled about. I didn't dream how seriously he was injured because he kept cheering us up with his motions (thumbs up and thumb and forefinger circled). When he noticed in his dazed condition what the excitement was about, he thought we were again being attacked so he tried to crawl to his turret to help ward off the fighters he thought were present. It was almost impossible to stop him.

Forkner had always seemed young and perhaps excitable but he was all there on this trip. He had completely stopped the flow of blood from all wounds; he had disinfected all injuries. He had calmed his patients with morphine. He had them all covered with blankets to lessen the shock of the approaching landing and the mental shock of their pain. He had encouraged them all during the crossing. Moreover, even though his key had been shot away he still managed to send out distress signals by pounding his finger on his throat mike! (Actually, Forkner sent messages by touching two exposed wires of the smashed radio.) Thornton cradled Via with his body in the waist since the latter's condition prevented his being moved. The rest of us cushioned ourselves as best we could for a landing we knew was going to be rough. And it was. The tail wheel hadn't come down. The brakes were gone. One elevator was useless. Nothing worked properly at all. Even the hydraulic system failed. And to add to it all, just as we hit the ground the frayed cables to the rudder snapped. From then on, even the pilots were just riding.

On the entire field there were two big trees together and the plane now completely beyond control, veered toward them. The largest one was hit while the plane was going about 50mph. Luckily it passed between the No. 2 engine and pilot's compartment so we were swung around instead of being jerked to a halt. Nevertheless, the nose compartment was completely destroyed. But we were on the ground. Even the triumph of this was negated when we learned that we had picked an unused field. The planes we had seen on the perimeters were dummies. And medical aid was still two hours away! We did everything we could. Aid was summoned immediately. The rockets we had fired had been seen from Coltishall so it wasn't long till some RAF medical officers arrived. We were extremely grateful to Flight Lieutenant Nolan of RAF Coltishall for his medical care. Two ambulances arrived and our four wounded men, all busily engaged in cheering each other up, were loaded into them and soon were under expert medical care at the Norfolk and Norwich Hospital.

When word reached Thorpe Abbotts that the crew of *Just A Snappin'* were still alive the sea of despondency that had descended on base operations was lifted. Everyone had thought that the crew were 'done for' and that they were yet more casualties on a day of high losses. Though the crew of

Just A Snappin' were not yet aware of it, the 'Bloody Hundredth' had lost seven B-17s and seventy-two combat crewmen. At least thirteen more were in hospital suffering from wounds. In all, the 8th lost twenty-six bombers, fourteen of them from the 3rd Bomb Division.[14]

The four surviving B-17s in the 'Bloody Hundredth' formation that made it back to Thorpe Abbotts owed their survival to the 390th leader, Major Robert O. Good, who encouraged them to move in tightly behind his twenty B-17s after the target. Silas Nettles' crew in the 'Snetterton Falcons' were also lucky to make it back in a new Fort called *V Packet*, which returned 'somehow' with over 100 holes and one feathered engine. Nettles' crew felt like veterans because 'no mission could be rougher than this'.[15] Co-pilot Jerry V. Lefors, who had just flown his first mission, told the crew chief that all the engines would have to be replaced because they had flown for about forty-five minutes at full rpm and maximum manifold pressure. The rule was that an engine should be replaced if run under such conditions for 'several' minutes. The crew chief laughed and said that they would fire the engines up and if they ran, 'the plane goes up again'. There were few extra engines available. Nettles' crew scrounged for armour plate the next day and discussed carrying more ammunition. They were a green crew but united in their determination to complete their missions. Perhaps Lefors was the greenest, having graduated from the Flying Cadet programme on 6 June 1943 as a single-engine fighter pilot. Though he had no desire to fly bombers his heart sank when he and thirteen other pilots had been sent to become pilots on Forts.

After the P-47 escort had withdrawn, low on fuel, the First Division encountered enemy fighters in strength. Altogether, twelve Fortresses in the First Division failed to return. The unfortunate 381st, flying as low group, lost seven of its eighteen B-17s, including the lead ship. Of the eleven that returned, several were shot to pieces. *Our Mom*, piloted by Lieutenant Miller, came home to Ridgewell with a shattered nose, which caused fragments of Plexiglas to strike Lieutenant Ed Klein, the navigator, who was on his first mission, in the face. Miller landed with the rudder almost blown off its mounting and an ambulance followed the aircraft as it rolled down the runway. When the aircraft stopped, Chaplain James Good Brown helped the navigator carry S/Sgt Stephen J. Klinger, the tail gunner, out of the plane. He had been killed instantly. They put him on a stretcher and into the ambulance. He still had his oxygen mask on. His neck was penetrated, leaving a big hole. The sight of all this was too much for the navigator who broke down and cried, saying in desperate tones,

'Jesus Christ and he was only twenty years old.' It was the boy's first mission.[16]

Tinkertoy made it home with a shattered cockpit after a fighter fired shells through the windscreen and destroyed the Plexiglas nose. This Fortress had been featured in a film, *Hers To Hold* as it came off the Vega assembly line and a number of crews who flew it later, met untimely and gruesome deaths. Neither man in the nose compartment was wounded but Lieutenant Hal Minerich, the pilot, was decapitated. Lieutenant Thomas Sellars, the co-pilot, was wounded by the exploding shells. Spraying blood froze on the top turret base and prevented Tech Sergeant Miller from manning his position. He assisted Sellars who against all odds managed to get *Tinkertoy* home to Ridgewell where he ground looped the badly damaged Fortress. Sellars later was awarded the Distinguished Service Cross.

'There was barely a square inch of the entire cockpit that was not covered with blood and brain tissue,' said the surgeon. 'One half of the pilot's face and a portion of his cervical vertebra were found just in front of the bomb bay. The decapitation was complete.' Chaplain James Good Brown wrote: 'To place his body on a stretcher with his head beside him is enough to make one conclude that war is not the best way of solving the world's problems.'[17]

The surgeon concluded:

> After this mission in visiting the many crews right after they hit the ground, the tense excitement of many was apparent and in many cases was border-line hysteria. This was the roughest mission experienced in some time and most of the personnel seemed to feel the losses keenly.

Next day the 381st put up sixteen Fortresses for the raid on the Arado aircraft component plant at Anklam near Peenemünde and three more crews failed to return. It was nearly four. Just as the formation was reaching the Danish coast a 20mm shell exploded in the cockpit of Lieutenant Doug Winters' B-17 and he was temporarily stunned or blinded by the flash. When he came to the bombardier and navigator had already left the aircraft, the co-pilot was jumping and none of the crewmembers gave him a farewell salute – and jumped. The B-17 was in a steep gliding turn and there was a fire in the rear of the cockpit. Winters righted the aircraft, put on the autopilot, went back and put out the fire, and brought the aircraft safely back to England.

The 1st and 41st Combat Wings had dispatched 115 aircraft to the

Arado aircraft component plant as a diversion for 263 bombers attacking the Polish port of Gdynia and the Focke-Wulf plant at Marienburg. The Anklam raid was the twenty-fifth and final mission of the war for Howard E. Hernan and two other members of Claude Campbell's crew in the 'Hell's Angels' at Molesworth. The night before the mission Campbell had been told he would lead the Anklam raid with Major Calhoun, the 359th Squadron CO, but on the morning of the 9th Campbell discovered to his dismay that he would miss the mission altogether. Calhoun would fly *The Eightball* with General Travis, the 1st Bomb Division commander, taking the co-pilot's seat. Howard Hernan and the rest of Campbell's crew would make up the complement. The news that Campbell would not be coming with them was a bad blow, as Hernan explains.

> I couldn't believe it and my morale dropped to rock bottom. It seemed so strange to fly twenty-four missions with this good man and all he had got us through to have his place taken by a general. When we finally got away from the crowded flight line we taxied *The Eightball* up to the end of the runway where the gas trucks met us. We topped off our tanks and took off. I was never so glad to get away. We circled the field until all the group had formed up. It was not until 0930 hours before we finally left the coast and headed out over The Wash towards Denmark and then we were supposed to fire a green flare to let everyone know that the mission was on. I looked at the dashboard and counted seventeen green flares and two red. I said I didn't think it a good idea for all those flares to be there. If one got hit it might start a fire. I couldn't very well throw them out of the plane because they might hit one behind. General Travis said, 'Fire 'em off.' I did and it caused uproar because the rest of the group didn't know what it meant!
>
> We flew out over the North Sea at probably only 5,000 feet; my lowest ever raid. After we had used our gas in the bomb bay tank I disconnected the hoses and told the bombardier to open the bomb bay doors and try to salvo it. Momentarily it hung up, so I kicked it and off it went. There must have been 115 tanks washed up along the coast that day. We made landfall on the Danish coast and turned south-east to make a feint towards Berlin. By this time the enemy fighters had hit us en masse. They tried to hit us in the lead plane and I had plenty to shoot at. (Later, when I saw the General's notes, he recorded that we had been attacked 114 times, 102 of those at 12 o'clock level, no fewer than two planes in each attack and one time as high as fourteen.) The fourteen came at us wing tip to wing tip,

firing rockets. There wasn't really much we could do about them, but I started on the one on the left and raked the entire formation.

Just before we reached the target a Ju 88 followed us out to our left at 10 o'clock, probably calling out our altitude. The General asked if I couldn't get him out of there. I informed General Travis that he was approximately 2,500 yards away and it probably wouldn't do any good to shoot at him. However, I did notice that once in a while we would make a one-degree turn to the left and I asked him if he would tell me the next time he was going to turn. This Ju 88 would not immediately correct his course as it took him a moment to notice we were turning. Consequently, that would narrow the gap. I really didn't think I had a chance of hitting him, but I set up the sight for his fuselage length. The General told me he was turning and I watched the Ju 88. He didn't correct right away and I had my graticules on him and figured he was probably 1,500 yards away. As my sight was pointed towards him, I looked at my guns and they were out to my right so I knew that the sight was computing. I began firing off short bursts of four or five rounds at a time. After about the third burst the Ju 88's right engine caught fire, black smoke poured out and down he went. I don't think he crashed but the General saw what happened and I got credit for the Ju 88.

On our approach to the target there was little flak, although there was a lot around Peenemünde. There did not appear to be many fighters either so I had an opportunity of watching the bombs drop. I very seldom did this but since we were only at 12,500 feet I figured I could follow them all the way down and see them hit. Our first bomb landed on a railroad car between two warehouses, blowing it to pieces, while others on either side of it turned flip-flops through the air. We completely saturated the target and started making our left turns to head back over Denmark and the North Sea.[18]

The Gdynia force led by Lieutenant Colonel Henry G. MacDonald, 40th Combat Wing Operations Officer, had continued on its 1,500-mile round trip to the dock area. Leslie C. Thibodeau, flying his third mission in the 388th, recalled:

Our group made two runs on the target area before we dropped our bombs because we were confronted by a great smoke-screen thrown up by German destroyers in an effort to protect the ships and installations. However, the 550-foot long liner *Stuttgart* was on fire and the docks, railways and workshops were hit.

Flak was heavy over the target area and on the homeward trip the *Luftwaffe* was waiting. Bill Rose, in the 92nd formation, said:

> It amazed me how the German pilots could fly through the hail of shells we were firing at them. Every fifth round was a tracer. The fighters came in straight through the formation and knocked down Bill Whelan's plane.[19] Then the fighters left the formation as if knocked down themselves. We realized that this was a game for keeps. They were out to kill us and we were going to kill them.

A third force of B-17s, which bombed Marienburg, achieved the greatest success of the day. The normally unfortunate 385th led the raid and lost only two aircraft, one through engine trouble. Major 'Pappy' Colby led the 94th, which followed closely behind. 'The target was completely demolished,' he wrote. 'As we turned for home one gun fired three bursts at least a mile away, proving that we had complete surprise. They just didn't believe we could bomb so far from England.' Anti-aircraft defences had been thought unnecessary so far from England and their absence meant that the force could bomb from between 11,000 and 13,000 feet.[20] Before the raid the Marienburg plant had been turning out almost 50 per cent of the *Luftwaffe*'s FW 190 production. The results were devastating. General Eaker called it, 'A classic example of precision bombing'.

When *The Eightball* arrived back at Molesworth, the crew was 'welcomed by the same throng, possibly more, than had seen us off.' According to Howard Hernan:

> I was overwhelmed and, of course, my good pilot, Claude Campbell, was there to greet us. Every man in the squadron was anxious for me to complete my twenty-five missions so they could tear my filthy coveralls off me. Everyone, including General Travis, six foot two and weighing 200lbs, who grabbed hold of my shoulder and yanked me clear off the ground, had a lot of fun tearing those coveralls off. General Travis told Campbell 'This is the best goddam crew I've ever flown with.'

At the Standard Oil Company of California in the Standard Oil Building in San Francisco, L. W. Peck, the editor of *The Standard Oiler*, received a two-page release from the headquarters if the 8th Air Force about Lieutenant Charlie Hudson being cited for heroism on his first four raids on Europe. He had immediately taken the liberty of writing to Hudson's wife in Bakersfield congratulating her and asking if she had a picture of him in uniform, preferably one taken in England. 'You see,' Peck wrote to Charlie Hudson. 'You are our only bombardier-gunner out of over 6,300 standard oilers now in the Services and here's a swell chance to make a swell story without making you the guy that's telling it.'

Charlie's third mission was the one to Bremen. Peck began the write-up saying that the ship, which was being flown by Lieutenant 'Bud' Evers, had a nude painted in the nose and was named *Hell's Belle*.

> Far out over the North Sea the pilot of the ship flying alongside the 'Belle' calls up on the radio: 'The door has come off your ball turret and the gunner is falling out head first. He's hanging out in the slipstream with his head, shoulders and most of his Mae West showing.'

Once again Charlie jumped out of his flak suit, grabbed a couple of walk-around bottles and headed back through the ship. Meanwhile, the ball turret gunner had managed to pull himself back into the turret and had rolled it up so that the open door was inside the ship. But he had caught his head in the mechanism on the way up. When Charlie reached the turret he found the sergeant hanging with his head in his lap and blood pouring over his face and into the bottom of the turret. His forehead was cut nearly from ear to ear, about an inch above his eyebrows and half of his scalp was laid back like a peeled orange. Charlie grasped him under the armpits and struggling against his own weakness due to lack of sufficient oxygen, slowly dragged him out of the turret. The blood running over the sergeant's face was freezing and he was choking on chunks of the ice. Charlie put his finger in the boy's mouth and removed the ice. Then he took off his own oxygen mask and placed it over the gunner's face. Charlie's face was covered with the other fellow's blood and he found that he too had been hit by something over the eye and that some of his own blood was streaming down his face.

A thousand jumbled reactions and thoughts rushed through Charlie's brain in a fleeting moment. He even recalled a recent newspaper story and considered parachuting the wounded gunner out over the enemy, hoping that a German doctor would find him before it was too late. Crawling into the radio room, Charlie got himself an oxygen mask and then passed out for a few moments from sheer exhaustion. When he came to he returned to the ball turret gunner, slit the arm of his jacket with a knife, administered a shot of morphine from a nearby first aid kit, dragged the boy into the radio room and plugged in his heated suit.

The ship was nearing the target and once again Charlie dragged himself up to the nose from where he already could see Bremen's dry docks. Once again a lot of hurried, minute adjustments and it was 'bombs away'. Then he manned one of the nose guns until the friendly fighter escort arrived on the scene, when he returned to the radio room to comfort the injured gunner as much as possible.

Back at base there were red flares and the sergeant was rushed to a general hospital and a few weeks later he was back on the base with a sear across his forehead little worse than another wrinkle, thanks to the skill of his doctors.

That was Charlie's third trip. Early next morning the map in the intelligence briefing room showed a string running halfway across Europe to the Pomeranian village of Anklam, only seventy-five miles north of Berlin. The target was a vital Focke Wulf component parts factory. This was the furthest the Forts had ever gone to date. Charlie was flying in *Lightning Strikes*. On the nose there was a cartoon showing a bolt of lightning 'knocking the shingles off a Chio Sale, with Hitler dashing out the door with his pants down'.

To the enemy this attack looked like a raid on Berlin. The *Luftwaffe* sent up almost 350 fighters of every description, which stayed with the Forts for more than three and a half hours. One of *Lightning Strikes*' engines was knocked out of commission going into the target and another was smoking. After Charlie got his bombs away there was a loud W-H-O-O-M and a crash as a flak burst wrecked the hydraulic system, making it impossible to close the bomb-bay doors. The trail of smoke, the open doors and the feathered prop were an invitation to enemy fighters and *Lightning Strikes* was flying 'tail-end Charlie' at the rear of the formation, down in what fliers called 'Purple Heart Corner'. It looked as though Charlie Hudson was due for his Purple Heart.

Charlie and Bruce Moore, the navigator, were sweating over their nose guns and the great bomber was vibrating as gunners throughout the ship poured out their protective fire. A flak fragment crashed through the nose glass, hitting Charlie on his left wrist. His feet flew up in the air and he was sent sprawling in a heap of shell casings on the floor. The fragment put a hole through his wrist the size of a silver dollar, breaking the bone. Moore helped him to his feet and attempted to give him first aid.

'Get back to your gun and keep firing at the bastards; I'm all right' Charlie ordered. Then he took out his knife and cut a slit from wrist to elbow through his leather jacket, flying suit, sweat short and pyjamas. After giving himself a shot of morphine, he used the low slung neck of his Mae West life preserver as a sort of a sling and returned to his heavy .50-calibre machine gun, manoeuvring it, aiming it and firing it with his right hand. He noticed that the Fortress on his right wing was gone. (It never returned to England.) Then a fighter attacked the bomber in his left wing, setting three engines ablaze. The ship pulled away to one side. Apparently the pilot had sounded the bale-out alarm. Four parachutes blossomed out and then the ship disintegrated in mid-air with a terrible explosion. It must have been the gas tanks. The tail spun crazily in one direction, the wheels in another and debris filled the air looking like a slow motion film. Bodies could be seen pin wheeling upward. Then, right in the midst of the smoke and debris, a parachute mysteriously opened up and floated away. Charlie looked away; he did not want to see any more. He resumed firing.

Again there was a W-H-O-O-M and Charlie felt a searing pain as another piece of flak came through the nose, burying itself in his wounded left arm. He was knocked sprawling again, but scrambled back to his gun and he tried to continue firing. But the Fort was going through violent evasive action, diving, climbing and slipping, one moment flying with the top element; the next with the lower. Then Charlie fired his last cartridge. Bruce Moore went back to the radio room to get some more ammunition. Too exhausted to carry a heavy boxful, he took off the lid, grabbed one end of the cumbersome 350-round belt and staggered back through the ship dragging the long chain of bullets behind him... across the narrow catwalk through the open bomb bay... over the base of the top turret where the gunner reached down between bursts to help inch the belt along...under the cockpit where the co-pilot leaned down to give a few tugs... up into the nose where it took both men to load the gun... and the firing resumed.

There was another explosion and pieces of metal came through the roof, lacerating Charlie's right arm twice, once above and once below the elbow. Charlie was down on the canvas for the third time in one round, but his fighting blood brought him back to his machine gun. The ship must get home to England!

Now the B-17 was out over the North Sea. The smoking engine stopped running altogether and *Lightning Strikes* fell further and further behind the disappearing formation; unable to maintain sufficient speed. Dropping down nearly to water level for protection against pursuing fighters, they headed for home barely skimming the whitecaps. Moore pored over his maps and kept an eye open for check-points on the English coast. The fuel was low.

With no brakes due to the damaged hydraulic system, the ship landed at Bassingbourn firing red flares to attract the ambulance. 'Bud' Evers gunned the motor on one side taxiing the ship around in a big curve across the grass of the field and finally it came to a stop. Charlie was removed from the nose and speeded to a hospital. After twenty-eight days of stitching, skin grafting and bone setting, he was back on the base, ready to go on his fifth mission as soon as they took the cast off his arm.

The raid on Münster on Sunday 10 October heralded a surprising switch in bombing policy. For the first time in the war the 8th Air Force was to bomb a residential area to deprive the Germans of its rail workers, who were practically all billeted in the town. At Framlingham, home of the 95th Bomb Group, which would lead the 3rd Bomb Division to Münster, crews were told: 'Your MPI will be Münster Cathedral and you are going to bomb the workers' homes…' A maximum effort was ordered, with 264 B-17s from the 1st and 3rd Divisions being dispatched. Crews were told that approximately 245 single-engined and 290 twin-engined fighters could be expected to oppose the mission. Despite a planned direct route, the 1st and 3rd Division forces would be given a strong Thunderbolt escort and Liberators of the 2nd Bomb Division would fly a diversionary sweep over the North Sea.

At 1348 hours Colonel John K. Gerhart, the 95th CO, took off from Horham to lead the 13th Wing and the 3rd Bomb Division over the North Sea towards Münster. Following closely behind came the 390th and the 'Bloody Hundredth' led by Major 'Bucky' Egan and John Brady in *Mlle Zig-Zag*. Brady had been a saxophone player in one of Bunny Berrigan's bands. Egan, who was superstitious, had survived the Regensburg mission in August carrying two rosaries, two good luck medals and a $2 bill from which he had chewed a corner for each of his missions, plus he was wearing his good luck jacket and his sweater back to front.[21] By the time the 3rd Division crossed the Dutch coast at 1416 hours no fewer than twenty-seven aircraft had aborted with mechanical problems. The 'Hundredth' for instance, had lost seven of its original twenty-one aircraft, including one that had failed to take off from Thorpe Abbotts. Fog over England prevented the next relay of Thunderbolt escorts from taking off and the B-17s had to continue alone. Then the diversionary force of B-24s was forced to abort and as the formation turned for home the German controllers redirected their fighters towards the 3rd Division instead. The *Luftwaffe* picked up the leading 13th Wing and concentrating on the low group, proceeded to tear the 'Hundredth' apart. *Mlle Zig-Zag* was hit by a rocket and went down. 'Bucky' Egan baled out and was eventually taken prisoner. The 'Hard Luck' Group reeled under the incessant attacks and eleven aircraft were shot down before the target was reached. Only *Royal Flush*, *Pasadena Nena* and *Stork Club*, which was flown by Captain Keith Harris in the 390th who was flying in the 'Hundredth' formation, reached the target. (*Pasadena Nena* and Lieutenant John 'Jack' Justice's crew was shot down on the homeward leg.) Over Münster *Royal Flush*, which was being flown by 2nd Lieutenant Robert Rosenthal because *Rosie's Riveters*, his usual aircraft, was still under repair following *Rosie*'s debut on the disastrous mission to Bremen, lost two engines and a rocket shell tore through the right wing, leaving a large hole. Despite this, Rosenthal completed the bomb run and instigated a series of violent manoeuvres to throw the aim of the flak guns.

The eighteen B-17s in the 390th also felt the full impact of the *Luftwaffe* attacks. In about twenty-five minutes the Group lost eight of its bombers as the rockets exploded among them. Next, the *Luftwaffe* turned on the 95th. Five of the nineteen B-17s were shot down. The survivors continued to the target, desperately fighting off the intense *Luftwaffe* attacks. Beyond the target *Tech Supply*, flown by Lieutenant John G. Winant Jr, son of the US Ambassador to Great Britain, was hit by a rocket and exploded. It was Winant's thirteenth mission.[22] Shortly after *Tech Supply* went down, *The Eightball* in the 390th formation was hit in the starboard wing by a rocket. 'The rocket sheared a path through the top half of the right wing (about 15 feet from the end),' recalls Richard H. Perry, the co-pilot. 'The wing tip flapped up and down in the wind-stream and caused us to lose the lift that we should have gotten from the wing.' The combined efforts of Perry and Bill Cabral, the pilot, were not enough to keep the bomber from falling out of formation, so Ferris was called to the controls. He stood between Perry and Cabral and managed, despite his injuries, to put a hand on each of the control wheels and help the pilots keep *The Eightball* straight and level in formation. It was a great relief to one and all when the white vapour trails of the Thunderbolt escort looking like the sky-writing advertising the boys used to see back in the States were seen directly ahead. There were few B-17s for the 'little friends' to protect. The 390th was pitifully down to ten bombers and even the survivors were not sure they would reach England. Those that did were badly damaged, with wounded crews and pilots and put down as best they could. Bill Cabral and Richard Perry landed at Thorpe Abbotts after bad weather prevented a landing at Framlingham. Despite the fog, all ten aircraft in the 390th made it to Suffolk. It had been a black day for the 13th Wing, which had lost twenty-five of the twenty-nine B-17s lost by the 3rd Division. The 390th had lost eight and the 95th five. Worst of all, the 'Bloody

Hundredth' had lost a dozen bombers. This brought its total losses to nineteen in three days.

'Rosie' Rosenthal got the badly damaged *Royal Flush* back to Thorpe Abbotts with two engines out, a large hole in the wing and two badly wounded waist gunners. After de-briefing, Rosenthal went to the officers' club. He found the place empty and deathly quiet. No one came over to talk to them. Lieutenant Clifford 'C. J.' Milburn, the bombardier, sat down at the piano and began playing. A couple of the crew gathered around him. Milburn, W. T. 'Pappy' Lewis, the co-pilot, Ronald C. Bailey, the navigator, and Rosenthal were summoned to Elveden Hall by General Curtis LeMay to attend a critique. 'Rosie' was the only one present that had flown the Bremen, Marienburg and Münster raids and his summation was well received by LeMay, so much so that one colonel who spoke to 'Rosie' afterwards said that he had never heard him give such lavish praise! A few days later Rosie's crew were sent to the flak house[23] but Rosenthal was upset. He wanted to keep flying missions.

Eaker made a broadcast back to America on Sunday night.

On Friday, we sent more than 4,000 Eighth Air Force fighting men against German industrial targets and again yesterday, more than 4,000 fought their way through the German defences to destroy vital Nazi aircraft factories. And here is a message direct from my combat crews, a message which they want me to give tonight directly to their greatest supporters, the working men and women in the factories at home who build our fine planes and the weapons they carry. This is the message. We have not yet won this battle. The battle has not yet even reached its climax. The fight is now on at white heat. We have just passed the fifth inning but we have not yet reached the seventh inning stretch. We are not going to relax over here. And you must not relax at home.

On Monday morning the London *Daily Sketch* headlines were: 'US Forts Shatter Munster – 814 Nazi Fighters Down in 40 Days.' In all, eighty-eight bombers had been lost on three successive days and the losses came at a time when intelligence sources revealed that *Luftwaffe* fighter strength was increasing. Some put the figure at around 1,100 operational fighters. In reality, the *Luftwaffe* could call upon 1,646 single- and twin-engined fighters for the defence of the *Reich*; 400 more than before the 'Pointblank' directive. The Allies' figures confirmed their worst fears. General Arnold in Washington sent Eaker a cable in which he said that since German air power appeared at a critical stage, it was necessary to send the maximum number of planes against the enemy. The decision was therefore taken to attack the ball-hearing plant at Schweinfurt for the second time in three months in the hope that VIII Bomber Command could deliver a single, decisive blow to the German aircraft industry and stem the flow of fighters to *Luftwaffe* units.

On the 12th fog mercifully rolled over the English countryside to offer a welcome respite. Wednesday the 13th dawned in pea soup weather and the crews could sleep late, as the mission was scrubbed. At High Wycombe that afternoon in a square, large room with a high ceiling buried beneath thirty feet of reinforced concrete, Brigadier General Fred Anderson, Commanding General of VIII Bomber Command, a position he had held since June, gathered for the daily Operations Conference. Anderson and the five senior staff officers were told that good weather was expected for the morrow. At once a warning order was sent out to all three Bomb Division headquarters with details of a mission, No. 115, to Schweinfurt. The orders were then transmitted over teletape machines to the various combat wing headquarters. Anderson hoped to launch 420 Fortresses and Liberators in a three-pronged attack on the city and he composed a message to be read to all crews at mission briefings that morning:

> To all leaders and combat crews. This air operation today is the most important air operation yet conducted in this war. The target must be destroyed. It is of vital importance to the enemy. Your friends and comrades that have been lost and that will be lost today are depending on you. Their sacrifices must not be in vain. Good luck, good shooting and good bombing.

Nowhere were the sacrifices greater than at Ridgewell, where the 381st had lost thirteen Fortresses on 8 and 9 October and at Thorpe Abbotts where the 'Bloody Hundredth' was still licking its wounds after the severe maulings of 8 October, when it lost seven crews and 10 October when it lost another dozen crews. On 10 October the 381st surgeon at Ridgewell noted that: 'The mental attitude and morale of the crews is the lowest that has yet been observed'. Three days later he noted: 'Captain ———— a squadron leader and a brave man, informed the commanding officer that he had no desire to continue flying.' Despite these extremely serious losses the 381st and the 'Bloody Hundredth' were still expected to contribute to the tonnage of bombs to be dropped on Schweinfurt.

At Horham on the night of the 13th 'Maggy's Drawers' were flying from a squadron flagpole. Thus they were alerted for a mission the next day.

Leonard W. Herman laid out the various layers of his combat clothing and shaved before going to bed. In the morning it would be the same routine: a flashlight stabbing its way through the dark hut; men dressing while half-asleep and boarding a truck or jeep to the mess hall. After Sunday's raid, his third in three days, George 'Bud' Moffet, a gunner and the others in his crew in another hut at Horham had slept like 'dead men' all day Monday and Monday night. After 'eating the Army out of house and home', they had bathed, dressed and visited Kane at the 12th Evacuation Hospital. Seeing all the pretty nurses, they almost wished that they had been hit too. Kane was giving the prettiest ones a big line, gesticulating with his hands and going 'rat-a-tat-tat'. They should have known better than to worry about him. Kane showed them that when he drank coffee, it leaked out the back of his neck on to the pillow! When he got back to his hut Moffet wrote some letters so that the folks back home would not worry about him. They checked the bulletin board; they were alerted for a mission the next morning. They hit the hay early. Another alert had been issued for the morning of the 14th. The men knew that they must have a very 'hot' target.

When the order came at Polebrook during the night of 13 October, 1st Lieutenant Jim Bradley, the lead bombardier in his Group, got out his maps. Bradley's original crew, without Walter Stockman and himself went down on the mission to Schweinfurt on 17 August and he really wanted to 'get' Schweinfurt. A lead bombardier, Captain Bill Winters, told Bradley that he had a perfect bomb run on that tragic and frustrating August day and he could not believe it when all the bombs fell short and south of the target. Bradley had already studied all approaches to the target and was confident that he knew it like his hometown. On the way to his barracks a couple of crewmen asked him where they were going on the 14th.

He told them that it was a real 'milk run'.

Notes

1. Further radar bombing was delayed because the 482nd Bomb Group had insufficient aircraft and crews to participate in a major mission and there were several days on which conditions were suitable for visual attacks in western Germany.

2. Seay and his crew had fallen to what the RAF knew as a *Wild Boar* tactic where day fighters were used in conjunction with searchlights. It was highly successful. Five crew were KIA, 5 PoW. B-17F 41-24616 *Sam's Little Helper* survived the war and was flown home to the USA in 1945.

3. 2nd Lt Paul H. Keilman who was from Missoula, Montana, was the bombardier in Lt Nolan B. Cargile's crew in the 68th Squadron who were all killed.

4. *Mac's Sack/Filthy Annie* and Lt Orval S. Morphew's crew and *Satan's Flame* and Lt Brian T. Smith's crews went down in the North Sea with no survivors from either crew. The low squadron, containing the 44th and 93rd flights was well worked over by the fighters because they did not have the new nose turrets. American gunners claimed nineteen fighters destroyed.

5. *The Big Square A drops in on Thanet* by Joe Kovac.

6. *Eighth Air Force: The American Bomber Crews in Britain* by Donald L. Miller (Aurum 2007).

7. Thayer manned one of the waist guns in *Our Baby*.

8. *Gee* was a British navigational device that involved a special aircraft radio receiver working on pulsed signals received from three ground stations. It was limited to a range of about 400 miles. By late 1942 *Gee* had been rendered almost ineffective by German jamming, and it was replaced by *Oboe*. *Gee-H* was a development of *Gee*, giving more precise fixes to aircraft and *Micro-H* was a further development of the *Gee* system using ground stations' signals, but combined with *H2X* for bombing.

9. After the P-47 escort had withdrawn, low on fuel, the B-17s, which approached Bremen from two different directions in an attempt to fool the German controllers, were met in strength. The ruses and feints and the use of airborne *Carpet* radar jammers aboard some of the B-17s for the first time, were not enough to prevent the loss of twenty-seven B-17s and three B-24s. P-47s, before they had to return, low on fuel, took on *Geschwaderstab* JG 1 over Nordhorn and accounted for *Geschwaderkommodore* Major Hans Philipp, a 206-victory ace. *Oberst* Walter Oesau, previously *Jagdfliegerführer* 4 Brittany and forbidden to fly operationally, assumed command two days later. Physically and mentally exhausted, he was shot down and killed in combat with P-51 Mustangs and P-38 Lightnings on 11 May 1944. He had 125 victories.

10. *Eighth Air Force: The American Bomber Crews in Britain* by Donald L. Miller (Aurum 2007).

11. FW 190 A-6 Black 5, flown by 29-year-old *Leutnant* Hans Ehlers, *Staffelführer* of 2./JG 1, collided with *Marie Helena*, piloted by 2nd Lt Raymond J. Gormley, in the low squadron of the 100th BG. All 10 men, including Gormley, were KIA. Ehlers survived the mid-air collision and baled out with various facial injuries and a double fracture of the right thighbone. On 11 November 1943 Ehlers was promoted to *Staffelkapitän* of 3/JG 1 and became *Kommandeur* of 1/JG 1 in May 1944. In July 1944, when Ehlers received the Knight's Cross, he had been shot down no fewer than twelve times and was credited with the destruction of twenty *Viermots*. Robert J. Cupp, manning one of the nose guns

on *The Zoot Suiters*, the lead aircraft in the 95th BG's low squadron, saw Ehlers and a second FW 190 pass through the 100th BG formation. This second FW 190 passed over the formation and crossed his path. The pilot, probably Johannes Kreimeyer of 1/JG 1, was killed when his FW 190A-6 exploded after receiving several short bursts from Cupp's 50 calibre. Following the collision between Gormley and Ehlers, 1st Lt Frank H. Meadows' *Phartzac* was torn apart from what appeared to have been an explosion in the bomb bay area (eight KIA, two PoW). Minutes later 2nd Lt Arthur H. Becktoft's *War Eagle* was observed by Owen 'Cowboy' Roane and Robert N. Lohof leaving the formation under control with its No. 3 engine on fire. It crashed with the loss of radio operator T/Sgt Floyd A. Lowe who was hit between the shoulder blades by a 20mm shell and probably died instantly (nine PoW). The encounter reports from the 95th and 390th BGs reveal that between the European coast and the beginning of the bomb run (a period of about thirty minutes) these two groups were attacked by no fewer than forty-two fighters, of which all but eight were FW 190s or Bf 109s. Also, from the perspective of the 3rd Division's surviving crews, the level of German fighter interception was more prominent than had been the situation throughout most of September and early October, but did not match the vigour endured by those who survived the 'double strike' mission on 17 August.

12. 'Bucky' Cleven baled out at about 2,000ft and landed about ten miles northwest of Osnabrück where he and Benny DeMarco were surrounded by irate farmers before being taken promptly to a *Luftwaffe* airfield west of the city where all the crew gradually filtered in. All eleven reached the ground safely but three suffered slight injury on landing. The radio operator's parachute canopy caught in a tree and he fractured several ribs when he swung against the trunk.

13. Incredibly, almost all the crew of *Salvo Sal* (one Evd, one KIA, 8 PoW) managed to bale out of the doomed aircraft, which turned over, spun slightly and burst into flames before it crashed near the Zuider Zee in western Holland. The left waist gunner, Douglas Agee, was struck by a 20mm shell about thirty minutes before the crew baled out and bled to death in the aircraft. The rest of the enlisted men were captured by German patrols shortly after landing. 2nd Lt John J. James, co-pilot, had jumped with a parachute that had been holed by a cannon shell and broke his leg in a bumpy landing. He was taken prisoner by German soldiers and hospitalized. 2nd Lt Carl L. Spicer evaded capture and made it home to England via France and Spain. MacDonald and McGlinchey also evaded capture and travelled along the evasion lines through Holland and France into Spain, only to be caught at a crossing point on the Pyrenees. They were sent to *Stalag Luft 1*, Barth. 42-30840 (Herbert Nash, pilot and two crew KIA). On *Piccadilly Lily* Captain Thomas Murphy, Captain Alvin L. Barker, 351st BS Operations Officer, co-pilot 2nd Lt Marshall F. Lee, who was riding in the ball turret, Derrell Piel,

Elder Dickerson and S/Sgt Aaron A. David, tail gunner, were KIA. The five other members of the crew survived and they were taken prisoner.

14. The 100th had lost seven B-17s. The 390th had lost three B-17s including *Devil's Daughter* and *Blood, Guts and Rust II*. The 96th contributed three B-17s to the division's loss. If it had not been for the installation of *Carpet* blinkers aboard some 96th and 388th BG B-17s, losses might well have been much higher. *Carpet* was another British invention, which used radio signals to interfere with radar-directed flak guns. Over the next two months *Carpet* devices were fitted to all Fortresses. Experienced crews could not be totally replaced, but new crews were now passing through the Combat Crew Replacement Centre at Bovingdon daily. Since 1 March 1943 the 398th BG had assumed the duties of the CCRC and by December that year would have trained over 300 B-17 crews.

15. They would be proved wrong on 14 October when he and the Nettles' crew were shot down on the mission to Schweinfurt.

16. *The Mighty Men of the 381st, Heroes All: A Chaplain's Inside Story of the men of the 381st Bomb Group* by James Good Brown (Salt Lake City: Publishers Press 1994).

17. *Tinkertoy* would only last until 20 December on the raid on Bremen when it was involved in a collision with a Bf 109 and went down with seven of 2nd Lt Leo Dorman F. Lane's crew killed.

18. The Anklam force lost fourteen B-17s; all from the 1st Combat Wing.

19. Five KIA, five PoW.

20. At such heights accuracy was almost guaranteed and 60 per cent of the bombs dropped by the 96 Fortresses exploded within 1,000ft of the MPI and 83 per cent fell within 2,000ft.

21. *Eighth Air Force: The American Bomber Crews in Britain* by Donald L. Miller (Aurum 2007).

22. Winant and five of his crew were taken prisoner.

23. A number of private manor houses and a few small hotels were under the control of the 8th AF. They had been acquired for usage as rest homes or 'flak shacks' as they were familiarly known, for AAF personnel. These were assigned for the use of combat crews for rest and recuperation either late in their combat tours, or after a significantly traumatic mission or series of missions.

CHAPTER 4

The Long Fall

I met a doughboy from the Third Army Group that moved through Southern Germany. He said that when they moved through Schweinfurt the troops could not stand up where the ball bearings littered the area. [1]

Joseph Christie, deputy group radio operator-gunner, 351st Bomb Group

After weeks of intense operations tired crews at bases in East Anglia were trying to sleep in the early morning of Thursday 14 October as best they could. At Rougham, Hal Kowal had been on a few missions – Emden on the 2nd and then Hanau, Bremen, Marienburg and Münster. Coming home from the long journey to Marienburg on three engines with a runaway prop had been a 'white knuckle flying trip'. The 8th carried out raids to Bremen on the 8th, Gdynia on the 9th and Münster on Sunday, the 10th. At Horham radio operator E. A. Beans in W. V. Owens' crew thought that they were 'already dead' after their first three rough raids in three days, 8–10 October. At Bremen they endured the heaviest flak up to that time in the ETO. On the way back from the long trip to Marienburg they saw a crew bale out of a B-17 with their chutes on fire and fall into the North Sea as smoking dots. At Münster they saw twelve out of the thirteen B-17s in the 'Bloody Hundredth' Bomb Group go down in fourteen minutes. Owens' crew would sight fifty enemy fighters at close range and shoot one down on 14 October mission. They were used to rough ones by this time!

At Horham, 'Bud' Moffet was among those awakened at 0200 hours, with the weather cold and the wind howling but he was in good spirits. At the rate they were flying missions they should be through by Christmas and home by Easter he thought. And he had been credited with shooting down two Me 210s over Münster on Sunday. At Polebrook, Joseph Christie was awakened at 0430 hours and pulled from his crew. He began quizzing the orderly about the mission. His only reply was, 'You'll find out at the briefing.' At Thurleigh a flashlight woke radio operator George Roberts in the 'Clay Pigeon' Squadron from a restless sleep. A soft voice said, 'Breakfast at six, briefing at seven.' Jim Harris in W. W. Thomas' crew had heard the sounds of big engines being run up and pre-flighted on the hardstands around the perimeter of the airfield. As it was raining quite hard he figured that the mission would be scrubbed. He was not feeling up to par, so he remained in his warm sack while the others left for the mess hall. The CQ (Charge of Quarters) soon returned and told him to get to the briefing. He lost no time getting dressed and riding his bicycle on the shortest route to the flight line and the briefing! At Molesworth, Bill Bergeron and his crew shared quarters with Bill Heller's crew. The other crews in the 360th Squadron that lived with them kept being shot down with unnerving regularity. Bergeron and Heller wondered who would be next. Heller recalled the advice given by John Pastello, the squadron operations officer. 'If you fly good and tight formation, you will come back. The Germans pick on loners.' It was the best advice he ever got during the war. Over at Kimbolton Sam Mehaffey, a spare ball turret gunner in the 379th Bomb Group, did not expect to fly. The 525th Squadron was loaded with spare gunners so he did not get a chance to fly too often. His first assigned aircraft was *Ensign Mary*, named by the engineering officer who was dating a Navy nurse. When the CQ woke him he knew that he would fly the mission.

At Horham, Leonard W. Herman knew that they were in for a 'real tough' mission. Fresh eggs on the breakfast menu were always the indicator; the better the chow, the rougher the mission. At the briefing 'Bud' Moffet and the others were laying bets on the day's target. When Major 'Jiggs' unveiled the map, everybody groaned as usual. Schweinfurt – and it would be a long haul. They would be in the second combat wing over the target. Fighters would be heavy, flak intense and temperature — 48° at their altitude. Moffet and Herman and the rest knew that they were in for a very tough day. The intelligence officer's comments about knocking out the ball-bearing plants were, 'Shorten the war! All vehicles, all engines manufactured need ball bearings. Factories will be closed down! The cost will be worth it! It was Herman's twenty-fourth mission.[2] At Polebrook Joseph Christie learned that he was to fly and fight as the deputy group radio operator-gunner. He briefly met the crew before they took off.

At Rougham, Hal Kowal sat through the 94th Bomb Group briefing. On the Münster raid when the group had the 'pleasure' of destroying ten

German planes and damaging two, *Carolee*, his aircraft, lost two engines to enemy fire; the third had the supercharger shot out with about a quarter. The third engine had failed just prior to home base but they made a successful landing. The aircraft needed considerable maintenance work and everyone worked around the clock to fix his Fortress. The 94th had three squadrons with a fourth squadron as a fill-in for the lead, high and low locations with the Group. Tail end or 'ass end' on a mission to Schweinfurt was not the place to be. Kowal knew that no place would be a picnic on this raid. The 333rd was the fill-in squadron.

At Snetterton Heath, Staff Sergeant (later Colonel) Marshall Hamer, a ball turret gunner, who was down to fly his second mission, was one of the crewmen who sat nervously in the quiet briefing room that morning because they had heard rumours of a big raid coming up. When Colonel James L. Harris, the Group Commander, pulled the curtain back and with a pointer directed their attention to the target, the stillness was broken by gasps of disbelief. Hamer and the others knew that many of them would not be making the return trip to England. Later that day his crew would make the decision to continue to the target even when the engineer and navigator calculated that there might not be enough gas to get back to England and land. For Hamer and most of the men shot out of the sky this day it was the beginning of nineteen months of suffering and privation in PoW camps such as *Stalag Luft* XVII, a former Russian labour camp that was turned overnight in to an American PoW compound.

At Grafton Underwood, Frank Fitzpatrick, who normally flew in Lieutenant Joseph P. Hurley's crew, walked into the briefing room past the sign, posted in large letters, that said, 'LET'S GET THE SHOW ON THE ROAD'. Fitzpatrick, who flew with another crew, felt that maybe they were all actors and the good ones would go to Heaven and the bad actors would go to Hell. By the end of the day Hurley and four others in the crew were dead. (When Fitzpatrick went to see Hurley's father later he had never been at such a loss for words as he was that day.)

When he learned that the target was Schweinfurt, Staff Sergeant Don Gorham, the ball turret gunner on *Stella*, flown by Captain Randall 'Jake' Jacobs, was sure that his heart stopped. The former electrical engineering graduate knew that the last raid there had cost the 8th 'plenty of planes and crews' and he was 'not exactly crazy' about returning to this target. Gorham's hobby was amateur radio and flying was very low on his list of preferred occupations. But the choice between going to gunnery school at Las Vegas, Nevada, and becoming a staff sergeant with a shiny pair of wings or to radio operator's school at Boca Raton, Florida, and being a

PFC had not been a difficult decision to make. *Stella* would make it back to Grafton Underwood early after being hit by two FW 190s and being forced to abort far inland.[3]

The plan called for the 1st and 3rd Bomb Divisions to cross Holland thirty miles apart, while the third task force, composed of sixty Liberators, would fly to the south on a parallel course. The 923-mile trip would last just over seven hours and this meant that the B-17s of the 1st Division, which were not equipped with 'Tokyo tanks' would have to be fitted with an additional fuel tank in the bomb bay, with a consequent reduction in bomb load. A P-47 group would escort each division, while a third fighter group would provide withdrawal support from sixty miles inland to halfway across the Channel. Two squadrons of RAF Spitfire Mk 9s were to provide cover for the stragglers five minutes after the main force had left the withdrawal area and other RAF squadrons would be on standby for action if required. Despite these precautions, 370 miles of the route would be flown without fighter support. The 'Snetterton Falcons', which would be flying in the van of the 45th Combat Wing, would lead the 3rd Division, while the 92nd at the head of the 40th Combat Wing, would lead the 1st Division. The air commander was former 384th Bomb Group CO, Colonel Budd J. Peaslee, now deputy commander to Colonel Howard 'Slim' Turner of the 40th Combat Wing. Peaslee's pilot on the mission was Captain James Kemp McLaughlin in the 92nd. A native of Charleston, West Virginia, McLaughlin graduated from West Virginia University in 1941 and USAAF Flight School and had joined the Group at MacDill Field, Florida, in May 1942. He recalls:

> I shall never forget the many target briefings that Ed O'Grady, my bombardier, Harry Hughes, my navigator and I went through preparing for this famous raid. We had led our squadron on the first Schweinfurt raid on 17 August and along with the others, did a pretty good job of missing the target too. We had all been apprehensive of the second raid because we'd been flying missions since we'd arrived in England in August 1942. And we had first-hand experience of how the *Luftwaffe* would punish us, particularly when we failed to knock out a target for the first time and attempted to go back.

At Ridgewell the mention of the word 'Schweinfurt' shocked the crews completely as on 17 August the Group had lost so heavily on this same target. Also conspicuous by its omission was the estimated number of enemy fighters based along the route. Upon checking with the S-2 later, it was found that this omission was intentional and that the entire German fighter force of 1,100 fighters was based within eighty-five miles of the route. The implications were obvious. As the surgeon went around to the crews to check their equipment, sandwiches, coffee etc the crews were scared and it was obvious to him that many doubted that they would return.

At the end of the briefing at Chelveston Lieutenant Joe Pellegrini, from South Philadelphia, the Group Bombardier, one of fourteen children born to Italian parents, stood up. He had a question for the CO, Lieutenant Colonel Donald K. Fargo. Pellegrini, who had joined the Army in 1941, had married a hometown girl during final phase training in Idaho. He had flown his first raid on 17 April, to Bremen. Over the target he discovered what the veterans meant when they reported that 'flak was so damn thick, you could step out and lie on it'. Pellegrini's ship came home with the whole left stabilizer shot away and 128 holes in the fuselage 'from nose to tail'. The Italian-American would feature later in the Office of War Information film, *Welcome To Britain*, narrated by Captain Burgess Meredith, a one-time Hollywood star. Meredith recalled:

> That's Joe Pellegrini. He was leading bombardier of his group on the big Schweinfurt raid. Going into the target, they run into pretty heavy flak and rocket-firing fighters and they're pretty badly shot up. And Joe says to the pilot, listen, if we get knocked off our bombing run, we're gonna go around again and make another run. The pilot says are you crazy Joe? There's only two planes left in our whole damn group. And Joe says, okay, if there's only two of us left, all the more reason to go around and get it right.

But that was not the way it was, of course.

Joe's pilot was 2nd Lieutenant Joseph W. Kane and Major Charles G. Y. Normand, the Command Pilot, would ride in the co-pilot's seat. When it was announced that Schweinfurt would be the target for today there was instant whistling and nervous laughter and wisecracking. One captain solemnly performed a ceremony that was reserved for tough targets like Schweinfurt; he took out a roll of toilet paper, tore off ten squares for each man and passed them out. Pellegrini was one of the few that did not have 'butterflies' in his stomach. There was electric silence when he stood up and put his question to Fargo. As the target was so important could he take the sixteen B-17s of the group over the target again if clouds obscured the aiming point on the first run? Pellegrini just stood there and asked his question a second time. Fargo said, 'Yes

Pellegrini – you can go around a second time and a third and a fourth today. This is one target you must hit.'

Quietly Joe said, 'Thank you sir.'[4]

At Thurleigh Colonel George L. Robinson, the 306th commander, told the assembled crews that they would be bombing the most important target to date. The name had no meaning to George Roberts, who would be the radio operator on *Cavalier*. When the route map was uncovered Jim Harris said that the 'damned red line' led to Schweinfurt and recalled that 'you could have heard a pin drop'. The red string on the map told them that they were in for a long flight over heavily defended territory. Was this trip necessary? Harris knew that it was. 'Theirs is not to reason why; theirs is to do and die' he thought. He and the crew learned that their regular pilot, W. W. Thomas, was hospitalized and grounded and so they would fly with Richard Butler's crew. Harris knew that a good crew could be compared to the precision of a fine watch or a good ball team whose members know their plays and anticipate each other's moves and act accordingly; with no mistakes. It was especially hard for a crew to accept a replacement pilot therefore. (Butler's crew would be among those picked off one by one; they would bale out and become guests of the *Luftwaffe*.[5])

Nineteen-year old John E. Corcoran, the ball turret gunner in William Tackmier's crew in the 'Clay Pigeons' Squadron, who was flying his nineteenth mission, learned that he and the rest of the crew would lead the low squadron of the low group. Corcoran thought that his 23-year-old pilot, all of 6 feet 3 inches and 215lb, who was an above average basketball player, was a great guy. Tackmier was from Taft, California, and was used to better weather than the overcast, drizzle and gloom outside. He and the rest of the crew knew that there would be a lot of B-17s ahead of them in the formation, if they got off. The weather over England would remain marginal but would be clear over the continent. They could expect serious fighter opposition, moderate to intense flak and a long cold ride. With this dire information crews donned their flying gear, checked out parachutes, oxygen masks, escape kits and the codes for the day and went by truck to their hardstands where the B-17s waited.

After the briefing at Horham Leonard W. Herman reported to intelligence, as his crew were flying alternate lead. They studied an enlarged map of the target and the surrounding countryside, the IP, target approach and the target. He memorized the landmarks and the important terrain features and visualized what he would see from the nose and jotted down any references that he wished to make. 'Then you got your ass out to the ship!'

When 'Bud' Moffet checked out his new guns in the crew's new *Liberty Bell II*, he found that the ground crew had painted two swastikas on his turret door. He did not know whether to cuss them or kiss them. He and the crew talked in low voices (for security reasons) about the raid until it was time to start the engines. Moffet got a bright idea. He wrote on the topmost bomb, *To Adolph mit luf – Owen's Angels*. They had a new radioman, Gotleib, a short, burly kid with a big smile. He was killed about a week later.

Shortly before start engine time at 0900 hours word came of a one-hour weather delay. It remained foggy with a 200-foot cloud ceiling. Unpredictable weather, which intervened before take-off, hampered the B-24s' assembly, finally ruling out their participation. It seemed that the Fortresses' participation was also ruled out but an American-crewed Mosquito, 35,000 feet over the Continent, radioed back that all of central Germany was in the clear. At Thurleigh, promptly at ten the green flare was fired from the control tower and the engines came to life. George Roberts' pilot, Captain William S. Kirk of Richmond, Virginia, moved in line down the taxiway. Pilots did their engine run-ups but the end of the runway was not visible through the fog and rain and most crews expected word that the mission would be cancelled. Unbelievably, the command for take-off was given and bomb and gasoline loaded bombers taxied to the runways. Under full throttle they began the dash down the concrete strip. Very near the end of the runway Roberts felt the heavy plane leave the ground and ascend into the low hanging clouds. As they climbed through the undercast, pilots wondered how they were going to land when the cancellation order was given. They would not break out of the overcast for another thirty minutes. Their assembly and climb appeared normal, though other groups were having difficulty getting organized.

Captain Kirk's crew was in the high group of the 40th Combat Wing, which led the 1st Division over the coast of England, 20,000 feet above Orford Ness. The 381st was late in assembling and Major George G. Shackley decided to cut for the English coast in order to pick up the 1st CBW, which was achieved. However the unenviable low position or 'Purple Heart Corner' was already occupied by the 305th in the 40th CBW, which had screwed up royally and mistakenly latched onto the wrong wing and the wrong low group slot so Shackley pulled his formation up and happily flew high on the high group – a much safer haven. The move would produce a lucky outcome for the Ridgewell Group but the opposite would be true for the Chelveston outfit.

Further south, the 45th Combat Wing led the 3rd Division over the Naze. Behind them came the 4th Combat Wing, followed by the 13th Combat Wing. Fifteen of the 164 aircraft in the 1st Division and eighteen aircraft of the 160 in the 3rd Division either turned back with mechanical problems or became lost in the cloudy conditions. The long and complicated assembly also diminished the Fortresses' vital fuel reserves, especially in those aircraft carrying bombs externally to compensate for the internal tonnage lost to bomb bay fuel tanks. Many of these crews were forced to dump their wing-mounted bombs in the Channel or abort the mission. George Roberts listened on the radio for a possible recall but all he heard was the steady call sign '7MT' and the regular time check. They test fired rounds over the Channel and noted a few P-47 Thunderbolts as they crossed the French coast. The 'Little Friends' did not remain with them for long. The next fighters the crew would see would be Germans at 3 o'clock high.

After flying twenty-three missions Leonard Herman's combat routine was familiar:

> Take-off, climb, rendezvous and circle for altitude, join other groups and head out across the Channel. You sweat out the flak and pray that you will not meet too many fighters. You have checked in all the gunners and instruct them to go on oxygen at critical altitude. Test fire the guns and you are all set up. We were a 'chatter' crew. We didn't get this far without being sharp. Previously our pilot had been killed and many of us wounded but the majority of the original crew were still together because we were good at our jobs. Flak you can't do anything about. You fly course, stay in formation and pray you don't get hit. At least with fighters you can shoot back. You are busy watching fighters as they line up to attack, busy following them as they come in, crazy busy short bursting them to death! You are on 100% oxygen and can feel the adrenaline flowing through you. There is no fear at this time because you are too busy to think about anything except doing your job and shooting back. You see planes hit, you count the chutes as your buddies bale out and wonder, 'When the hell are they going to stop coming?' You're on the bomb run, flying straight and level and then, 'Bombs away!' Bomb bay

doors coming up; let's get the hell out of here! You peer down and hope to see the flames and explosions when the bombs hit.

William Tackmier's crew never got to the target as the minute they hit the enemy coast they were jumped by fighters and shortly lost an engine. They continued under heavy fighter attacks, with planes going down or leaving the formation. Clarence Munger in the 'Grim Reapers' high squadron formation was the first of three planes to turn back. Twenty minutes later when supercharger problems resulted in his inability to keep the squadron in group formation, Tackmier was also forced to turn back. Badly shot up, he came home harassed by fighters and gunners shooting at them from the ground. With over eight hours' flight time they got credit for a mission. Sam Mehaffey never got to the target either. His ship had taken the place of an abort at the French coast where they were hit by a flak barrage.

The navigator called on the interphone, 'The bombardier's hit; he's hit'.

The pilot asked, 'How bad?'

'Pretty bad' was the reply.

The bombardier had lost an arm. The pilot signalled to drop out and made a 180° turn. Sam Mehaffey swung his ball turret to the 6 o'clock position to watch the formation go on. Their replacement became a black puff of smoke where they had been. Mehaffey thought that it must have been a direct hit in the bomb bay. On board was his friend Francis S. Chard from Minnesota.[6]

Over Germany 'Bud' Moffet saw trucks creeping along like pin pints on the roads below. The farmland and low hills looked warm and beautiful. His eyelids were covered in fine frost. He broke ice away in chunks from the valves on his oxygen mask. They crept on for hours. He was stiff and his eyes strained from looking. They made an 80° diversionary turn near Aachen while the 1st Division continued on as briefed. After about sixty miles they turned left toward the target. A terrific fight was going on over Schweinfurt, about thirty miles away. The flak looked 'heavy as hell'.

Someone called, 'fighters 3 o'clock high.'

Moffet called 'FW 190s at 12 o'clock low.'

The fighters stabbed at them and Whitey began firing the top turret. He called Moffet.

'Coming under at 10 o'clock.'

Moffet swung around and waited. As he swooped under him, he followed him firing both guns. Whitey and Moffet had good teamwork:

Four FW 190s from 12 o'clock low were coming up on their noses and Moffet flailed away at them.

He called to Whitey, 'Up and over at 5 o'clock.'

He heard his guns chime in with his. Galba, in the tail, also got in a good burst. Thurston hollered, 'Bombs away!' Moffet watched them go down. They landed to the right of the already devastated city into a factory area.

I told the navigator the results and went back to work on those stinking Krauts. There were a few 'Jerries' also flying in the thick flak. As we came out they hit us again. We had already lost many ships to flak and fighters and would lose more. A ship below us went down about a thousand feet in a dive. Then an amazing thing, he started up again, did a complete loop, levelled off and exploded, leaving only a large puff of black smoke. Our attackers continued in groups of three and four, firing rockets. I could receive only on the interphone, so I could not hear anyone calling fighter positions. I watched for guns firing from other B-17s. Then I swung around to see what they were firing at. Whitey got a Me 109 about this time. I was pouring all hell into a two-engine jet fighter when one of my guns jammed. Ammunition caught in the baffle plates and I'd have to get out of the turret to do anything about it. Things were too hot, so I stayed put and hoped to God that the other gun didn't screw up on me. I cracked off some more ice from my oxygen mask. I wished I were a chaplain's assistant or something, as I cursed the war. We had two more hours of fighter attacks. A B-17 lagged behind on two engines and was shot down in flames, taking one fighter with it. Two chutes came out.

For the crew of Captain Kirk's Fort in the 'Clay Pigeons' Squadron intense battle had begun with Bf 109s flying right between the squadrons, ignoring the fire from the bombers. It was the most daring attack George Roberts had seen to date.

The Germans were determined to stop the formations at any cost. The *Cavalier* was being raked with enemy fire. Quite suddenly, the plane shuddered from an explosion in the waist section. Sergeant Eugene Kelly called to say that a 20mm shell had hit his partner Sergeant Webber. I went back and noted Webber was bleeding from the upper right leg and the pelvic area. We moved him to the ledge near the ball turret. Kelly injected morphine, applied a sulfa pad and covered him with a blanket. As I was returning to my gun, an explosion in the radio room ruined my transmitter. At the same time my oxygen supply dropped to zero. I plugged into an emergency tank, which I turned on about once per minute. This fifteen-minute supply was to last me for two hours. Ball turret gunner Hill called on the interphone that he was out of ammunition and needed his guns reloaded. Kelly told him that he also was out of ammo in the waist and a little too busy to come to his aid. I told Hill, that there was no spare ammo and no way that I could help him reload.

He replied: 'Load me up or I'm coming out of this tin can.'

I said to stay in, move his guns around and pretend to be firing to discourage fighter attacks.

His return words were, 'Like Hell, these guys are checked out and they are going to press the attack without fear of fire!'

Kirk gave Hill permission to leave the ball and take over the waist gun left by the injured Webber. An ammo check revealed that all gun positions were nearly out of bullets. Kirk told us to conserve our ammo and fire only short bursts. As the fighter from the rear got close he would take evasive action when it had lined up on us. Sergeant Poff in the tail and I in the radio room called each time we saw tracers coming from lined up fighters with the advice to: 'Kick it sir.' This manoeuvre probably did more than anything to save us.

I noted several planes with smoking engines and/or feathered propellers. As we approached the bomb run I saw seven chutes at 9 o'clock low and a B-17 in a slow spin. The fighters left. Ahead and low, I saw several white puffs of flak, which became darker and more accurate as we approached the target. The barrage did not seem as heavy as that over Bremen. But I could feel the concussion and hear the 'Woof' and the peppering of the fuselage. When the bombardier called 'Bombs away', I checked the bomb bays to see that all bombs were out. The bomb-bay doors did not close, so the navigator, Lieutenant Pleasant, spent several minutes correcting the malfunction. Very few B-17s were left in our formation. I thought the fighters could easily finish us off. Luckily, we had only thirteen minutes of new attacks, which were not as intense as before. Evidently, the German fighters had gone to attack the incoming bombers.

The 3rd Division encountered some fighter opposition and lost two Fortresses before the Thunderbolt escort withdrew but, by the time it entered the target area, the 1st Division had lost thirty-six bombers shot down and twenty had turned back. Although the 1st still had 224

Fortresses, most of the groups had been torn to shreds and some were barely skeleton formations. The 306th had lost ten of its twenty-one Fortresses. At 1520 hours after bombing the target, 1st Lieutenant Ralph T. Peters in the 'Fightin' Bitin' Squadron gave the order for his crew to bale out. Their Fort was riddled with 20mm bullet holes, hundreds of flak fragments and had received a direct hit by a rocket launched from a Ju 88. With the propeller on No. 3 engine running away they had no choice but to abandon ship. The plane exploded shortly after the last man jumped. 1st Lieutenant James V. Vaughter, the bombardier, cried as he floated down in bright sunshine, twenty miles south-west of Schweinfurt. Tears came because he immediately thought about his mother, how she would worry, cry and pray about her baby boy. Crying was also result of the realization that he was helpless, was going to become a prisoner, was not going to make it back to Thurleigh and because he was so mad that the enemy had got the best of them. He never did consider himself a good loser; at times nor even a good winner.[7]

Another of the 'Fightin' Bitin' squadron to go down was the Fortress flown by 1st Lieutenant Willard H. Lockyear, which was hit by rockets in the nose, killing the navigator and bombardier. When another rocket exploded just outside the right waist window, Ernest J. Gilbert knew that his flight had reached the end of the line. A fire started in the No. 3 engine and soon there was a fire in the radio room also. Gilbert turned to see the other waist gunner and ball gunner already at the open door, watching him. Gilbert put on his chute and went out. The descent through the sunlit autumn sky was by no means peaceful. He saw only one other chute. German fighters strafed the helpless airmen in their parachutes. Several panels of Gilbert's chute were shot away and he was hit by a bullet in his back. The only thing that saved him from death was that he fell into the River Rhine, near Andernach. Staff Sergeant Alfred H. Weiland Jr, the ball turret gunner, was not as lucky. In his damaged chute he fell with a shattering impact among the rocks at the river's edge and he received massive and mortal injuries. Both men were taken to a first aid station and later transported to a hospital several miles away. Weiland died that night. Gilbert's back and head wounds were treated at the hospital for several days before he was sent to *Dulag Luft* at Frankfurt for interrogation and eventual transfer to the PoW camp at Krems in Austria. At Frankfurt railway station several *Luftwaffe* pilots, noticing the American's sorry condition, asked Gilbert if he had been shot down on 14 October. They too had been shot down the same day.

By the time the 305th could see the city of Schweinfurt, twelve miles distant, it had lost its entire low squadron of five aircraft and parts of the high and lead squadrons. Minutes from the IP Lieutenant Victor C. Maxwell's B-17 became the eleventh Fortress in the Group to be lost. Only *Sundown Sal'*, which was on fire, Barney Farrell's *Rigor Mortis* and the lead ship flown by Joe Kane remained from the original eighteen aircraft and a Fortress from another group joined them. There were not enough aircraft for effective bombing so Major Charles G. Y. Normand, the group leader, decided to join the depleted 92nd and 306th formations for the bomb run. Of the thirty-seven Fortresses in the 40th Combat Wing, which had crossed the Channel, only sixteen remained. Worse was to follow.

At 1439 hours the 91st began dropping its bombs on the streets, houses and factories of Schweinfurt and would claim the best overall bombing results for the 1st Division though the 351st was the most accurate. Jim Bradley, in the composite group lead ship flown by Major John R. Blaylock, was of the opinion that the 351st had had great fighter protection to Aachen but when the Spitfires and P-47s left, the *Luftwaffe* had been ready with 'a fighting welcome'. The group to their rear was wiped out by the time they started the bomb run at Würzburg. When one German unit left, another took its place. Bradley was a voluntary non-shooter, explaining to the crew that his hands were like those of a 'fine concert pianist' and he could not get his bombing fingers tight from the recoil of the fifty calibre guns. Actually, he had grazed a couple of B-17s on a prior mission. For the good of the 8th Air Force, Bradley had decided that he was too 'lousy' in his shooting to risk the lives of the other crews. Blaylock was a perfect pilot, cool and poised. Bradley had trained with him a number of times over the Irish Sea just to give him practice in turning a group or wing.

Another group tried to cut in front of them on the bomb run but they won in a game of 'Chicken' with them and did not change course. Bradley always took from five to seven minutes to set up the course and rate to drop the bombs. At the last second, the lights did not come on so he had to salvo six bombs and the bomb bay gas tank. The cross hairs never moved after the bombsight clicked and the bombs were dropped. On the final run Paul Post lost an eye and the other waist gunner lost a leg. As they turned away from the target and headed back to England Bradley went to the waist of the ship and closed the two side gun ports and tried to comfort the wounded. He felt badly that he was not a better medic who possibly could have saved Post's eye. He couldn't tell him what was wrong with his eye, since there was no blood. The other gunner's wound was in the upper groin area, so it was necessary to wrap it in telephone cable to stop the blood.[8]

After flying through flak the deputy Group lead aircraft had lost their No. 1 engine and then they had lost their Group commander's ship and crew from the formation so they led the thirty-five Forts over the ball-bearing factory buildings. Captain H. D. Wallace placed all his bombs within 1,000 feet of the MPI (Mean Point of Impact). Joseph Christie tapped out 'Bombs away' on his telegraph key. He knew that the bomb aimer had done well. Then they lost two more engines.

At the head of the three Forts left in the 305th formation Joe Pellegrini could see the target in his bombsight and knew he could hit it but Command Pilot Normand did not think they could hold it on the run. Pellegrini, who had already set the cross hairs of the bombsight on the aiming point, begged Normand, 'Major, please let me continue this run. Visibility is perfect; we can't miss!' But Normand decided to follow the 91st and ordered Pellegrini to bomb with them. The eighteen 1,000lb bombs dropped from the bomb bays of the three B-17s fell in a civilian neighbourhood. Immediately after 'bombs away' *Sundown Sal'* flown by Ray Bullock became the unlucky thirteenth and final victim in the 305th formation. Bullock's crew all baled out successfully. Joe Kane and Barney Farrell turned their Forts away from the target and followed the lead group home.[9]

The 40th Combat Wing dropped its bombs and headed in the direction of the 1st Combat Wing, which was now making for the French border. The third and final wing added its bombs to the conflagration and turned off the target to allow the 3rd Bomb Division, flying six minutes behind, to take its turn.

First over the target was the 'Snetterton Falcons' at the head of the 45th Combat Wing. The target was obscured by smoke from the preceding bomb runs but crews had not flown this far to be thwarted and they released their bomb anyway. The second group in the wing was the 388th, with sixteen aircraft. The lead bombardier was unable to identify either the Kugelfischer ball-bearing works or the marshalling yards located to the south, so he set his sight on the bridge over the River Main and released his bombs slightly to the right of the ball-bearing plant. The bombs cascaded down into the southern half of Schweinfurt and the western end of the marshalling yards. In the 4th Combat Wing the leading 385th led by the CO, Colonel Elliott 'Vandy' Vandevanter, from Baltimore, a graduate of West Point, headed for the target too. Robert Bennett, Norm Weiden's co-pilot, who was flying on the left wing of the high squadron leader, was doing most of the flying as it was easier to fly on the left side of the formation from the right seat. Their gunnery officer was flying with them as observer. Just before they got to the bomb run they saw a Ju 88 flying alongside at about 1,500 yards to their left. The gunnery officer was at the waist window and he squirted off a burst in front of the German twin-engined ship. The next burst was slightly behind. The third burst was right on the money as the Ju 88 exploded. It was generally accepted that a flexible .50 gun was inaccurate beyond 1,000 yards. Bennett was willing to bet his bottom dollar that after that the gunnery officer got the attention and respect of every gunner at Great Ashfield.

To Hal Kowal it seemed like the 94th, going and returning, had the 'honour' of seeing all of the German fighters on 14 October.

It felt like the inside of a bee's nest with enemy fighters swarming from all directions. The 94th did not see a friendly fighter plane. The crew of the *Carolee* expended all of its ammunition. On the way home the gunners were picking up the individual bullets pulled through their guns on the floor. I don't know how many times the waist gunners, Lew Digby and Eugene Painter, landed on their fannies trying to shoot on a bed of spent casings on the floor. After the ammunition was exhausted they were throwing empty shells through the open waist window at German planes. Digby was part American Indian and Painter a typical American teenager going into his twenties. Frank Tamburrino our 'hot shot' card player was in the tail having a three-ring circus with the Germans continuously attacking from the rear and they came, wave after wave. From the call outs of the gunners, I skidded or slipped within the limits of the formation in order not to be in a German's gunsight at the closing range of the gunfire. Good flying gave way to any conceived manoeuvre to prevent a sitting duck position for the attackers to shoot at. At the rear end, you are always trying to catch up to the formation with plenty of space to try evasion. In a four-engine B-17 that responds slowly at altitude this is rather difficult but every bit helps. A few feet out of line would help us survive. Even the gunners were rooting the aerial pilot movement.

This reminded me of the Clown Act (or Stolen Airplane Act) when I flew a Piper Cub at airshows: slip until the tail was in front of the nose. The B-17 wouldn't react that way but I sure tried when the German Air Force was on my tail with their firepower nipping at our heels. The 94th lost six planes out of 21 for a 28 per cent loss. Brennan's crew ditched in the Channel and the crew were fished out. Mullinax, Roy Davidson and Reed crews went down. Beal and Dodge were lost.[10] We came home somehow – five planes and fifty men lost. The 94th claimed twenty-one destroyed enemy aircraft, nine damaged and two probables. The target was bombed well by the 94th.

Sherman Hart, my co-pilot (besides God), helped me out considerably, especially when the prop wash from the group ahead tried to throw *Carolee* out of formation. At one time we actually climbed to the top of our seats with our feet on the steering column to keep from being thrown out of the formation, which could toss us up to four miles to the side and all alone. This happened on a previous raid, so we knew the consequences. 'Herbie' Freidman, our navigator, had to be watched. He would shoot anything that approached, including a B-17. Maybe it was his Chicago cab driving background. His cohort in the nose, bombardier 'Charlie' Vance, raised by a Mammy, just pecked away with his 'pea shooter' and kept giving us an artistic panoramic conception of the titanic battle. Cool Benjamin Roberts, engineer/top turret gunner, and Leland Neiswander in the ball turret, just 'merry-go-round' with their turrets. Any compass direction had a German to pick on as they rotated. Steve Olenik in the radio room had the unlimited roof top view of Germans swarming overhead. The little butcher-boy from Pennsylvania gave them a taste of his 'Top Round' 50 calibre.

The 13th Combat Wing was the last wing in the 3rd Division to cross Schweinfurt. Captain John B. Miller was leading the high squadron of the 95th, the second from the last group over the target.

I really had a panoramic view of the whole bloody mess. I saw wave after wave of *Luftwaffe* attackers – FW 190s, Me 109s, 110s, 210s and Ju 88s. They knew we were coming. Long before the IP I could see a cloud of black smoke over the target at our altitude. There were Forts going down with *Luftwaffe* fighters making sure of their job to destroy them. We held tight formation and continued into the carnage. We made our bomb run, which seemed forever. Flak was accurate and thick, coming in barrages. After bombs away I saw Angus McPherson's ship, which was leading the low squadron, peel off to the left and the landing gear drop down. His was the first in our group that had volunteered for a twenty-sixth mission. After that there were no more volunteers for more than the required twenty-five missions. I really thought that most of us would be wiped out. Once we were committed to do the job, there was no retreat.

The city of Schweinfurt had soaked up over 483 short tons of high explosives and incendiaries. The 3rd Division had dropped the most bombs on target and the 390th was the most successful. Although the lead ship had experienced difficulty, all 15 aircraft placed 50 per cent of their bombs within 1,000 feet of the MPI. The B-17s turned off the target and flew an almost complete 180° circle around Schweinfurt. A group of FW 190s headed for the 1st Division formation and singled out the trailing 41st Combat Wing. The leading 379th lost four B-17s in the first pass. A German plane crashed into Lieutenant Samuel A. Gaffield Jr's B-17 and split it in half. Only one of the crew survived. Arvid Dahl's crew flying *Dangerous Dan* on their ninth mission came through the maelstrom, happy in the knowledge that they had dropped their bombs on Schweinfurt. One of them was a 'Blue Pickle' practice bomb painted with 'nasty sayings' on it and filled with the product of the nearest outhouse to their hut at Kimbolton. They had rigged it with a fuse and a small amount of explosive. In retrospect Dahl thought that the good citizens of Schweinfurt would probably thank them for their gift of fertilizer. He wondered where it hit.[11]

Both divisions headed for their respective rally points and began forming into combat wings again for the return over Germany and France. Approaching the French coast, the two surviving aircraft in the 305th sighted the 92nd and 306th Groups for the first time during the mission. Luckily, the two B-17s had met little fighter opposition on the way home, as they had used almost all their ammunition before reaching the target. The Fortresses' return to England was hampered by the same soupy weather that had dogged their departure. At 1640 hours the 1st Division bombers crossed the Channel coast and were followed, just five minutes later, by those in the 3rd Division.

Budd Peaslee's pilot, James McLaughlin, recalled:

The trip back was far from uneventful, for we had again almost continuous attacks and lost four more of our group. Then to top it all off, the low ceilings and poor visibility loomed as an almost insurmountable problem on our return because most of our aircraft were damaged and at least two had wounded aboard who needed immediate attention. One of these landed in East Anglia, while the other stayed in formation. Harry Hughes directed me to the landing end of our home runway at Podington, using for the first time an intersecting Gee line as an instrument approach system. With our wounded wingman, Lieutenant Moke McKennon, we tracked into a descending approach to the runway. When we had it in sight, by prearrangement, we pulled up and let him land. Then we led the other two remaining aircraft around and back to the final approach and landing. Nine aircraft got back to England – four back at home base – out of a full group of twenty-one. It was a long tough soul searing day I'd not soon forget.[12]

Clouds covered the Channel on the return. Captain William S. Kirk in the 'Clay Pigeons' squadron, opting to return over the clouds, found the break he needed over England and circled the *Cavalier* to below the ceiling. George Roberts fired a flare as they approached the runway at Thurleigh to signal the medics for the injured Webber. In bad weather, with a damaged plane in descending darkness, Kirk and Flight Officer Clyde K. Cosper made a good landing. Medics met them at the hardstand. Only five out of the eighteen planes in their Group had reached the target. Kirk's was the only one from the 'Clay Pigeon' squadron. They had over 300 holes in the *Cavalier*, one of them large enough to fall through. Sergeant Webber, in serious condition, was taken to a regional hospital. It was his second Purple Heart in four raids. This was his last mission. Roberts concluded:

> One hundred of our friends did not return to Thurleigh that afternoon. It was indeed a 'Black Thursday' for those who had given their all on this 14th of October, 1943.[13]

It was with a big sigh of relief that 'Bud' Moffet's crew reached the Channel. At the English coast he admired the White Cliffs of Dover, threw them a hearty kiss and crawled stiffly out of his turret. His first cigarette was worth its weight in gold. On landing at Horham Bud Moffet and the rest of the crew heard that sixty B-17s had been lost but it seemed an understatement. Moffet's attitude was, 'Well, the job was done, at any cost.' Six hundred chairs would be empty at chow that night. However, his chair was going to be filled and in a hurry!

Crossing the Channel and with the danger of flak and fighters gone, Leonard Herman knew that he would live to fight another day. He was lightheaded and asked the gunners for a couple of their special renditions of some favourite barroom ballads. He was ready for his shot of whisky. As they crossed the Channel, Joseph Christie in the 351st deputy lead ship noticed that they were so low he could almost feel the waves. They could not live in the cold water more than a few minutes but the good old B-17 made it back to Polebrook. He knew that a B-24 could never have made it. When the 'Hells Angels' returned to Molesworth Bill Bergeron had to make three circles of the airfield in order to give priority to the many badly damaged ships, several with wounded men aboard. It looked like a Fourth of July fireworks, so many flares were being shot off by the landing aircraft in distress. *Carolee* brought Hal Kowal's crew back to Rougham. Kowal would name his first born daughter Carolee after this B-17 that took them through twenty-three successful and most eventful missions. The crew earned the Presidential Citation with Oak Leaf Cluster along with the rest of the Group. During their missions each gunner on the crew earned a destroyed German fighter plane. Kowal kidded that some of them must have had more than one but handed it over to another crew member for credit. The whole crew survived and they were awarded their DFC medal, along with the Air Medals. Olenik, who must have got on top of the radio room opening to get hit, got a Purple Heart.

Altogether, the 1st Division had lost forty-five Fortresses on the raid. The 305th had suffered greatly. Of the eighteen participating, one returned unable to find the Group and two others had to abort due to mechanical problems. Of the fifteen remaining; only three survived long enough to reach the target. One of the three, *Sundown Sal'*, flown by the Raymond P. Bullock crew, burning fiercely, was abandoned after releasing its bombs and exploded immediately afterwards. Left waist gunner, Harold E. Coyne, recalls:

We knew what to expect having been to Schweinfurt on 17 August. That morning was overcast and we did not think that we would take off. When we did and got above the overcast and headed for the coast it was good to see our escort but knew they wouldn't be there for long. As we were heading for Germany, Curtis in the tail called over the intercom that our escort was leaving. He no more than said it when Brunswick in the top turret called out, 'Fighters coming in from the front.' We were really getting hit by fighters. They were coming from the front side and tail. Curtis would call out as planes behind us were going down. Just before the IP the togglier said he was out of ammunition. The ball turret gunner's guns had jammed and shortly after that we were hit in the left wing. I looked out the left waist and saw that the left wing was on fire. I guess we were hit in the gas tank. The pilot said we were approaching the bomb run. Then the fighters started to leave and I saw the plane on our right get hit and start to go down. All I could see was the lead plane. We dropped our bombs on the target and made a right turn. Ray said that he could not hold the plane much longer and that we would have to bale out. The wing was burning. He finally told us to bale out. I motioned for the ball turret gunner, who had come out of the ball when he saw we were on fire, to bale out. He and I went to the side door and I took off my flak jacket and helmet. I pulled the emergency release and kicked out the door. I remember pulling on my ripcord and I must have passed out because the next thing I knew I was floating to the ground. A FW 190 buzzed me but did not fire. I started to float towards the target and I could see it burning. That was one place where I did not want to land.[14]

Thirteen of the Group's Forts were lost at a cost of forty killed and twenty wounded. Of the eighty-three that baled out and survived, seventy-nine were taken prisoner, four evaded and a crew that had to head for neutral Switzerland was interned. Two remaining ships, one badly damaged, survived a hazardous journey home and tucked in with the 92nd formation, which lost six Forts on the mission. A seventh was written off in a crash-landing at Aldermaston.

The 379th and 384th had each lost six B-17s in combat and three crews in the latter group had to abandon their aircraft over England,[15] making nine losses in all. Among those missing were *T.S.* , *The Joker*, *Me and My Gal* and *Sad Sack*. Stanley Mazarka, the ball gunner on *Tallywhacker* flown by Robert L. Robinson, said 'We shot our way in and we shot our way out.' Radio operator Howard Stumpf said that at one time near the target he had counted thirty-five fighters flying parallel to them off their left wing and that he owed his life to a tremendous pilot and crew.

Worse, the 306th had sent out eighteen B-17s and had lost ten. William Tackmier's crew had been one of the first back after aborting with engine problems and they were surrounded by 'brass', in jeeps, who wanted to know how the mission had gone. John E. Corcoran saw Major George Buckey, the 'Clay Pigeons' Squadron Commander, Major Ken Reecher and Colonel William Raper who asked where the others were. Tackmier's men told them that as far as they knew they were all that was left. Corcoran could see tears streaming down George Buckey's face. He had sent them out and had lost many friends.

So too had Corcoran. How many of the hundred men on the ten planes had survived he wondered. William Bisson, who was from Athens, Georgia, was his original pilot. He was killed and buried on the continent. Waist gunner Constantine 'Gus' Lamb, a New York City police officer, and four other crewmen from the aft section of the plane had survived. Amazingly he must have probably been less than 50 feet from him when he went down. Corcoran had seen nine chutes leave Lieutenant Dick Butler's plane. Some of them belonged to Alexander Hayburn, Ernest Henderson and Jim Harris (who before going down recalled that the intercom was bedlam with crew members calling out fighter attacks and that it had got so bad that it didn't do any good to call them out). Another belonged to Tech Sergeant Alexander M. Mayburn Jr, who was from a prominent family in Louisville, Kentucky. Ernest H. Henderson, waist gunner, was a tall, lean, taciturn westerner with a pencil moustache. Amos R. May, radio, and Marcel St Louis, a handsome dark Frenchman who had been previously wounded in the back and had a flak punctured A-2 jacket to prove it, had also survived. Later Corcoran heard that Edward DeBuyser Jr, a fellow ball turret gunner and good friend from Rochester, New York, had survived too, though he broken both legs on landing.

Corcoran found out too that Lieutenant Douglas H. White's crew, the first plane shot out of formation by a swarm of fighters, had gone down with gunners, Charles Adams, Francis Pulliam and togglier, George Toney Jr, 'a small dark guy' from Miami. Reportedly, Toney was a gambler who always made a lot of money at cards and dice. The only survivor was Tech Sergeant Joseph C. Bocelli, the radio operator. A few days later at 11th Avenue in Portland, Oregon, the Rasmussen family received a telegram telling them that Emil O. Rasmussen, the co-pilot in White's ship, was missing. His Group CO sent a letter encouraging them not to give up hope since there was a good possibility that he was a prisoner. The family would have to wait until the end of the war before they learned of Emil's fate. Corcoran felt that the 306th, due to its position in the wing, had no chance. On 17 August the Group had a relatively soft touch and the guys behind them were pounded. On 14 October the group was so far back that they had no chance and the Germans had plenty of time to jump on them.

The 'Hell's Angels' lost two aircraft, including *Cat O'Nine Tails*, which crashed near Riseley after the crew had baled out in the Aylesbury area. Captain George V. Stallings' crew had picked up the brand new B-17F in Bangor, Maine, and a commercial artist had carefully painted her nose decoration, a cat with nine barbed tails. The crew had intended to add dual automobile horns but on arrival at Molesworth in February the *Cat O'Nine Tails* had been given to another crew. The 91st and 351st each lost one B-17, as did the 381st. Ironically that one ship that failed to return to Ridgewell was *Flak Foot Floogie* – old 803 – that had come from the 305th, which had taken the 381st's slot with such disastrous consequences. *Floogie* did not come close to finishing her tour.

At Bassingbourn no word was received from '741' flown by 1st Lieutenant Harold R. 'Chris' Christensen of Eagle Grove, Iowa. The ship that had no name had been hit on the bomb run by a fighter, which put one of the engines out of action. Further attacks by three Bf 109s wounded the ball turret gunner, Staff Sergeant Walter J. Molson of Jersey City, New Jersey. Molson called 1st Lieutenant Homer E. Chatfield the bombardier, on the interphone. 'I've been hit' he said. 'I'm coming up to have you dress the wound.' Chatfield, of Hartford, Connecticut, administered first aid and Molson went back to his turret and manned his guns. For protection, Christiansen headed for some clouds, but before he reached them, three fighters attacked. One Bf 109 stayed on '741's' tail with guns blazing. The rear compartment of the Fortress looked like a sieve, but lucky Staff Sergeant James J. Sweeley of Tracy, Minnesota, the tail gunner, was not seriously wounded. The pilot threw the ship around like a kite to evade the fighter and eventually slipped into the clouds. Down in the nose the navigator, 2nd Lieutenant Kenneth C. Homuth, of Laurens, Iowa, was looking at his maps of Switzerland. 'Chris' Christensen called the crew on the interphone and asked if they wanted to bale out over Germany, try for Switzerland or attempt to make it home. 'Home, James home!' shouted one of the gunners and the rest of the crew agreed. They dropped down and despite poor visibility, raced for England at tree top level.

But hedgehopping over France to avoid being spotted by fighters, a nest of machine guns and light flak opened up and a shell tore a big hole in the side of the cockpit. Chatfield later explained:

> We swept over one small hill and there was a city in the valley. A nest of machines guns and light flak guns opened up on us as we passed over. A lucky shot made a big hole in the side of the cockpit and hit 'Chris' in the upper arm. He stayed at the controls until the ship was over the next knoll and out of range of the German guns, which actually were firing right through French homes at us as we left them.

Then 2nd Lieutenant Stuart B. Mendelsohn, of Cleveland, Ohio, the co-pilot, took over and his pilot crawled down from the cockpit, collapsing in the entrance to the nose. The bombardier and navigator made Christensen as comfortable as possible, applied a tourniquet to his arm, which was severely lacerated and spurting blood, and then they injected a shot of morphine to deaden the pain.

Visibility was getting poorer and the Fortress clipped off the top of one especially tall tree, smashing in the plane's Plexiglas nose. They were fired on again at the French coast by machine gun and anti-aircraft fire and one of the engines was set on fire but Mendelsohn banked the Fortress slightly and the radio gunner, Tech Sergeant Lloyd DeRousse, of Portageville, Missouri, who was the only one left with ammunition, picked off three or four of the German gunners standing along the cliff. The ground fire ceased. Crossing the Channel only a few feet above the waves, the co-pilot watched the fuel gauge and there was doubt whether they would have sufficient gasoline to reach England. Old '41' finally hit the English coast and despite a flat tyre and poor visibility, Mendelsohn made a safe landing at RAF Tangmere. One engine was on fire as the bomber landed and there was only about four minutes' fuel left in the tanks. Christensen was well cared for at the station hospital but he died early the next morning. When the badly damaged Fortress was put back in active service again, the crew painted *Corn State Terror* on the nose in memory of the Fort's gallant pilot.[16]

Three crews in the 379th that returned safely landed at Little Staughton, a repair depot ten miles from Kimbolton, their home base. Colonel Louis W. 'Rip' Rohr who led the 40th Wing and Captain Bill Hawkins, knowing where they were, went on to land at Kimbolton. Walter Bzibziak's crew were delivered home in the back of a GI truck about four hours later! Lieutenant Corson ground-looped *Gay Caballeros* at RAF Biggin Hill. Staff Sergeant Dominick Cemante, the ball turret gunner, saw workers who were laying the runway, come running up to the plane and wanting to know 'How many were killed? The plane was in bad shape. There were three big holes, one right behind the No. 1 engine, one in the right horizontal stabiliser and one a little forward of the main door. Although all three holes were thought to be from 20mm cannon the engineer said that he saw an aerial bomb hit the left wing. The 20mm that hit the waist had made 'hundreds of small holes' but no one had got a scratch.

Arvid Dahl landed *Dangerous Dan* at Kimbolton with just one hole in the left stabilizer, put there by his left waist gunner. Dahl said that there was so much to shoot at that 'he got carried away'. Richard Simmons miraculously put down at the base after being hit in an attack by two formations of Bf 109s attacking twelve abreast. Jim Foster, right waist gunner, who was on his thirteenth mission saw the lead Fortress on the element to his left go down and then the right wing ship and the last ship in their formation went down. The last the former office worker and would-be pilot remembered was seeing a very bright yellow spinner on one of the Messerschmitts and all hell breaking loose. (Foster's paperwork had got lost before pilot training and being impatient for action he had trained as a gunner.) He was lifted gently out of the bullet-riddled Fort with a fractured skull, his left eye gone, right eye badly damaged, right hand broken and frostbite and numerous other injuries. Left waist gunner Ron Britten, who saved his life by holding an oxygen mask to his face was also injured and suffered severe frostbite.[17]

Robert E. Haughy, a pilot in the 526th Squadron, who was on mission No. 22, had a better homecoming, although he could not get as far as Kimbolton. He and his crew had been to Schweinfurt on 17 August as well as the 'Bloody Münster' raid on 10 October but never 'had I been on such a raid! The good Lord certainly rides in our plane'. They saw more German fighters than ever before. Haughy had to leave the formation on return to the English coast, as they were pretty low on gas. Haughy proceeded to find any airfield that he could set down on. On landing at a RAF fighter field he found two other crews from his squadron were also there. Since the weather closed in, they had to stay the night. The RAF and the Fortress crews were glad to have a change from the normal routine. The 'Yanks' got a little intoxicated in the officers' mess at the expense of their hosts and 'Jolly well raised a little Hell.' Their hosts enjoyed and joined in the gaiety. Although the British treated their officers royally, it seemed to Haughy that they did not seem to know how to enjoy their good fortune, so the Americans proceeded to show them how. They soon let their hair down and learned quickly. Pretty WAAFs served them. Ringing a bell brought a drink with promptness and great courtesy. After a full evening and a night's rest in their assigned quarters, a sweet voice saying, 'it's 9 o'clock sir' pleasantly astounded Haughy. A pretty WAAF was standing in the doorway with a cup of tea. After she set the tea on the bedside table, she took his shoes, pants and shirt. He asked her what was going on. She replied that she was going to shine the shoes and press the clothes. She returned in about ten minutes. Haughy learned that she talked only when spoken to. RAF officers were normally awakened in this manner and the visitors were thinking of starting a drive to get this kind of service in the USAAF by their WACs! After lunch the B-17 crews departed. Though glad to see them land, Haughy suspected that their hosts were also glad to see them go. They had demolished the dignity of their domain by talking to and kidding the WAAFs – strictly taboo in the RAF. However, Haughy noticed that wherever they went they seemed to turn a lot of heads.[18]

The 3rd Division had lost fifteen aircraft. One of the seven losses in the 'Snetterton Falcons' was twenty-one-year-old Lieutenant Joseph X. Brennan, who was from Germantown, Philadelphia, and his crew flying *Larrupin' Lou'* a ship borrowed from the 94th. The first engine was shot out about ten minutes before the target was reached. After five minutes of futile struggling to keep up with the rest of the formation Brennan and his co-pilot, 2nd Lieutenant Gordon E. White, twenty-two, of Parsons, Kansas, decided that their only chance lay in lightening the load. The bombardier, 2nd Lieutenant Joseph E. Genone, twenty-four, of Macon, Georgia, was told to drop his bombs before reaching the target. But the bomb bay mechanism had also been hit and put out of commission and the bombs didn't fall. 'I decided right then that we had to peel off,' Brennan said. 'We were far behind the rest of the formation by then and the fighters were making terrific passes at us. We were at 25,000 feet when I swung her over and let her go.'

Shaking and shivering, the Fort went down in a dive at 350mph. The German fighters followed it down, slugging their shells and rockets into it. Tech Sergeant Willard R. Wetzel, twenty-three, a radio operator gunner from Aldernon, Pennsylvania, flying on his twenty-fifth mission, had one of the worst moments of his combat career just then.

> The pilot kept circling as he went down because if we'd gone down in a straight dive, all a fighter had to do was get on our tail and stay there while he was letting us have it. As it was, the Jerries managed to hit another engine, the prop began to run away at such a speed it made the most horrifying noise I have ever heard. I didn't know then it was the prop. I thought that the wings were falling off. I was all alone in the radio compartment and didn't have my headset on. I thought, with the wings falling off, the pilot had ordered us to bale out and I hadn't heard him. I opened the radio compartment door and looked to see if the bomb bay doors were open. They were. I thought then that I was left all alone in the ship with no one at the controls. That really hit me. I turned to ice. I fumbled around, finally managed to plug in my headset and call the pilot. There was a minute before he answered and I think I kept holding my breath. Then he said, 'Stick with us.' Boy, was I relieved.

Staff Sergeant Norbert P. Loupe, the twenty-two-year-old ball turret gunner, who was from Reserve, Louisiana, recalls:

> In the vicinity of Luxembourg, large numbers of Me 109s and FW 190s were coming at us from all directions. I kept firing at the one coming directly at us and those others within view from my ball turret. Brennan said, 'Stick with us boys.' The earth was getting closer and closer as I prayed and thought, 'this is the end'. I lost my vision momentarily but was able to see again as we were coming out of the dive. The waist gunners immediately got me out of the ball turret. We were very low; the rooftops just below us. Germans were

shooting at us from the ground. I could see projectiles hitting the rooftops of the taller buildings. We were shot up badly and under heavy fire as we approached the coast. Bullets were hitting us with a sound like popping corn.

The bombardier, in the meantime, had finally succeeded in releasing the bombs. As the ship levelled off, the navigator, Lieutenant Verne D. Viterbo of Beaumont, Texas, received a fix from Wetzel and set a course for home. Brennan, in a last desperate effort to shake the German pursuers, brought the bomber down to within 15 feet of the ground. The fighters finally turned back. Brennan maintained his low altitude and with only two engines left, hedgehopped so low over fields and towns that frequently he had to lift a wing over a tree or rooftop. By the time they reached Holland and Belgium, the worst of the air attacks had passed. The Fort was not fired upon except as it passed over a small aerodrome. The crewmen could clearly see civilian inhabitants of occupied territory waving and cheering and raising their arms in V-for-Victory salutes. Near the coast however, they ran into a heavy barrage of fire from enemy pound troops that cost them their third engine.

'They fired everything they had at us,' said Staff Sergeant Denver A. Nowlin, twenty-nine, of Longview, Texas, the right waist gunner. 'We were so close to them that the noise was terrific. They used pistols, rifles, machine guns – everything they had.' 'That ground fire knocked out one of the two good engines we had left,' added Staff Sergeant Severin H. Rodeschin, twenty-nine, the waist gunner from Newport, New Hampshire. 'It must have been machine gun fire. It was real heavy.' The ground volleys continued as the Fortress sped out to sea and from his tail gun position, Staff Sergeant Roy R. King, twenty-nine, of Robson, West Virginia, could see the bullets splashing in the water behind him as they curved out over the land.

Wetzel had sent out an identifying signal to British shore stations, thinking that the ship was still capable of making the English coast. But a few minutes later Wetzel changed over to a SOS when Brennan called back and ordered the crew to prepare to ditch. Loupe, Norman Nelson (top turret gunner), Nowlin, King (tail gunner) and Rodeschin went into the radio room. Loupe recalls:

Wetzel set the transmitting key and got into position with us. Brennan said, 'This is it!' We hit the water only five miles from land. Everything got dark then light again. It was some landing. We came in as smoothly as if we were coming in on a runway. We quickly opened the top hatch of the radio room and started releasing dinghies on each side. I was having trouble getting out of the aircraft, when suddenly I was lifted up and out. We got into the dinghies and started paddling to a nearby rescue boat. The rescue crew lifted us into their craft. Just after we got aboard we removed our helmets in a salute to the Fort, as it sank into the waters of the English Channel. It was a very emotional moment for me. I would always remember it as a time of dignity.

'We didn't even get our feet wet,' added Tech Sergeant Norman W. Nelson, twenty-two, of Lindsborg, Kansas, the top turret gunner. The tail gunner had been brought into the radio compartment where the crew gathered and as the big ship began to settle, the dinghies were loosed and the men went aboard. A short time later they were picked up and brought safely ashore.[19]

Emery R. Chesmore's crew in the 'Snetterton Falcons' who were flying *Charlene*, a B-17 borrowed from 'Van's Valiants' at Great Ashfield, got their badly shot-up Fort back to England before baling out.[20] Thomas Parks flew *8 Ball*, a ship borrowed from the 94th, which was like a 'race horse' to the target but could not keep up with the stragglers coming back. They landed south of London at a fighter station and were a week late getting back to Snetterton Heath.[21] Lieutenant Richard M. Jerger, a pilot in the 'Snetterton Falcons' from St Petersburg, Florida, put *Big Dick* down at a fighter field on one engine after five red-nosed Messerschmitt 110s had knocked out the other three. His gunners had repulsed every attack without a man being injured. Bombardier Lieutenant Henry E. Tessien of Oakland, California, was on his twenty-third and toughest mission. He asserted that the target caught 'simple, unadulterated hell'. He saw fires all over the area and smoke rising to 15,000 feet. And he claimed a Ju 88, which came in at 11 o'clock level. Tessien gave him two long bursts when he got up close and he saw a sheet of flame widen out from the fuselage and it went down trailing blue smoke. Tessien noted that the *Luftwaffe* was using Stuka dive-bombers, which were scarcely faster than Fortresses.[22]

The 95th and 390th had each lost one B-17. At Horham Captain John B. Miller had a 'good but sad feeling' to land at our home base after what he had seen and felt. 'The real heroes never returned. Only the good Lord knows what happened to them.' He hoped that it would never happen again. Leonard Herman went to see his commanding officer. Herman was in a quandary. He did not know whether to go back to his quarters and sack out or wash up and change for chow or go to the club. Or he could write a letter or two. It was time to give thanks for a safe return to home base. Of one thing he was certain. He wanted to propose to Colonel Dave McKnight that since the Schweinfurt raid was tougher and longer than most, it should count as two. Thus he would complete his twenty-five missions and would be a 'free man' – a 'Lucky Bastard'. Herman thought that it was an excellent idea. McKnight however, did not and Herman would have to wait until 3 November to complete his twenty-fifth and final mission. A few days later he was on orders signed by Colonel McKnight, going home.

At Framlingham Robert Saunders who flew on *Royal Flush*, piloted by William Royal, was convinced that the crew survived because they were crew No. 13, had handstand No. 13 and the tail gunner was born on the 13th day and lived on 13th Street in Pine Bluff, Arkansas![23] The 'Hundredth', 385th and 388th Bomb Groups suffered no losses, although few aircraft, if any, escaped scot-free. Of the bombers, which returned to England, 142 in both divisions were blackened and charred by fighter attacks and holed by flak. Sixty Fortresses and 600 men were missing. Five battle-damaged B-17s had crashed in England and twelve more were destroyed in crash-landings or so badly damaged that they had to be written off. Of the returning bombers, 121 required repairs and five fatal casualties and forty-three wounded crewmen were removed from the aircraft. Only eighty-eight of the 1,222 bombs dropped actually fell on the plants. Production at the Kugelfischer plant, the largest of the five plants, was interrupted for only six weeks and the German war machine never lacked for ball bearings throughout the remainder of the war. As in many other German industries, dispersal of factories ensured the survival of the German ball-bearing industry and careful husbanding of resources meant that some forms of machinery needed fewer ball bearings or none at all.

At Thurleigh, which had suffered one of the worst three days in the combat history of the 306th and Chelveston, where fifteen crews were lost, morale was low. Men were physically and mentally exhausted; their emotions were strung as tight as possible and they needed rest and understanding. Lieutenant Colonel Delmar Wilson, who had been 306th deputy commander and had headed the 305th during the preparations for the raid, hurried down from 8th Air Force Headquarters to Chelveston to commiserate with his former command. There was little he could do.

Colonel Budd J. Peaslee sums up the second Schweinfurt:

It was my questionable privilege to witness the greatest air battle of the ages fought by massed men and machines engaged in a mortal and lethal confrontation from which there was no victor and no vanquished. There were only the quick and the dead. It was my official assignment to participate in this awesome spectacle of flaming violence, death and mayhem that was to result in the greatest loss in men and machines ever suffered by a nation in a single aerial effort. I was not a volunteer for this mission; it was simply my turn to act as Air Commander of the leading task force of the 1st Bomb Division. This was to become an incident of war that can never again be visited upon a military force due to the outmoding of tactics and techniques of military hardware.

The bomb run was a torment in time. Never have five minutes seemed so long, like waiting for the sand in an hourglass to fall one grain at a time. As we entered the flak fields, the heavy gunfire was intense and accurate and so near, the crackling explosions were audible above the sounds of the engines and defensive machine guns. At long last our B-17 surged with the release of our bombs and we were on our way home. Miraculously, though holed by many fragments, our aircraft was without critical damage. We turned toward the nearest French border, where the chances of evasion would be better if we were forced to abandon ship. The target area had become obscured by smoke from our bombs, renewed time after time as succeeding formations struck home with massive bombs.

Devastation visited Schweinfurt but at a terrible cost. Never again would American bomber formations be dispatched to targets without friendly fighter escort as long as the *Luftwaffe* had an appreciable fighter defence capability. Officially we lost sixty bombers and over 600 airmen: the highest price ever paid for a single mission against a single target. The assessment included only those lost over the continent and not fifteen more written off when returning crews crashed while attempting to land or were forced to abandon ship. The total cost was one of every three of the 230 attacking aircraft. On the return flight, no friendly fighters met us as we expected to drive off the Germans who harassed us all the way to the English Channel. The reason was revealed when we found our bases covered by 20,000 feet of dense clouds reaching to the treetops.

The brave young Americans who took the 'Long Fall' were a section of a generation that established the traditions of the US Air Forces and the criteria of great courage and dedication that guides airmen of the Armed Forces to the far flung heavens and surrounding space.[24]

All heavy bomb groups were stood down to lick their wounds. At Bovingdon, Bill Rose went out to his bullet-riddled B-17 to see for himself how much damage had been caused.

We had two of our machine guns hit and bent back ninety degrees. I thought, 'now we could shoot around corners'. The skin of our ship had holes all through it and was so badly damaged it became a 'hangar queen'. In the afternoon a bomber came down to pick us up and we got back to Alconbury to find only three planes on the field. The officers' mess was completely empty.

The story was the same at every base. 'Pappy' Colby returned to Bury St Edmunds after a 48-hour pass and looked over the damaged B-17s.

Most of our aeroplanes were spattered with flak holes and the Lockheed boys were busy patching them up. Eight replacement crews were sent in but due to heavier losses in some of the other groups five of them were re-assigned and we only kept three.

At Widewing General Ira Eaker had tried to put a brave face on losses. Next day he wrote an optimistic report to Washington where General 'Hap' Arnold wanted 'more planes over the target on more days of the month' and where there seemed little appreciation in the capitol for the battle that the 8th Air Force men were waging.

Yesterday the Hun sprang his trap. He fully revealed his countermeasure to our daylight bombing…We must show the enemy that we can replace our losses. He knows he cannot replace his. We must continue the battle with unrelenting fury. This we shall do. There is no discouragement here. We are convinced that when the totals are struck, yesterday's losses will be far outweighed by the value of the enemy material destroyed…Yesterday's effort was not, as might at first appear, contrary thereto. I class it pretty much as the last final struggles of a monster in his death throes. There is not the slightest question but that we now have our teeth in the Hun Air Force's neck.

The losses and a spell of bad weather restricted the 8th to just two more missions in October. After Schweinfurt all heavy bomb groups were stood down to lick their wounds and replacements were sent in. Sam Laface arrived in England in October, as a spare assigned to the 349th Squadron in the 'Hundredth'. Although he was a product of the gunnery school at

Las Vegas, his CO asked him to join a cadre training to be toggliers. In short order, he learned how to handle the apparatus which dropped bombs. After several practice missions, he set up office in the Plexiglas nose of a B-17. Throughout his tour he flew with various crews.

> Before I got to my Group, they flew a raid and then continued on to North Africa. Many of the GIs made deals with the local Arabs for trinkets and clothing, but two guys from my squadron traded for a miniature donkey. It was dark brown and had big ears and big eyes. How they thought they'd be able to sneak it on board a B-17, I don't know. The legend has it that they wrapped her in a blanket and slipped back to their tent. When it was time to depart, they shoved the little donkey through the hatch and into the waist. 'Little Mo' quieted down while the plane took off and headed back for England. But the real problem was how we were going to keep her safe at 12,000 feet, with no oxygen and the temperature at fifty below. It was going to be a long trip and they had to bomb Marseilles on the way back! Well, they strapped a mask on her nose. The two gunners and the donkey shared their oxygen all the way home. What a sight that must have been! When they landed, there was still the problem of getting off the plane and back to the barracks. Discipline was pretty tight at this time and they couldn't be sure what would happen if they were caught. By the time I got to the Squadron, 'Little Mo' roamed all around with a boot in her mouth, quite at home.

On 3 November 555 bombers and H2X ships from the 482nd Bomb Group were dispatched to Wilhelmshaven. H2X, or *Mickey Mouse* (later shortened to just *Mickey*), was a recently developed American version of the British H2S bombing aid. Some groups carried incendiaries and, in the words of Captain Claude Campbell, flying his twenty-fourth mission in *The Eightball*, 'intended to burn up the city'.

Cliff Hatcher was a recent replacement co-pilot in a new crew in the 94th captained by Johnny Pyles.

> We took off in *Lil' Butch* and flew in 'Purple Heart Corner'. A new crew always flew in the tail-end of the formation. 'Purple Heart Corner' was on the left wing of the second element leader of the low squadron. We were the lowest 'plane in the formation. The opposite was tail-end-Charlie, which was in the top position off the right wing of the second element leader in the high squadron. During the

mission a German fighter passed under our left wing less than fifteen feet below us. He was so close I could make out the features on the pilot's face and could see that he was wearing a light-coloured scarf. His guns were blazing and the black swastika stuck out sharply on the tail. Flying was in my blood. My father had been a pilot in the First World War but had joined the Air Service towards the tail-end and had not seen combat. After the war he had his own aircraft. I remember Eddie Rickenbacker, Colonel Elliot Springs, Mike O'Leary and other aces. That camaraderie of World War One was still there when the German fighter came by. I was right in combat like Captain Elliot and the others. I sat there like a kid. This feeling persisted for two or three missions until I realized what I was into. Then I wasn't a kid any longer. A Bf 109 hit us and knocked out our number two engine. There were lots of contrails and we hid in them, flying behind our group. It proved successful and we got home although later our ground crew chief at Bury St Edmunds told us he found a .50 calibre bullet in the inverter beneath my seat! Obviously one of our boys in the 94th thought we were a German fighter! The Group lost only one aircraft, *Margie*, Lieutenant William L. Brunson from the 332nd Squadron being set on fire by a combination of flak and fighters. One to six chutes were reported.

The P-38 escort all the way to the target kept losses to a minimum and crews were quick to praise their 'little friends'. Claude Campbell recalls:

I saw about twenty-five enemy fighters, but our boys kept them at bay. They came in real close and gave good protection to the stragglers. My hat's off to them and I hoped we could get more of them over to England. The target was covered by clouds and bombing results could not be determined. There were no casualties in our group and I thought, 'Bring on the next one (my twenty-fifth and final mission).

At Hardwick Staff Sergeant John W. Butler in the 'Travelling Circus' flew his fifth mission, in the *Tennessee Rambler* as Theron U. Collins' left waist gunner. Collins, who came from Houston, Texas, was a Ploesti veteran. Butler had begun to philosophize about things. He hoped that Wilhelmshaven would be a 'milk run' just like his fourth trip, when *Valiant Virgin*[25] and the rest of the Group bombed Pisa in Italy during their sojourn at Tunis in North Africa. There was no flak or fighters, the day had been 'nice and warm' and they had 'knocked hell' out of their target.

When you don't make it back the fellows divide up anything they wouldn't send home to your next of kin. Combat, especially the money, was pretty good if you made it back but the raids were very tiresome, as the oxygen and the cold temperature really tired you out. A lot of my good friends went down. At first it bothered you but later I didn't mind it so much. To think I used to be afraid of the dark and I wouldn't even ride the roller coaster. But I can say with truth that I'd rather face fighter than flak as fighters you can shoot back but flak you couldn't. You just had to ride through it and hope for the best.

We took off at 1015 to bomb the docks and submarine pens. There were 600 planes on this raid, as it was the biggest US day raid on Germany. We had P-47s as escorts. Boy, did they look good. Before we got to the target we had to feather No. 4 engine on account of an oil leak. Four FW 190s attacked our formation and the right waist gunner fired some rounds and then the fighters' barrel-rolled right through our formation. I saw a B-17 go into a spin and explode. No chutes. We had to fall back so another ship fell back with us to help us in case of a fighter attack. Flak was pretty good and there was plenty of it. They had our range but not our deflection. It was minus forty and pretty damn cold. The weather was very clear and the fighter looked very pretty as they left their vapour trails in the sky. I also received the Air Medal so I was pretty happy over it as I certainly sweated it out long enough combat. Wouldn't be too bad if you could get a mission a week. That way you got in the habit and it would be just routine.

Daisy Elmar who with her husband Jimmy ran the 'Three Nags' at Fritton would never forget the men of the 'Travelling Circus':

They were wonderful boys. At first we weren't sure what to expect. But in a few weeks it was like having one big family. They didn't like our bitter to start with but soon they got used to it. It was the same with darts. Most had never played before so we had to teach them. Then it became their game. Our pub is in the path of what they called 'Bomber Alley'. All the 'planes used to fly overhead to get to the airfield after bombing the Germans. But not one of our 'regular' boys got killed. One 'plane went down in Switzerland, but they all got back later. The nearest thing we came to losing anybody was Scottie. We were all sitting around with long faces when we heard that he hadn't got back to the airfield. Nobody had a drink. Nobody spoke. It was like a funeral. Then the door burst open and in walked Scottie with a huge bunch of carnations. All he said was, 'I'm back.' Some of the boys married the local girls they were going out with.

The 8th was again out in force on 5 November when 374 Fortresses were dispatched to the iron foundry works and marshalling yards at Gelsenkirchen. Five *Oboe*-equipped B-24 pathfinders in the 482nd Bomb Group led them. The Liberator bombers meanwhile, went to Münster. Staff Sergeant John W. Butler in the 'Travelling Circus' flew his sixth mission as left waist gunner in *Q for Queenie*,[26] which was flown by Theron U. Collins and carried ten 500lb incendiary clusters.

> We took off at 1040. Our job was to burn the town and transportation system. Münster was a very important target and the Jerries did their damnedest to keep us from hitting it. Visibility was damn good and the weather was 37 below. We ran into heavy flak three or four places along the way. There was plenty of it. Our supercharger on No. 3 engine was broken so we had to drop back. Three Me 109s came up and Haggerty, the right waist gunner, fired a short burst at them. They threw their bellies up and dove downward. A Me 110 came in at nine o'clock. I gave him a short burst and he lobbed a rocket into the formation ahead of us. I then gave him another burst of about twenty rounds and he started to smoke. He then peeled off and came in at 7 o'clock where I got in another short burst. A P-38 then jumped his tail and he started down when I lost sight of them. We had P-47s and P-38s for escorts and they sure did their job well.

Gelsenkirchen, located in the Ruhr, an area with a reputation of being one of the most heavily defended in Germany, was not an ideal mission to finish on. But Captain Robert E. Nichols, of Garden Grove, California, who had finished the number of raids required to retire a man from combat piloted his Fortress over Europe five more times, was doing just that. Before the war Nichols had an orange grove on Route 1 near Garden Grove. His sister, Edith Nichols, lived there now and he hoped to return there after the war was over.

During his tour of operations in the 91st Bomb Group at Bassingbourn Nichols flew through the flak and fighters to bomb some of Europe's toughest targets. For meritorious achievement on all these daylight raids, he was awarded the Air Medal with three Oak Leaf Clusters. Nichols was separated from his crew and went alone on his first five combat missions as co-pilot with a different crew. Consequently, when he finished his tour, the members of his crew still had five raids to go. That is why he went on five additional missions. 'I wanted to finish up with my crew,' Nichols smiled.

I figured that they'd be split up and farmed out to other pilots if I left them. They didn't want me to, but when I said I was going to stay with them they felt good. You see, we trained together back in the States. Of course, I'm not so crazy about flying that I like going over to Germany every day, but I felt that I owed it to the boys to stick with them.

Nichols' crew members would swear by him as 'the swellest guy we've ever known'. A short, mild-mannered boy with a black moustache and a ready smile, in combat he always wore the same clothes and a sloppy sun-tan officer's cap he had picked up in the States. His men had confidence in him because he 'knew his airplane'. Nichols had studied aircraft, built them, trained in them, ferried them and flown them in combat against the Germans. After graduating from Garden Grove Union High School, he studied Aeronautical Engineering at Fullerton College. He then went to work in the tool and die department at Vultee Aircraft's Downey plant. When the war came along, Nichols went to Canada and in September 1940 enlisted in the RCAF where he trained and later ferried aircraft across country. In June 1942 he transferred to the 8th Air Force and went to work on bombers. Then they sent him to England. His third raid fell on his thirty-first birthday. He went to Villacoublay aerodrome in France that day and almost got hit by pieces of glass when his cockpit windshield was hit. His trip to Kassel, Germany, was a memorable one.

We encountered a large number of enemy fighters prior to the target and heavy flak at the target. My engine control cables were damaged and the gasoline ran short and we were just able to make it back to the English coast for a landing. All in all it was a mission that will long be remembered by my entire crew and myself. We were glad to see the English coast again.

After Gelsenkirchen Nichols probably would have been sent to the States for a rest. But if they had other plans for him and wanted him to go to a flyers' rest home on the English south coast, he said that he'd prefer to go to college in Oxford for the week and 'learn something'.

It was not until 11 November that the 8th was in the air again, this time to Münster, the scene of such devastation a month previously. Major 'Pappy' Colby led the 94th and Lieutenant Pyles' crew flew their third mission this day, in *Lil' Operator*. (This B-17 had the face of 'Esky', the little man who appeared on the cover of *Esquire* magazine, on its nose.) Pyles' crew was assigned the tail-end-Charlie slot in the high squadron. This was reckoned to be the most dangerous position after 'Purple Heart Corner'. Everything went well until shortly before bomb release. *Lil' Operator* was rocked by an explosion just forward of the engines on the left side. Oil began pouring out of the number two engine and streaked back across the cowling and wing area. Pyles told Hatcher to keep an eye on the oil pressure and feather the number two propeller if necessary. Quickly the pressure dropped to nothing and Hatcher punched the feathering button. *Lil' Operator* continued its bomb run and Lieutenant Adolph J. Delzoppo, the bombardier, released his bomb load over the target. The loss of one engine had considerably reduced their speed and they were now alone. 'Bandits at two o'clock' crackled over the intercom and Hatcher peered into the strong sun. Suddenly, out of nowhere appeared a Bf 109 that dived so close that for a moment the crew feared they were going to be rammed. The German pilot opened fire and several explosions occurred in the cockpit of the B-17, filling it with smoke. *Lil' Operator* fell off to the right and dived for the ground at alarming speed. Hatcher and Pyles opened their side windows to let out the smoke and for the first time realized they were going down fast! Straining on their steering columns, they managed to right their bomber. Hatcher was sure the number three engine was windmilling but three and four engine instruments had been shot out in the fighter attack. Pyles levelled off at 15,000 feet and applied full left rudder to keep the bomber on course. Three and four engine throttles were dead, so he decided to shut down number three engine. Then Ervin Smith, the ball turret gunner, called up on the intercom to say that the undercarriage was in the 'down' position. Ross Andrews, the engineer, discovered a large hole in the right forward bulkhead of the bomb bay, which had been caused by two 20mm shells exploding in that area. It had cut off all the electrical supply to the right-hand side of the aircraft and only the armoured pilots' seats had saved Hatcher and Pyles from flying shrapnel. Amazingly, the top turret gunner had escaped injury after fragments had whistled around his legs. Pyles headed for some clouds. One and a half engines out and a lowered undercarriage were more than an open invitation to any enemy fighter pilots. It was certain death. Soon five fighters had ganged up on the crippled bomber. Harold Norris, the tail gunner, saw them first, approaching from the rear. *Lil' Operator* dodged in and out of cloud and was soon down to just 500 feet. Over towns and villages they flew, at roof top height. Milburn Franklin passed up the temptation to strafe the streets and instead the

B-17F-25-DL 42-3082 *Double Trouble* in the 333rd Bomb Squadron, 94th Bomb Group. The pilot, Lt Bill Winneshiek, aborted the mission to Bremen on 25 June 1943 after fighters knocked out two engines and he landed in England despite a full bomb load. On 4 October 1943 during a mission to St-Dizier, France, fighters knocked out the No. 3 engine and the propeller refused to feather but the crew managed to crash-land at Margate. Vance Van Hooser, the assistant engineer-waist gunner, who was on his twenty-third mission was hit in the head by 20mm shell fragments and never flew again. *(USAF)*

B-17s in the 388th Bomb Group crossing Bremen on 8 October 1943 at 23,000 feet. The target below is obscured effectively by German smoke pots. None of the twenty-three Fortresses despatched by the Knettishall group were lost but twenty-one were damaged by flak from the 260 AA guns at Bremen. *(USAF)*.

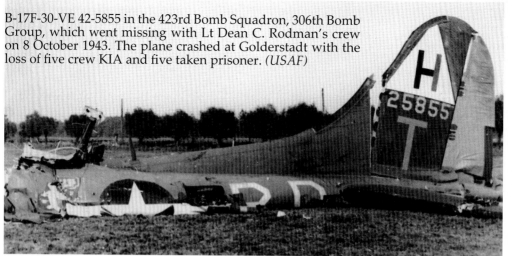

B-17F-30-VE 42-5855 in the 423rd Bomb Squadron, 306th Bomb Group, which went missing with Lt Dean C. Rodman's crew on 8 October 1943. The plane crashed at Golderstadt with the loss of five crew KIA and five taken prisoner. (USAF)

B-17F 42-30157 *Dirty Gertie* (formerly *Hell's Bells*) which Lt Van der Heyde crash-landed close to Bassingbourn on 30 July 1943. The aircraft was salvaged soon after. (USAF)

B-17F-50-DL 42-3393 *Just A Snappin'* in the 418th Bomb Squadron, 100th Bomb Group, lies wrecked beside a tree at RAF Ludham after returning from the raid on Bremen on 8 October 1943. (TAMM)

Air battle over Bremen, 8 October 1943: an FW 190 dives away after a frontal pass at the 95th Bomb Group formation. Sixteen of the Group's Fortresses sustained battle damage, mostly minor, but aircraft had to crash-land on return to England. The 95th lost no aircraft, while its gunners made claims for twenty-four of the enemy. It is possible one fighter did fall to the defensive fire of this formation: two dozen is probably greater than the number of attackers involved.

B-17F 42-5846 *Tinker Toy* in the 381st Bomb Group after the 8 October 1943 mission. Men point to holes made by 20mm cannon shells that decapitated the pilot, Lt Hal Minerich. Lt Thomas Sellars, the co-pilot, was wounded by the exploding shells. Spraying blood froze on the top turret base and prevented T/Sgt Miller from manning his position. He assisted Sellars who against all odds managed to get *Tinker Toy* home to Ridgewell where he ground looped the badly damaged Fortress. Sellars later was awarded the Distinguished Service Cross. *(USAF)*

Flying Fortresses in the 390th Bomb Group leaving the burning Focke-Wulf factory at Marienburg on 9 October 1943. *(USAF)*

Crews in the 385th Bomb Group at Great Ashfield back from the mission on 9 October 1943.

B-17F-55-DL 42-3413 *Hard Luck!* in the 350th Bomb Squadron, 100th Bomb Group, with Captain Loren Van Steenis ('The Flying Dutchman') and his crew. When Crew 13 had joined the 'Hundredth' on 13 October 1943 they were told, 'You fellers are Crew 13. This is the 13th Wing. You're assigned to airplane #13. Oh yes, your airplane is named *Hard Luck!*' (Its name derived from the date of its arrival – Friday 13th August 1943 – and the last two digits of the serial number). Van Steenis' crew flew the plane for seventeen consecutive missions. On 7 May 1944 while on the bomb run over Berlin *Hard Luck!* was hit by a flak burst, which killed the navigator, Harold Becker, and wounded the bombardier, Lester Torbett. In the ensuing confusion and with no navigator Van Steenis and his co-pilot, Jack Ogg, lost the Group but a P-47 rescued them and guided them home. Seven of the crew finished their tour. *Hard Luck!* held what must have been a record in the 8th Air Force, its first fifty missions being flown with original engines. Ground Crew Chief 'Zip' Myers was extremely proud of 'his ship' and refused to allow inexperienced pilots to fly it – 'that is if it could be avoided!' *Hard Luck!* flew missions for a year and a day, being lost on its sixty-second mission, on 14 August 1944 when 2nd Lt Donald E. Cielewich's crew baled out and all nine men were taken prisoner. (*via Michael P. Faley*)

B-17F 42-39789 in the 526th Bomb Squadron, 379th Bomb Group, which was badly damaged by enemy action on 19 October 1943. The Fortress was repaired by BAD 1 and in July 1944 was re-assigned to the 487th Bomb Group. It survived the war. *(USAF)*

B-17F 42-39789 in the 401st Bomb Group at Deenethorpe on 19 October 1943. This aircraft was transferred to the 351st Bomb Group at Polebrook on 18 November 1943 and named *Little Twinkle*. It crash-landed at Hawkinge on 30 December. It was salvaged the following month. *(USAF)*

B-17F-70-BO 42-29803 (seen here earlier in its career when it was assigned to the 365th Bomb Squadron, 305th Bomb Group, and was named *Flat Foot Floogie*) was the only 381st Bomb Group aircraft that FTR from the Schweinfurt raid on 14 October 1943. Four of Lt Bernarde M. Yorba Jnr's crew were KIA and six were taken prisoner. *(USAF via Bill Donald)*

B-17F 42-30719 *Shatzi* in the 390th Bomb Group with a damaged ball turret. This aircraft went MIA with Lt Harold W. Schyler and crew on 20 October 1943. Seven men were taken prisoner, one evaded and second were KIA. *(USAF)*

A number of B-17s and B-24s were lost through the inability of the pilots to feather propellers on failed engines. The degree to which this was occurring over enemy territory was not fully apparent for some months. If sump oil was suddenly lost, the pitch of the propeller blade could not be altered, causing the propeller to 'windmill', setting up extreme vibration and threatening the security of the whole aircraft. Eventually, the friction created in the drive gears would cause the propeller to break away. This 390th Bomb Group B-17F experienced this problem with the No. 1 engine during the 20 October 1943 mission to Duren. Fortunately the crew were able to bring the bomber back to home base at Framlingham, drawing a small crowd to view the damage.

B-17F 42-3327 *Tet T'Mote* in the 390th Bomb Group, which belly-landed at Framlingham on 21 October 1943. *(USAF)*

B-17G 42-39813 *Yankee Rebel* in the 390th Bomb Group, which crashed at Mount Pleasant on 16 November 1943. One of Lt Elbert R, Hoover's crew was killed. *(USAF)*

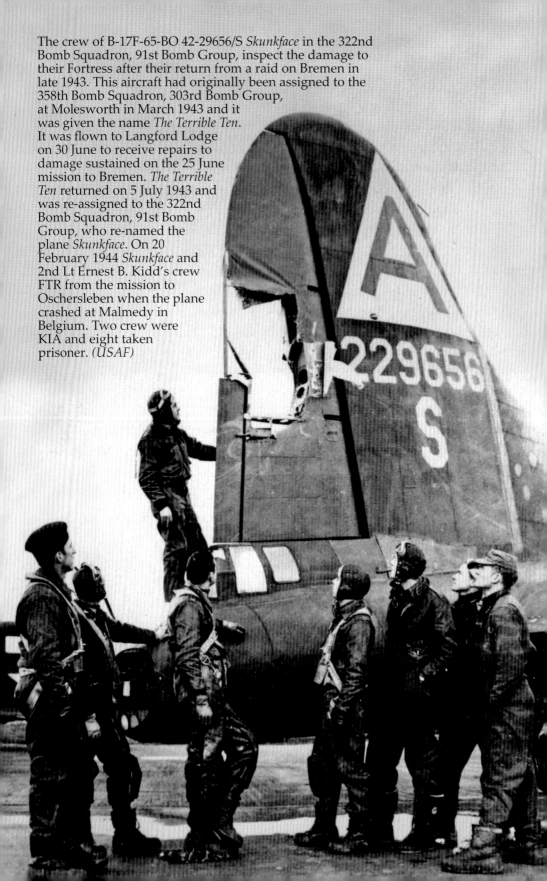

The crew of B-17F-65-BO 42-29656/S *Skunkface* in the 322nd Bomb Squadron, 91st Bomb Group, inspect the damage to their Fortress after their return from a raid on Bremen in late 1943. This aircraft had originally been assigned to the 358th Bomb Squadron, 303rd Bomb Group, at Molesworth in March 1943 and it was given the name *The Terrible Ten*. It was flown to Langford Lodge on 30 June to receive repairs to damage sustained on the 25 June mission to Bremen. *The Terrible Ten* returned on 5 July 1943 and was re-assigned to the 322nd Bomb Squadron, 91st Bomb Group, who re-named the plane *Skunkface*. On 20 February 1944 *Skunkface* and 2nd Lt Ernest B. Kidd's crew FTR from the mission to Oschersleben when the plane crashed at Malmedy in Belgium. Two crew were KIA and eight taken prisoner. *(USAF)*

Liberator 42-7535/U *Peep Sight* of the 68th Bomb Squadron, had seven wounded crew members, a disabled No. 4 engine, large cannon-shell holes in the fuselage, tail and right wing, damaged control cables and instruments and a flat tyre when it put down at Shipdham after the Munster mission of 5 November 1943. Flying on the outer side of the formation, it had been picked out in an attack by FW 190s. Pilot Lt R. A. Parker managed to bring the cripple home and is seen (with back-pack parachute) talking to other members of the crew while the three more seriously injured men are removed. The bomber was repaired and later used for transport work. *(USAAF)*

Five Medal of Honor awards, three posthumously, were awarded for the 1 August Ploesti operation. Colonel Leon Johnson received his decoration at a ceremony held on the 44th Bomb Group base at Shipdham, on 22 November 1943. On hand were General Devers, senior US Army commander in Europe at this time, and General Eaker. Here Johnson (by now commanding the 14th Combat Wing at Shipdham) indicates the horizontal bomb symbol for participation in this low-level mission on B-24D 41-23813 *Victory Ship* in the 68th Bomb Squadron. The unofficial 'Flying Eightball' insignia is hidden by a taped white sheet. *Victory Ship* and Lt Alfred A. Starring and crew were lost on 21 January 1944 when they were shot down over France; it was the last of the Group's original aircraft. *(USAF)*

Men of the 401st Bomb Group about to fly their first mission, on 26 November 1943. (USAF)

Tyre trouble at the start of the 401st Bomb Group's first mission on 26 November 1943. (USAF)

Norwich Cathedral, where men such as 'Staff Sergeant William J. 'Billy the Kid' McCullah sought solace and inspiration. (*Allan Healy*)

Both images below: American servicemen arriving in East Anglia were shocked by what they saw in cities like Norwich, which suffered terribly during the 'Baedecker Blitz' in 1942. (*George Swain*)

B-24D-90-CO 42-40738 *Fightin' Sam* in the 566th Bomb Squadron, 389th Bomb Group, at Hethel. (*John Driscoll*)

Lieutenant Lowell Watts, a pilot in the 562nd Squadron, 388th Bomb Group, at Knettishall. *(Watts)*

Colonel Myron Keilman (right) in the 392nd Bomb Group receives the Distinguished Flying Cross from General Leon Johnson, CO, 14th Combat Bombardment Wing. *(Keilman)*

B-17 42-31090 *Nasty Habit* in the 613th Bomb Squadron, 401st Bomb Group, returning from a mission on 1 December 1943. This aircraft was salvaged in January 1944. *(USAF)*

B-17F 42-39825 *Zenobia-El Elephanta* in the 613th Bomb Squadron, 401st Bomb Group, which crashed on 5 December 1943. After repairs by 2 SAD the aircraft was returned to flying status but it was wrecked in a take-off accident on 5 December 1943 and was salvaged. *(USAF)*

B-17F 42-29891 *Dangerous Dan* in the 379th Bomb Group, which crashed on 22 December 1943 and was salvaged two days later. *(USAF)*

gunners took it out on the enemy fighters that continued to harass them until they were clear of the coast. Two enemy fighters were claimed destroyed.

At the coast Pyles eased up to 1,000 feet and the crew began throwing out all excess equipment. As a result, the airspeed picked up a little and *Lil' Operator* flew on over the English Channel without getting her feet wet, thanks to the gentle manipulation of the number one throttle. As they approached the Bury St Edmunds control tower, Cliff Hatcher tried calling but the radios were dead. Luckily, the ADF was operating and they were able to home in on the airfield. Pyles put *Lil' Operator* down on the concrete runway but the number four engine resisted all Hatcher's attempts to kill it until the last minute. Both pilots hit their brakes hard and the aircraft stopped just short of the end of the tarmac. Smoke and dust shot into the air and the crew sat there for a few seconds until the very real threat of fire prompted them to evacuate the ship. Then came the distant scream of vehicles and the 'blood wagons' with Colonel Castle at the helm. Castle made sure no wounded were on board and then demanded to know why Pyles had stopped on the runway. Other aircraft were about to land with wounded on board. Pyles explained their situation and pointed out that they could not taxi away on one engine. Colonel Castle walked across to *Lil'Operator*, rubbed his chin and returned to the crew. He said, 'You boys have had a trying day but you had better head for debriefing and then perhaps you can get some well deserved rest.'

The next day Pyles' crew were given a three-day pass to London, courtesy of the Colonel. At the end of their leave and while waiting for their train at Liverpool Street Station, the crew decided to drop into a small cinema nearby. Just after the lights went out a British newsreel feature appeared on the screen. It began, *American Flying Fortress Shot Down Over Münster*. At debriefing Pyles had been told that his crew had been reported missing after being seen going straight down over the target. Now they sat there in the dimly lit London cinema watching a re-run of *Lil' Operator* going down over Münster. As it reached the frame showing the large 'Square A' and the lowered undercarriage the crew jumped out of their seats as one man, startling their fellow cinema goers with cries of, 'Hey, that's us!' The manager finally persuaded the 'rowdy', 'drunken' and 'obviously combat-fatigued Yanks' to leave his premises and they never saw the movie again!

For the first two weeks of November England was blanketed by thick, woolly fog and airfields were lashed with intermittent showers and high winds. The weathermen predicted that the bad weather would lift on the morning of 16 November. However, crews were told to make ready for a special mission to Norway, where visual bombing could be used to advantage. Colonel Myron H. Keilman, CO of the 579th Squadron at Wendling recalls:

> Enthusiasm generated by this intriguing mission was paramount. That night (15th November) the Division Field Order specified that the target was the secret German heavy water plant situated near the little town of Rjukan. It was a small target located in the mountains, about 75 miles from Oslo and was difficult to identify. Bomb loads had to be reduced because the distance involved a round trip of about 1,200 miles. Only ten 500-pounders were carried in each aircraft, which were to bomb from an altitude of only 12,000 feet.

At all 1st Bomb Division bases Fortresses were rolled from their muddy dispersal sites and lined up for the green light at the end of the runways. The division was assigned the molybdenum mines at Knaben and the Third was to attack a generating plant at Vermark in the Rjukan Valley. Intelligence sources indicated that both targets were connected with the German heavy water experiments, which would help give the Nazis the atomic bomb, but crews were not told this at the time. At Molesworth, the occasion was of special significance for *Knockout Dropper*, in the 'Hell's Angels', which was flying its fiftieth mission. If it completed the raid it would set a new record for a B-17. *Knockout Dropper* was something of a 'good luck' ship but the same could not be said of *Shady Lady II*, a B-17 that had flown with the 351st at Polebrook on the Group's first mission, to Schweinfurt on 14 May 1943. Repairs to damage sustained on a recent mission had only just been completed and the original crew refused to fly it any more. It was decided, therefore, that it be assigned to a new crew, led by Lieutenant Joseph Wroblewski. As he recalls, *Shady Lady II* was the first aircraft assigned to the 351st to have a chin turret. This reduced the airspeed by 10mph and made it a very clumsy and difficult aircraft to fly in formation.

Wroblewski recalls:

> Knaben was my crew's first mission of the war. I didn't expect to go with them on this one. Normally, an inexperienced pilot performed duties as a co-pilot with another crew on his first mission. The plane was heavily loaded with 2,500 gallons of gas and twelve 500-

pounders but she made take-off easily. After forming we headed for Knaben, almost 700 miles distant. Groups of formations were scattered around in every direction, leaving vapour trails. All I could see of Norway were the mountains covered with snow. This mission was flown at 15,000 feet and it was very cold. All but the co-pilot and I wore heated suits.

Twenty B-24s had taken off from Wendling and had joined with the rest of the 2nd Bomb Division over the North Sea. Landfall was made at Langesund Fiord, where *Luftwaffe* fighters could be expected from Denmark. The formation flew past the city of Skien and north-west to the target. The 392nd lead crew overcame navigational problems caused by scattered and broken cloud, which blotted out the landscape, and the Group made the IP on schedule. The bombing run was made using Automatic Flight Control Equipment. Bombardier 'Doc' Welland and the formation dropped bombs simultaneously on the nuclear energy development plant. The 'Sky Scorpions' however, encountered opposition, albeit weak, about 100 miles from the target. Three flew alongside the formation at 3 o'clock and each made three passes but the 'Sky Scorpions' suffered no serious damage and continued to the target. Only 40mm cannon-fire greeted them as they left the target at about 15,000 feet.

Meanwhile, the 3rd Division struck at Rjukan, about 75 miles due west of Oslo. As the formation approached the target area there was opposition, confirming the belief that the Germans would not be expecting a raid so far north. The 94th arrived ten minutes early and had to make a 360° turn. Crews had been told to make certain that Norwegian workers were not on their shift when the bombs were dropped. As the Fortresses crossed the target for the second time thick cloud obscured the plant from view and the formation was forced to make a 360° turn in the hope that it would clear. Ruben Fier, the bombardier in Edward J. Sullivan's Fortress in the formation, recalls:

While doing our 360° turns off the coast, a 17 from the 390th began doing slow gyrations in the sky without the benefit of anyone shooting at us. It felt like we were sitting in the balcony of a theatre watching an actor perform before us. The B-17 finally sliced into the water in an inverted position. We did not see my parachutes, nor could we understand what caused the unfortunate accident. Small ships were seen to head out towards the crash site but were unable to see survivors or what happened when the boats arrived on the scene. Our plane, momentarily attached to the 'Hundredth', began our run into the target behind other planes in formation before us but due to the cloud they were unable to drop their bombs. When the 100th approached the target the clouds drifted away and we dropped the first bombs on the target, which were what appeared to be large concrete buildings nestled in the mountains, with flat roofs. As we later described to the *Stars and Stripes* reporter on our return to Bury, I could see the bombs mushroom into the flat roofs and after a short period of time, flames of many colours escaped through the roofs. By the time we turned off the target and began flying out to sea, parallel to the course we flew in, the target area was engulfed in black smoke rising to the sky. The following groups were seen to be dropping their bombs into the smoke and licks of flame were seen coming up from the target area. Little did we realize at the time that the heavy water was essential to the Germans in their early stages of nuclear research.[27]

The round trip to Norway was slightly shorter than the 1,800-mile circuit to Trondheim on 25 July 1943 and the 1,600-mile round trip to Heroya. Joe Wroblewski returned to Polebrook at 1500 hours with 750 gallons of fuel remaining.

We were lucky to draw an easy mission first time out, although the going was rough coming into the English coast, with rain, snow and low ceilings. We gained some idea of what to expect for the future.

Lieutenant John P. Manning brought *Knockout Dropper* back to Molesworth to become the first B-17 to complete fifty missions in the ETO. Crews told waiting newsmen that the only anti-aircraft fire they had encountered had come from a single flak-ship in one of the fords. Crews in the 3rd Division rejoiced over their accurate bombing of Rjukan, saying that the explosion had lifted their aircraft suddenly, '...as if a giant hand was pulling them upwards. As it was we hit it right on the nose.'

On the fog-bound and icy morning of 18 November when the briefing curtains went up to reveal Norway again, crews were more concerned about the long time over cold weather than about enemy opposition. This time the Liberators received a 'frag' order for a mission to bomb the Ju 88 assembly plant at Oslo-Kjeller and industrial targets in Oslo, eighteen miles to the east. Another 127 B-17s were dispatched to Gelsenkirchen. However, the *Oboe* sets aboard the leading Fortresses gave trouble and directed the formation too far north of the target. After an unsuccessful battle with the elements the B-17s were forced to return to England. The

'Flying Eightballs' were unable to accomplish its formation assembly. Tail-end B-24s starting late for Norway expected to assemble en route. Because of this when the *Luftwaffe* fighters did arrive it was difficult for the bomber crews to identify their own damaged aircraft.

The twenty Liberators in the 'Travelling Circus' completed formation and headed across the North Sea for Norway. There was a low lead section and a high section on the right of the lead. Luther S. Bird was the pilot of *El Toro* and co-lead in the high section. He and most of the crew had flown with 1st Lieutenant Roy G. Martin on the low-level raid on the Ploesti oilfields on 1 August, in *Bomerang*, until Martin became 328th Squadron Operations Officer and Bird continued as first pilot.[28] Earl Wayne 'Rocky' Hill, an American transferred from the RCAF, became the co-pilot. Luther Bird flew the crew's fourteenth mission in *Bomerang* as pilot and George Bailey, co-pilot of the original *Bomerang* crew, flew his twenty-fifth mission as his co-pilot. When freeze-up problems with *Bomerang*'s high-pressure oxygen system began occurring at altitude where the temperature was often minus 50 to 60°C, the Bird crew was assigned a new B-24D, 42-63982, which had a low-pressure oxygen system. By majority vote the crew named the new B-24 *El Toro*. The William F. Stein crew in *Jerks Natural* was lost on the mission on 1 October 1943 to Weiner Neustadt and the ground crew took over *El Toro*. At this time *Bomerang* was close to having fifty missions and later completed these and returned to the States on a war bond selling mission.

Luther S. Bird recalls:

My Form 5 listed the November 18 target as Oslo and nine and a half hours' flying time. Our route and bombing altitude was 12,000 feet. It was extremely cold with the cockpit centigrade thermometer registering below minus 50. Periodically the group had to pass through scattered clouds and on these occasions some ships left the formation to return to base. About halfway to Norway, we passed through clouds and more ships, including the lead, aborted. At this point, the remaining ships formed on *El Toro* and we became the group lead. Except for seeing a *Stuka* dive bomber off towards Denmark, the flight to the IP was uneventful. But then our problems began. At the IP we turned on the bomb run. Immediately the bombardier called notifying that the bombsight was frozen – a disturbing message meaning we were useless in contributing to a successful mission. There wasn't time for the radio or flares. I rocked the wing tips a few times and went into a left turn to circle and return to the bomb run. About halfway around, another ship cut inside and took the lead. All ships formed on the new lead and the run from the IP to the target continued. No flak or fighters were encountered in the target area. The new lead bombardier did a good job and all ships released on his bomb drop. The men in the back reported that the bombs were all on target. The target, a hangar, literally disappeared from the earth! A mission that could have been a failure became very outstanding for the Circus.

General von Falkenhorst, the German commander of forces in Norway, was watching a defence exercise from his command car on a hill overlooking Kjeller and he had dismissed civilian workers from the base. When the Liberators came into view at about 12,000 feet, von Falkenhorst asked one of his aides who they were. The answer was roughly translated, 'My general they must be ours.' A few minutes later the first of 838 500-pounders started blasting the target. At 12,000 feet the 392nd lined up for the bomb run. Lieutenant Jim McGregor, in the lead aircraft, held his B-24 precisely on altitude and airspeed and he and the twenty bombers following released the 210 500-pounders on the target simultaneously. Some 70 per cent of the bombs dropped by the Liberators fell within 2,000 feet of the briefed aiming point. General von Falkenhorst and his aides had to run for their lives to seek cover. They survived but only by a few seconds before the bombs fell. A bunker nearby filled with German soldiers was hit and several bomb craters dotted the hillside. Only three Norwegians died in the raid.

On the return leg the same scattered to broken clouds lay across the Skagerrak beneath the formation. Suddenly the gunners spotted German fighters skimming across the cloud tops opposite the B-24s' line of flight. A dozen-plus Ju 88s climbed to make fast diving passes as they circled in behind the bombers. Liberator 'outriders' moved into a tight formation providing the mutual protection of concentrated firepower. Diving in pairs, the German twin-engined fighters lobbed rockets and 20mm explosive shells into the 392nd. Tail and top turrets responded with bursts of machine gun fire and the ball turret gunners opened up below as the fighters broke off the attack. Sergeant T. E. Johnson, flying with Lieutenant Wyeth C. Everhart, shot up one fighter so badly that it burst into flames and was last seen in an uncontrollable dive.[29] Two Liberators were hit and began to lose power. They could not keep up with the rest of the formation and as they fell behind the Ju 88s concentrated their fire on them. The B-24 pilots dived for cover and sheltered in the clouds. For a time they played hide and seek, as the fighters circled and eventually the bombers were lost from view.

Wave after wave of enemy fighters pressed home their attacks and three B-24s in the 44th that brought up the rear of the formation were shot down. In the 67th Squadron *Touch of Venus* piloted by 2nd Lieutenant Earl T. Johnson of Montgomery, Alabama, and *Raggedy Ann* flown by 2nd Lieutenant Edward M. Dobson of Merrick, New York, crashed in the North Sea with no survivors. A third Liberator, piloted by Captain Edward R. Mitchell, an original 67th Squadron pilot who had just transferred to the 68th Squadron, was shot down in the Skagerrak south of Oslo prior to the bomb run. All the crew perished. The bodies of the sixty-two Americans were never found after their B-24s crashed into the sea off Norway. Three more Liberators were forced to land in Sweden. *War Baby* in the 'Travelling Circus' landed at the small airstrip south of Örebro, as did *Bakadori* in the 392nd. *Helen Hywater* in the 'Flying Eightballs' circled the airfield at Trollhättan, firing signal flares to inform the Swedes that it was about to land. US policy at that time called for the burning of any aircraft that landed in neutral territory and Captain Baxter W. Weant's crew set fire to their Liberator shortly after landing.

Sergeant Forrest Clark, the tail gunner in Lieutenant Rocky C. Griffith's Liberator in the 'Eightballs', shot a Ju 88 down. He recalls:

Sitting in the tail position I could look back and see a line of seven to ten fighters lining up to attack our rear. 'They're waiting in line to get at us,' I called over the intercom, pressing the mike to my throat. Suddenly they attacked from all sides. Two shells went through the turret directly over my head, missing me by inches. I followed one after the other as the *Luftwaffe* pilots zoomed in at our tail and then dove beneath us to come up in front and swing and line up for another pass. One after another they came; closer and closer. I tracked them with my twin .50-calibre guns but could not get a good lead on any until they passed under us and then shot up again for the waist gunners to get shots at them. Finally, I fixed one in my sights as he levelled out and came in faster and faster. 'So close,' I said to myself. 'He's going to hit us: he's going to ram us.' I gripped the triggers of both guns, levelled them out and pressed down. I kept holding the triggers down, hoping they would not jam the belts. I could see my tracers going out in long lines right into his wing roots. Bright flashes of fire and traces kept boring into his wings until he came so close I could see the outline of the German pilot's head in the cockpit. Just as he slipped under us I saw a thin trail of smoke coming from the engine.

Clark was almost completely out of ammunition and a 20mm shell hit Sergeant Bill Kuban, the ball gunner, who was bringing him more rounds, in the head, knocking him unconscious and bleeding to the floor. Clark heard the bale-out bell but at first he had difficulty in getting out of his shattered turret. Two men, Sergeants John Gibboney and L. J. McAndrews, were getting ready to jump through the open camera hatch. Clark prayed, because he knew he would not survive long in the ice-cold sea if he jumped. 'I actually went down on my knees and prayed. Much to my surprise, just about that time the fighter attacks suddenly stopped and the Germans left us to what they must have thought was our death.'

In the 67th Squadron Lieutenant Joseph L. Houle's B-24, which was severely damaged, tottered gallantly to within fifty miles of the English coast with safety in sight. But by now his fuel indicators were reading zero and he was forced to ditch. The aircraft seemed to break in two and four minute figures were seen to slip into the icy waters of the North Sea. Griffith, himself flying on three faltering engines, circled over the scene while his radio-operator called ASR. His own fuel supply running low, Griffith dipped his wing in salute to his fallen comrades and turned towards his base. ASR found no trace of the Muskegan, Missouri pilot's crew or the aircraft. Griffith's Liberator spluttered on, just above the sea. Clark adds:

> More than once the call went out from the pilot to prepare to ditch but we had a wounded gunner who would surely die if we ditched in the icy water. We limped on and more than once it seemed all engines quit and the 'plane stuttered as if in its death throes. But the 'plane would not die.

Griffith made it back to Shipdham, where the landing gear failed to work. The flight engineer, Earl Parrish, tried desperately to crank it down by hand but this failed too. Griffith ordered everyone to bale out. Forrest Clark was certain he had landed in Holland but a Norfolk farmer holding a pitchfork soon reassured him. Clark fell to the ground and gripped it with both hands in a gesture of relief and thanksgiving. Griffith managed to land the badly damaged B-24 on one wheel and Kuban's life was saved. Two hours later repair crews checking the wreckage found two unexploded German shells in the one good engine that had brought the crew home.

Luther S. Bird again:

> After leaving the target area and heading for the North Sea, our armourer-gunner called with the news that we had a bomb hanging

by one latch in the right rear compartment. The decision was made to leave the bomb alone until we were over the North Sea. However, the bomb didn't wait as it dropped knocking the right rear bomb bay door off its tracks. The door was hanging down for the flight back. This did not interfere with the flight characteristics of the plane, flopping in the breeze. But we were concerned about our 'stray' hitting civilians. Despite our flapping bomb bay door, we made a successful landing and when we reported to interrogation, the Norwegian underground had already reported the success of the mission. The Norwegians did also report that some stray bombs caused some minor damage to their civilians. We immediately reviewed and estimated that our stray bomb would have hit in unpopulated country. It was good to be back at the home base with the warm feeling that another successful mission was completed, even though this time we had to make two bomb runs!

The bad weather continued over the next few days but did not prevent RAF Bomber Command bombing Berlin on the night of 22 November. This led to rumours of an American follow-up raid being mounted on the capital the next day. Bill Rose was in the 92nd Bomb Group, which would lead the raid.

We were on stand-down and consequently we stayed in the bar and drank more than we should have done. The bar closed at 12 o'clock and we hit the sack. Two hours later there came a guy waking us to go on a bombing mission! Of course we were in no physical shape to go but we managed to get through breakfast. Imagine our surprise and sobering effect when the curtain was pulled back to reveal the target. It was Berlin! We felt that, given such a target, even if we managed to survive the fighters and the flak on the run-in we would be lucky if there was anything left afterwards. There was not too much thought about being able to return so long as the bombing part of the mission could be completed. The *Luftwaffe* would certainly be waiting to finish off anyone coming back. As it turned out, the weather was as lousy as expected on the 23rd and you could hardly see. But we went out to the planes and started the engines before the red flare was fired cancelling the mission. It proved one thing though; that security on the base was very poor, because it was well known that the target would be Berlin. We were very thankful that the mission was scrubbed because we would certainly not have survived.

Meanwhile, replacement crews arrived to replace losses. At Knettishall on

20 November, just four days after Lieutenant Lowell Watts' crew reported to the 562nd Squadron, they were assigned a new B-17G, which was now beginning to come in to replace the older B-17Fs. Major improvements were the chin turret with its two .50 calibre guns, electronic turbo controls and enclosed waist windows. Lowell Watts named his B-17G *Blitzin' Betsy* in honour of his wife.

We were immersed in ground school and in checking everything about our new plane. We spent time with our ground crew headed by Harry Allert, a crew chief I would come to respect and value as a friend and one upon whom our crew could depend with utmost confidence. By this time I had met the other pilots in our squadron. I did not feel they conveyed a sense of superiority. Nor did they show enthusiasm for us either. We were just there, a part of a big machine and it would be up to us to earn our place in the system. I had the impression that I would make only a couple or three close friends and the rest would be seen as spots in our formation that were important to the strength of our group. The primary thought of most of the air crews was survival. There was little place for long-term friendships. Eventually I would come to know all the pilots in our squadron, but would never really know those in the other three squadrons.

We had been assigned to a Nissen hut and acquired a couple of oil burning heaters and two candles for night-time light. The officers on Monty Givens' crew were in our hut. Now we finally had another crew to relate to. The airmen on my crew got in so we could begin serious crew briefings. On our second day on the base we got to fly a two-hour group formation practice mission. It was good to get back in the air again. I got to meet some of the other pilots, but it was on a business-come-first basis. I was more concerned with learning what was expected of me and where everything was located than in anything else. We located the mess hall, Officers' Club, quarters for our airmen, the briefing and personal equipment room, the Flight Surgeon's office, link trainer and the hangars, control tower and flight line. I was interested in the posting of crews, pilots' names and number of missions each had.

On 23 November I was briefed for my first mission. I would fly as co-pilot with Lieutenant Duncan since it was customary for each crew commander to fly his first mission as co-pilot to get some sense of the techniques of aerial assembly and the combat environment. I slept poorly the night before that mission. I would be the only one in our hut flying and was afraid the CQ might not find me to wake me in time for briefing. I did not need to worry about that. We were briefed to bomb the Air Ministry in Berlin. I knew from the groans and comments that this was a super tough mission. I did not know at the time just how special and how difficult a mission it could have been, we would have only short-range fighter cover. The mission could be deadly, but I tagged dutifully along with Lieutenant Duncan as we checked the plane and taxied out for take-off. Then came the red flares from the tower and the mission was scrubbed. I've often wondered what our losses would have been had we actually flown that mission.

On November 26 we were again alerted. This time Major Goodman asked if I'd feel okay flying as first pilot, which of course I replied in the affirmative. The 8th wanted maximum effort and there was little time to waste getting crews in the air. Our new plane was still being refitted and we were assigned a B-17F named *Quarterback*. I felt that our training had been as adequate as could have been expected in the time frame of the war. I did not yet consider our crew as a real part of the Group. We needed combat to achieve that relationship. But I felt that the Bovingdon ground school had given us as much knowledge as possible of what we would face and what was expected of us. I thought the formation practices with the Group had been adequate and was comfortable with the personnel who were in command positions at the 388th. Now it would be up to us to prove we could carry out the tasks expected of us.

'B. J.' Keirsted's crew in the 563rd Squadron had also been alerted the night before that they would fly their first mission. 'Goldie' Goldstein recorded in his log:

Finally, we had the experience which should only come to a man once in his life. To me and all of my crewmates it came twenty-five times. That is, the early morning call for a combat flight.

It was a cold November morning, the barracks were dark. At 0330 the light was switched on. The CQ read off the names of the crews for the mission and added, 'the briefing is at 0600 hours'. We tumbled out of a warm bed, dressed warmly, shaved in cold water and boarded a GI truck in darkness to the mess halls for a breakfast we were not sure we could eat because of our nervous stomachs. Each man was wondering, 'Will we make it back today?'

Briefing was cold and matter of fact. The target: Bremen.[30] After the main briefing each man had his special briefing. I went to a communications briefing where radio operators received their special codes for the day. We checked out our parachutes and the sign over the door 'If it doesn't work, bring it back' was intended to lighten the tension. We dressed again in our flying clothes. First some warm underwear, some GI clothes and the famous blue heated suits. We removed all of our personal jewellery, wallets and rings, wearing only our dog tags. Then it was out to the trucks in the cold dawn for the ride to the plane. Nothing was more ominous than a B-17 standing in the early morning light, loaded with bombs, ready for its crew. Finally, we boarded the plane for a 0800 hour take-off after each of us has installed our machine guns in their place. The metal was cold to the touch and at that time of the morning our nerves were tense and our stomachs unsettled. All in all we weren't ready for what was to come.

The take-off and climb to altitude to get into formation was routine. There was much more flak and fighters always ready to knock the bombers down. The first flak I saw was just after we crossed the enemy coast. Talk about awesome; that was. The burst of black smoke was terrifying. A crewman commented over the intercom, 'The ones you see are OK. It's the ones you don't see you have to worry about.' A sick joke, but true.

We saw two mid-air collisions of '17s and to a crew on its first mission it was an awesome sight. To lose an aircraft in non-combat situations seemed to be such a waste.[31]

Lowell Watts was given one of the easiest spots in the Group; a slot on the left wing of the CO, Colonel William B. David, of Calhoun, Georgia.

Assembly was easy for our position and everything went along as briefed. As we climbed to altitude and crossed the enemy coast it became more difficult to keep up with our lead plane. At our new altitude our number three engine simply would not draw the manifold pressure we needed. Very slowly we slipped behind, dropping back to fly with the second element of our Group. Then we were back with the low squadron and still falling behind. One dominant theme drilled into new pilots was that we must never, never become a loner. Your protection is with your buddies. Fly alone and you are dead meat for the *Luftwaffe*. So here I was on my first mission unable to stay up with the formation. Reluctantly we turned back, hoping for clouds that were not quite as solid as we wanted. Luck rode our wings that day. We saw only one fighter and he did not press a serious attack. It was the first mission for all of the crew.

Murphy, our navigator, was next put on notice that I needed a heading for home. After all our jockeying and no longer in sight of our Group, Murphy gave me a heading. When we saw the coastline, nothing seemed quite right. It turned out to be the coastline of Scotland, well north of our intended landfall. Finally we got squared away and landed at Knettishall after all the other planes were in. Ah, the joy of a first mission.

The skies were unexpectedly cloudy and the 3rd Division was forced to return with its bomb loads intact.

'Goldie' Goldstein concluded:

We landed okay and were quite exhausted from being on oxygen for five hours. Although there were no enemy fighters encountered, the flak was heavy over the target. It was very close and I did quite a bit of 'sweating it out'. We flew under extreme conditions, the excessive cold, the use of oxygen for six-hour periods, the scene of fellow airmen being shot down and lastly the ever present enemy anti-aircraft fire and fighters waiting to knock us out of the sky. It was not until we returned to our home base and we began discussing the day's events that I realized how scared I was, but then again so was everyone else and not embarrassed to say so. Only twenty-four more to go.

The 1st Division, en route to Bremen, encountered persistent fighter attacks by up to 100 German fighters. Claude Campbell, flying the twenty-fifth and final mission of his tour with the 'Hell's Angels' that day, recalls:

Focke-Wulfs jumped us before we reached the enemy coast but I did evasive action and the boys shot 'em off. All kinds of enemy fighters were in the air, including old *Stuka* divebombers; a perfect illustration of Hitler's shortage of first-line fighters. We ran into a typically heavy barrage of flak over Bremen. The target was covered with clouds and bombing results could not be determined. P-47s picked us up and escorted us from the target so the enemy stayed away.

The 8th lost twenty-nine Fortresses and five fighters. The Third Division's mission to bomb industrial targets in Paris was aborted on arrival because of complete cloud cover that totally obscured the objectives. A navigator on the raid recalled:

Our target was another ball-bearing factory in the centre of Paris and only one 'wing' was going on this raid. Our group led this one and we flew the number two position in the lead squadron. We were 'loaded for bear' with six 1,000 demolition bombs in the bomb-bay. We took off at 0630 to rendezvous with the group, but it was 1030 when we left England. The formation was flying at 23,000 feet. It was 35 below zero and we had a high tail-wind. Our escort of about eighty P-47 fighters joined us and we were over at Paris at 1115. We had flown from 'peace to peril' in less than an hour and a half. Paris was completely covered by clouds; the only thing visible was the Eiffel tower sticking up through the clouds. One bomber was hit by flak over Paris. It dropped down and crashed into one in our formation and both went down; I saw only three chutes. We headed home without dropping our bombs and were hit by over a hundred Me 109s. I got three good shots with my nose gun. One B-17 went down in flames. Five minutes later a fighter knocked out another Fort and followed it down. A third bomber went down and I saw three chutes before it crashed in the forest below. We reached the Channel and Smith's plane dropped out of formation with two feathered engines, but got back to base later.

German fighter pilots had new planes and attacked our formation from out of the sun. Our P-47 escort fighters were a big help and had a lot of 'dog fights' with our attackers. We lost six B-17s and had to drop our bombs in the Channel before we landed shortly after noon. It was a short mission, but definitely not one to build our morale!'

After two days' rest the 8th Air Force returned to Bremen on 29 November for a raid on the centre of the city again. Larry Goldstein wrote:

Here we go again. Awakened at 3:30am and was surprised when there were no eggs for the 'last meal' as it is sometimes called. Had flap jacks instead. We took off okay and were soon headed out over the Channel, straight for Adolf's palace. We had some oxygen trouble and had to restrict our use to a minimal flow rather than 100% flow. The target was a 100% cloud covered and we had to return to Knettishall with our bomb load. This was never a comfortable feeling to men with ten 500lb bombs on board. At least I have adopted my mission preparation: the right clothes, the right routine. It was extremely cold today. 50 below zero. I say 'God bless the guy who invented heated flying clothes'. We had many P-47 escorts today to give us a feeling of comfort also. At least today I knew what to expect. A few more and I will be a combat veteran.

'Pappy' Colby was a combat veteran and on 30 November he flew his twenty-fifth and final mission. He said:

As long as I live I will never forget the first glimpse of the English coast, which told me I was coming home for good. I remember saying to myself, 'Pappy, with God's help you made it'.

The mission to a steel mill in Solingen, Germany, on 30 November resulted in an abort for 'BJ' Keirsted's crew as Larry Goldstein recalls:

We had a runaway propeller and the engine threatened to catch fire and engulf the fuel cells. We aborted and made an emergency landing. As soon as we braked I heard over the intercom, 'Howie, watch the prop'. I went out the back with the rest of the crew and we ran across the field thinking our plane was ready to blow at any moment. As I looked over my shoulder I saw 'BJ' bending on one knee and I saw blood. I assumed he had been hurt but it was Howie Palmer who had been hit as the prop had kicked over on its last turn. Howie was hospitalized and then returned to the States. He was replaced by Eddie Kozacek, an immigrant's son and farm boy from Coxsackie, New York.

Lowell Watts, who had flown his second mission the day before but had been unable to drop his bombs because of the weather, recalls:

We were carrying incendiaries. Kelly, my bombardier, was grounded with ear trouble and we took a replacement named Mecum, a stocky bombardier I had not met before. Bad weather caused serious mix-up in our assembly. As we broke out above the clouds I failed to see any flares from our Group lead. Continuing to climb as briefed, I finally saw the flares of the 96th Bomb Group, which was part of our Third Division. I flew over to the 96th and found a spot in their formation. I'd begun to feel a bit more at ease about everything. But now I wondered what happened to green pilots who couldn't find their correct formation. Flak was fairly heavy over the target. Only few fighters bothered us. But then something else bothered me and it was a big something. Three of our incendiaries had hung up in the bomb bay. I called Mecum to cut them loose. As he struggled with the bombs be pulled his oxygen hose loose and passed out. His body hung over the catwalk chain. The bomb bay doors were open. The three bombs swung back and forth as wind gusts caught them, the air coming in that bomb bay at 26,000 feet was almost 60 degrees below zero and Solingen was way, way down there below Mecum.

Ramsey, our engineer, and Finkle, our radio operator, joined forces to haul Mecum back into the radio room get him some oxygen. Now Mecum was safe, but we still had those bombs. Ramsey finally cut them loose without setting one of them off. Now we were back together again, but coming home with the wrong group. After landing, we learned that our group had been unable to assemble and only ten of us had actually made a good mission. That made us feel a whole lot better.

Lowell Watts' next mission was a replay for formation assembly above the cloud deck.

The target was Emden. Our pilots were having to learn to hold a briefed heading and climbing rate until they broke above the clouds and could form together. We did better on this mission, but those of us in my group never did form into a group. Once again we had to tie in with another group. Weather would be almost a constant problem during the winter months. For me, the descent in low visibility when we came back at the end of a mission was a more demanding task than the take-off and assembly, but getting the formations together was an arduous and time-consuming part of any mission. By this time our crew was beginning to feel more comfortable with our assignments. We had seen fighters and flak. We had blundered through clouds to make a mission out of chaos. We had almost salvoed our bombardier. We no longer felt an outsider in our group. Now we felt ready to face the weather, the *Luftwaffe* and the flak during the winter of 1943–44. This was just as well since tougher missions were coming up.

Notes

1. The German flag that flew over the Kugelfischer ball-bearing factories was presented to the 305th BG at Chelveston by a representative of the Third Armoured Division that captured Schweinfurt in early 1945.

2. *In My Book You're All Heroes* by Robert E. O'Hearn. Privately published 1984.

3. They salvoed their bombs in the Channel and fired green flares to signal Spitfire escort fighters for protection. After volunteering for another tour, Jacobs was killed on his twenty-eighth mission on 31 December 1943 when he ditched *Sea Hag* in the English Channel. Two of the crew perished and one of the waist gunners who suffered a lung injury was later medically discharged.

4. Adapted from *First of the Many* by Captain John R. 'Tex' McCrary and David E. Scherman, 1944.

5. All of Butler's crew survived. But after capture Harris, who had a minor shrapnel wound in his shoulder and had injured his back when his chute had opened, learned that regular bombardier, Joe Lukens, who had flown the mission on 1st Lt William C. Bisson's plane, was strafed and killed in his chute. He also learned that others had been hanged and shot by civilians.

6. In the following months Sam Mehaffey flew many more missions with several crews. He flew just about every position in the formations from tail end Charlie to lead crew and he finished a tour of thirty-two missions on 23 July 1944.

7. *In My Book You're All Heroes* by Robert E. O'Hearn. Privately published 1984. Vaughter landed in a pine forest about twenty minutes distant from the target and hid there until dark. He was free for two days and walked to Heidelberg where he found civilian clothes and a bicycle. He was finally picked up between Heidelberg and Strasbourg, pointing up the limitations of evasion in Germany with no friendly natives or any kind of assistance. A civilian guard captured Vaughter and, having himself been treated well as an Allied prisoner of war in World War I, was courteous to him. He even took the downed airman to his home where Vaughter was fed soup, apple cider and two apples before being turned over to the *Polizei*. *First Over Germany: A History of the 306th Bombardment Group* by Russell A. Strong (1982).

8. After the mission Major John R. Blaylock's crew was ordered to report to the 8th AF HQ to receive a commendation for a job well done. Blaylock lost his life on the mission on New Year's Eve 1943. Captain Bill Winters was KIA in 1944. Jim Bradley finished his twenty-five missions on 7 November 1943. His last mission was a radar run and he did not know 'what the hell was going on'. He would probably have gone down with Blaylock on 31 December if Smith had not asked for a chance to lead.

9. See *Wrong Place! Wrong Time! The 305th Bomb Group and the 2nd Schweinfurt Raid October 14 1943* by George C. Kuhl (Schiffer 1993). Major Normand was promoted to the rank of Lt Colonel on 27 October 1943. He was shot down on 24 August 1944, survived and was taken prisoner.

10. James A. 'Pete' Mullinax baled out and fell about as far as possible before pulling the ripcord. He had passed out due to lack of oxygen. He landed in some apple trees, suspended three feet from the ground. He reached up to grab the shrouds and fell out of his harness! He had forgotten to fasten his leg straps before jumping. Fortunately, he did not raise his arms while in the air. All the crew was captured. Navigator Maurice Fridrich evaded for ten days before he was caught just before he was about to swim the Rhine at Strasbourg to get into France.

11. The crew flew their last mission on 21 February 1944 to Quakenbrück-Bramsche.

12. Captain (later Brigadier General) J. Kemp McLaughlin completed a combat tour with the 92nd BG in the autumn of 1943 and after thirty days' leave

(R&R) remained with the Group as its operations officer until March 1943. In March 1947 he became Commander of the West Virginia ANG. He had a twenty-one-month tour of duty in the Korean conflict and several to Vietnam.

13. Cosper was later given his own crew and was killed on 13 November when the mission to Bremen was recalled before leaving the English coast because of bad weather. Cosper flew through a thunderhead, went into a spin and lost several thousand feet of altitude in a few seconds. He recovered from the spin and was able to level the Fortress long enough for the crew to bale out. In a heroic effort to keep the plane, which was still carrying a full bomb load, from crashing to an English village, Cosper chose a clearing near Princes Risborough in Buckinghamshire and crash-landed his almost uncontrollable plane in an open field. The aircraft immediately caught fire and exploded within a few seconds, instantly killing Cosper. He was posthumously awarded the Silver Star for his heroism. *First Over Germany: A History of the 306th Bombardment Group* by Russell A. Strong (1982).

14. Coyne and six others were captured and sent to PoW camps. Two men evaded and one was KIA.

15. Ex-305th BG B-17F 42-3037 *Windy City Avenger* crashed at Wakerley Woods, Corby. 42-5852 *Natural* went down at Chetwode and 42-29784 *Smilin-Thru* crashed at Blaydon, Gloucestershire. Two B-17s in the 92nd BG were lost when they crashed at Shiplake and Winkfield. *Fortresses Of The Big Triangle First* by Cliff T. Bishop. (East Anglia Books 1986)

16. 1st Lt Stuart B. Mendelsohn was shot down and KIA on 31 December 1943 flying *Black Swan*. *Corn State Terror* survived the war.

17. Foster was told that he probably would never regain visibility in his right eye. However, the medics were amazed that he still had some vision in his eye when they took the bandages off. The 'good' eye still had small fragments in it that the doctors did not want to risk removing. The right eye continued to haemorrhage and more operations were performed but the shrapnel fragments remained. Foster returned to civilian life and was in and out of hospital for the next ten years. All five of Jim Foster's sons performed military service in Vietnam.

18. Bob Haughy (pronounced 'Hoy') finished his missions on 5 November 1943 and returned to the States.

19. All ten crew were picked up and they were sent to the Flak House to recover.

20. 2nd Lt Chesmore's crew were shot down over Holland on 13 December 1943 and they ditched *Dry Run IV* in the North Sea. All the crew were picked up and they became prisoners of war.

21. Lt Parks and his crew and *Ramblin' Wreck* FTR from the mission on 29 November 1943. All ten crew were taken prisoner.

22. *Big Dick* and 2nd Lt David D. Jarrett's crew FTR on 25 February 1944. Five men evaded and five were captured after baling out.

23. *Royal Flush* finally went down on 11 December 1943. Lt Clarence A. Gill's crew survived and they were all taken prisoners.

24. Peaslee participated in thirty-seven air battles as task force commander and formation leader. His war decorations include the Silver Star, Legion of Merit, *Croix de Guerre*, three Distinguished Flying Crosses, five Air Medals, service and campaign medals and a Presidential Distinguished Citation. Colonel Peaslee's post-war duty included service in Formosa as head of the Far East Air Force Section. He retired in 1953 after twenty-eight years of service because of physical disability and became director of the Salinas Airport. Colonel Peaslee died on Easter Sunday, 1983.

25. B-24 42-40765 was lost on 13 November 1943 when it was involved in a collision with 41-24226 over Germany. Seven of Lt Richard O. Sedevic's crew were KIA and three were PoW.

26. Q-for Queenie, otherwise known as 41-24105 Tupelo Lass YM-Q in the 409th BS, was salvaged after crashing at Hardwick on 11 December 1943 on return from Emden.

27. The raid by approximately 155 bombers destroyed the power station in addition to other parts of the plant, causing a complete stoppage of the entire manufacturing process. The Germans later shipped their remaining heavy-water stockpile to Germany but all 546 tons was sent to the bottom of Lake Timm when the ferry boat being used to transport the heavy-water was blown up by SOE agents over the deepest part of the lake.

28. Martin later completed twenty-six missions and became Squadron Commander and still later Group Adjutant.

29. Captain Everhart's crew and *Last Frontier* were lost on 22 April 1944. One evaded and eleven were taken prisoner.

30. Two new B-17 groups – the 401st and 447th – had just joined the 8th and on Friday 26 November the 401st made its combat debut. Colonel Harold W. Bowman's outfit helped swell the 1st Division stream to 505 bombers briefed for the port area of Bremen, while 128 B-17s of the 3rd Division was assigned industrial targets in Paris. It was the largest formation yet assembled by the 8th.

31. 2nd Lt William H. McCown's crew, who were also on their first mission, were lost when a German-manned B-17 weaved around the formation and sliced the tail off their ship, *Second Chance*. 1st Lt G. E. Branham's B-17 was the second 388th B-17 lost on the mission.

CHAPTER 5

Complete Your Tour with a Trip to the Ruhr

As I straddled the catwalk during the bomb run and pressed the bomb bay anti-creep lever, a chunk of shrapnel ripped through my bunny suit, nearly making an instant soprano of me as it shorted out my suit. It was a cold flight home. The two-ounce shot of 86-proof was especially welcomed at the end of that difficult day.

Technical Sergeant Donald V. Chase, 44th Bomb Group

A little old at twenty-six years of age when he joined the Air Corps, Lieutenant Wallace Patterson was a newspaperman when war began. He did not have to enlist. He had a wife, Bobbie, a new daughter and a war deferment as he was doing defence work for Lockheed in Los Angeles but he believed strongly in the Fourth Estate and was willing to put his life on the line for that principle so he tried to enlist but was told, because of his age, that he would be better aiding the war effort at home and so he joined Lockheed. But the feeling persisted that something important, something he needed to be in on, was passing him by. And being the man he was, he could not let that happen. Patterson reapplied, was accepted and because he had had some college credits, was made an officer and he trained as a B-24 bombardier. He was assigned to the 448th Bomb Group, which was activated on 1 May 1943 at Gowen Field, Idaho, and he joined 1st Lieutenant Albert L. Northrup Jr's crew in the 715th Squadron. All the Liberator crews in the Group went through second phase training at Wendover Field, Utah, not a regular airbase but way up in the hills. If ever a place could be classified as a sample of hell, this was the place. It was a dreary base, with no shrubs or trees of any kind. The only thing green was the Liberator aircraft and they were olive drab. The town was nothing more than a train watering stop with a gas station, a couple of houses and the State Line Hotel straddling the Utah-Nevada State line, which ran down the centre of the hotel so it was possible to gamble on the Nevada side but not on the Utah side of the line! Wendover was so remote that it was said that a man going AWOL for five days would only be charged for three because he could be seen walking on the salt flats for the first two days. There were nurses to be impressed in Elko, Nevada. Those who were unmarried and in search of excitement had to travel the 120 miles to Salt Lake City, or go west to Kimberley, Nevada.

Final phase training was completed at Sargeants Bluff, five miles south-west of Sioux City, Iowa. It was a small base by most standards, with a large population of civilian employees. By November 1943 the 448th was ready for combat and the air echelon left Sioux City on 3 November for Herrington Field, Kansas, for final processing. Finally, the Group flew to Morrison Field at West Palm Beach in Florida to fly the Southern Ferry Route and one hour out pilots opened their secret orders and learned that their destination was the 8th Air Force in England.

The ground echelon, meanwhile, got ready to sail for Great Britain. Wallace Patterson and two other members of the crew were detailed to go with them. Early in the morning of 21 November they left Camp Shanks, New York, with the Ground Echelon and entrained for the 42nd Street pier at Hoboken in New Jersey for passage aboard the *Queen Elizabeth* with 15,000 other personnel and their equipment bound for Scotland. Patterson and his fellow crew members, each carrying 60lb of equipment plus about 40lb of B-4 bag, boarded the mighty Cunard White Star ocean liner and found their way to a main deck cabin, number 101, which they were to share with fifteen other officers. At a meeting in the afternoon and at another in the evening, they were told their duties and assigned to their positions. They were to check enlisted men's quarters for the proper number and condition of bunks and life preservers, toilets and the like. They had to be sure the correct number of enlisted men got in their quarters or there would be 'hell to pay'. The enlisted men started coming aboard the next evening at about 2200 hours. They were dog tired, having been sweating out the embarkation all day. Patterson and his fellow officers packed them in quickly and filled every bed and then showed them the ropes before they were through. All the officers would have to do for the duration of the voyage was to stand regular watches in pairs with the men to see to their needs.

At 0330 hours on 23 November the *Queen Elizabeth* pulled away from the dock. Everyone was called on deck and Wallace Patterson had a good spot by the rail. When they were out in the Hudson River they were dismissed and they dashed below to hang out of a porthole in the bitter wind for a last view of the Statue of Liberty. 'Packed in' was not the word for conditions in cabin number 101, but they were warm and the officers could bathe. The lounge was always jammed except when it was emptied for a meeting. The men ate in shifts and the food was quite good but there were only two meals a day and everyone was soon constipated from too many cookies and Hershey bars. The *Queen Elizabeth*'s constant zigzagging movement every three minutes to prevent possible U-boat attack caused seasickness in the hot and cramped quarters below deck. It did not stop many whiling away the voyage playing endless rounds of blackjack, craps and faro that would rival gambling dens in Las Vegas and Atlantic City put together.

Finally, after eight days at sea, at 8:00 in the morning, while it was still nearly dark, the *Queen* anchored in the River Clyde. Everyone was given debarkation instructions and at 1600 hours they all piled onto a tender and were taken to Greenock. Patterson noted that the harbour was beautiful in the evening light and the green hills and snow-covered Scottish highlands in the distance were a wonderful picture; and the dock workers walking home through the mist reminded him of a Hitchcock picture. They were cold and miserable in the drizzle and were marched into the train shed for an hour's wait while the Red Cross gave them coffee, doughnuts, gum and cigarettes. Patterson finished off a bottle of rye he had bought from a steward. They packed into the train at 1900 hours in a six-person third-class unheated compartment.

After a freezing, uncomfortable and sleepless night in the train the Red Cross in Lincoln gave everyone a cold breakfast and hot coffee. Late in the afternoon, after many false alarms, the train steamed into the village of Ditchingham in Norfolk and trucks took them out to the base, where, in a sea of mud they alighted and were herded into the theatre. They were told: 'This is Seething, your new home' and were given their new APO number before they were sent to quarters. Patterson wrote:

What a hell hole. Mud everywhere and nothing was finished. Our Nissen hut, the split garbage can, is so cold it sweats on the inside. The stove's no bigger around than a pencil and is limited to a small bucket of coal per day. We have enough blankets but when I crawled out in the night to urinate I damn near froze to death, even in my long woollies. There's no electricity, the can's 50 yards away and the baths are a special refrigerator unit of the club. This club is also cold and pitifully small. At our PX we get a ration once a week. It consists of seven packs of cigarettes (for me four 'Camels' and three 'Old

Golds'), one pack of gum, two candy bars, two razor blades, a bar of soap and two Cokes when they have any – all for one week. As my footlocker was filled with rationed items I bought back in the States, I think I shall do all right. I can always trade the OGs to an Englishman for something. The food's terrible but we expected even worse. There was too much of the kind of food that high-altitude crews should not eat. Getting acclimatized netted me chills and fever and with a temperature of 102, I had entered the hospital. At least there it was warm and I could bathe.

The Air Echelon, meanwhile, was en route via South America and North West Africa. After leaving Florida the Liberators had flown through a storm front over Puerto Rico to Trinidad and Belem, where a B-24 was lost and landed at Natal in Brazil on 17 November. At Natal the Ferry Command had a base to move all the bombers to Africa. It was an opportunity to go to the PX and buy Natal gaucho boots. And then it was off to the beach for a swim. The native kids had ripe pineapples they were selling for a US dime or quarter. 'Hey, Lootenants, you want pineap?' They all produced sharp table knives, probably stolen from the base mess hall, and sharpened them, razor-like, on a stone and then twirled the fruit by its fronds to tempt the swimmers. If men bought one the native kids twirled the fruit by its fronds while hacking off the outer skin with their knives. After enjoying the 'pineaps' men ran into the surf and washed off the juice.

Next the air echelon took off on the 2,100-mile long flight with full fuel tanks to Ecknes Field near Dakar in North Africa. Crews were told that if they were having fuel problems they could stop at Ascension Island in the middle of the South Atlantic. It was said that things were so bad there that the permanent party were drinking 'Aqua Velva', the after-shave lotion. The air echelon was flying into a rising sun and it was difficult to see land ahead. Looking straight down the men realized that they were over Africa. In a few minutes the Liberators were landing on the steel mesh runway at Dakar on a rocky plateau overlooking the Atlantic Ocean. They now qualified to become members of the 'Short Snorter' Club. The club consisted of pilots, crew members and passengers on a transoceanic flight. Paper currency of the countries visited were stuck together and signed by persons who had likewise flown across the ocean. The term came about because all this was usually done while having a 'short snort' at a bar. Dakar had the worst reputation of any city in West Africa for thieves. It was also the greatest malarial belt in Africa. Planes were sprayed with DDT bombs upon landing and after take-off on the next leg.

If they ventured outdoors crews were told to wear their trouser legs tucked in their boots, long-sleeved shirts and to button their collars. At night they slept on sheetless cots covered by mosquito netting. One pilot wrote:

> The beach was running over with natives from mere children to old men and women selling all kinds of things. These people are filthy in mind and body. Small kids who must be only 5 or 6 years old know what a woman is for. It's disgusting to watch them. The women are all over the place trying to sell themselves.

Local French currency that was handed out to the aircrews was put to good use as toilet paper. After use the native children would retrieve the soiled notes from the 'honey pits' to clean and re-use them!

Fortunately the B-24 crews' stay at Dakar was just one night. Before sunrise the bombers took off on the 1,300-mile flight over the desolate Sahara and mountainous country for Marrakesh, near Casablanca in French Morocco. The pilots were briefed to fly through a pass in the snow-covered 14,000-foot Atlas Mountains. Those who could not find the pass between the high shoulders of the range were advised to go on oxygen and fly over the mountains. With passengers and baggage aboard and not enough oxygen masks for all, the flight plan called for the route through the mountains. Peaks rose above the planes on either side. Camps and villages of nomads could be seen high in the mountains. Marrakesh, the ancient seat of the Moorish kings, nestled at the base of the Atlas Mountains. The red rocky terrain was dotted with green hills where there were date orchards. While the depot put the finishing touches on the B-24s for the long flight ahead, some of the crews went into the Medina (the walled city) and saw the way the Arabs had lived for centuries: streets barely wide enough for a carriage to pass through ... fresh meat displayed in stalls without refrigeration, silver handicrafts next to fancy rugs, and leather goods cured in manure. A native snake charmer played the flute, while a cobra stood up on its tail, hood flaring out, writhing back and forth, hypnotized by the music. All of a sudden, out of the corner of his mouth, in understandable English, the snake charmer said 'New York World's Fair, 1939.' vendors would chase the Americans if they showed interest in an item and failed to buy 'one last good prize, Lootenant!'

On the last leg to England on 1 December one of the crews hit a mountain peak on take-off and *Laki-Nuki* veered off course over France, was hit and just managed to cross a churning sea and the rugged Cornish coastline, cheerless and bleak, and crash-landed at Predannack.

Lieutenant William O. Ross and crew were grounded in Africa for ten days when a crew member went sick and then they stopped at St Mawgen in Wales for a week, sweating out a low ceiling. 2nd Lieutenant Paul Helander and his crew were held up at Marrakech awaiting a replacement engine part. When it finally arrived it was quickly installed and the crew left early that morning.

'We loaded our guns with live ammunition,' recalls Staff Sergeant William J. 'Billy the Kid' McCullah, the first armourer, ball/nose turret gunner, who was from Springfield, Missouri. He had turned twenty on 3 November.

My people had arrived in America in 1730. Alexander McCullah, Tennessee Militia, volunteered to fight the British in the war of 1812, fighting with Jackson, Colonel Blue's regiment in the Battle of New Orleans. For that he received a presidential land grant in Stone County, Missouri, signed by President James Monroe. The original land, added to by purchase of adjoining lands, resulted in big acreage, ten miles of black bottoms, clear running streams and big springs. During the Civil War both the northern and southern armies were encamped on our land at the same time, separated by 3½ miles. For four years both armies tramped up and down that road, pillaging and living off the land. Pillaging broke smaller neighbours who borrowed from my great-great-grandfather. When they defaulted on their loans, it broke him. We lost the land and never recovered. Through war, we won the land and through war, we lost the land. What goes around comes around.

Trained by a semi-professional gambler, Uncle George McCullah, a successful lifetime gambler, shooter and competitor, I was a good poker player but I had taken a $1,900 hit at Natal, Brazil! George held all of the rifle records at Camp Clark, Missouri. The Army wanted to make a sniper of him but George was legally blind. Extremely stiff-jointed, he nevertheless was a consistent winner in competitive endeavours, so good that he was barred from most competitions. Before he played, competitors knew he would win. This included craps, poker, shooting, horseshoes, bowling, pool, croquet, name it – he did it all! George was my role model. I loved that man! He was like a father to me. He made more money accidentally than most people make on purpose.

Flying well out to sea, we paralleled the coasts of Spain, Portugal and France carefully avoiding the French coast along the Bay of Biscay. German fighter units were stationed in southern France. We flew the French leg at full alert. At last, we were over England and then Seething suddenly lay beneath us. From the air the base was a widely scattered city of corrugated Quonsets. There were five big clusters of Quonsets and two runways, a long one, the one we would use most frequently, and a shorter one that butted up against a grove of trees. Helander made an uneventful landing. We followed a jeep carrying a 'FOLLOW ME' sign. We were home, our home away from home! It was a typical cold, damp, low-cast day. English workers waved their caps as we taxied past. Most of us stared at them and the passing scenery through our open waist windows. We followed the jeep to our permanent hardstand. Helander wheeled the B-24 onto the big concrete circle and shut her down. Our hardstand was 125 yards from base operations and the Seething control tower. We were close enough to walk.

First off the plane, I joined five English workers huddled around a fire that burned in an open metal barrel. We spoke. (I could hardly understand them and would guess they also had difficulty understanding me.)

'Hi Yank' the first man said. The term was new and strange.

'Would you care for an American cigarette?' I offered, in an attempt at cordiality.

'Don't mind if I do. I likes you blokes' cigarettes, I do,' the man said.

The men wore three-piece suits; matching coats, vests and trousers, with ties and each wore a woollen cap or a hat. Without exception, their suits were rumpled; legs, arms and trouser seats' butt-sprung, not a crease in them. (Working out-of-doors, the latter is expected but when performing rough labour?) Our suits were for dress-up, for formal or semi-formal attire. Outdoor work required rough clothing, denim, cotton trousers and overalls. Their suits and accents and the rosy cheeks of workers drew my attention. The ruddiness seemed artificial, cheeks appearing to be rouged.

The England of school history came to mind; 'The nation of shopkeepers', home of Shakespeare and countless kings and queens; a jumble of names and royal successions to be ever confusing. England; home of Kipling, my favourite poet and the vaunted British Empire on which, the sun never set, once mind-boggling in its scope and size; and of course, the conflict between Britain and a young America, as we struggled for our independence. As to closeness and kinship between our countries, there was never a doubt; the English were my cousins. The England I knew was connected to war – the longbow and the fabled British 'Square' that defeated Napoleon at Waterloo. Kipling said the Zulus were the only ones ever to break the square. I admired the British military precision and regimentation. Britain gave soldiering lessons to the world. Americans looked sick by comparison. But how could England lose a war against a rag-tag bunch of unregulated, unregimented American farmers? Squirrel shooters! Farmers took refuge behind hills, rocks and trees while British commanders marched their troops into our positions, at close-order, in open fields! Not only was that dumb, it was suicidal! I don't think Britain wanted to win that war. But it cost them dearly. They lost the United States of America!

After we had deplaned, we reported to base operations and signed in. There we inquired of food and billets. The enlisted men were sent by bus to the combat mess. After we had eaten, we were driven to the 712th Squadron orderly room, again signing in, drawing bedding and our assignment to barracks. We were bushed! Following our arrival, no time was wasted. Combat crews were assigned billets sequentially by crew number and we got 4A, a long, steel corrugated Nissen hut, which Crew 11 (us) through 17 shared. Squadron areas were spaced out at intervals to minimize damage and casualties from enemy bombing and strafing. The huts contained one coal burning stove, whereas six-crew huts like ours contained two. There was one steel-reinforced concrete, earthen-covered bunker in each squadron area. A single latrine combined commodes, wash basins and showers. The latrine stood alone, separate from other buildings. The latrine was a long walk from some of the barracks. During the cold months of winter, the latrine was usually visited on a dead run. It was a busy place. We had a makeshift base theatre but it wasn't much. It probably seated 200 people, maximum. The movies shown were old ones. There was an American Red Cross facility where music, dancing, donuts, coffee, tea and such were available to enlisted troops. American women ran the Red Cross. Our flying officers were constantly trying to put the make on them. Some succeeded. Though she was ten years my senior, I was attracted to one of the Red Cross women, a good-looking blonde, but I didn't have a snowball's chance in hell. I didn't have the horsepower (rank). She was a climber who liked the big brass. Sex was not a crass enlisted problem. Officers were more subtle and quiet about their affairs. Though officers and enlisted did not mix they were no better than we were. Maybe worse!

They had more money, were more sophisticated and consorted with the higher-class, university educated women. Despite 'holier-than-thou' remonstrations officers had the same desires, some aggressively pursued. A few discussed sex within my hearing. They would laughingly say, 'Going to town for some dual sack!' But they were invariably from other crews. My crew was more guarded, more reticent; more discreet.

Crew 11 was the first crew to enter the allotted six-crew Quonset thereby giving us first choice of bunks. The long room was filled with bunks, including several double-deckers, thirty-six in all. Each barracks contained two smallish tables, with several wooden chairs, at each end of the barracks. Clothes' racks beside each bunk consisted of wire hooks nailed to boards on the wall. That was the decor! Crew 11 selected bunks on the extreme opposite end of the barracks, next to a coal-burning stove. The stove was important. We thought it would be cold and it damn sure was! Crews in the middle of the barrack lived a miserable existence, as they never got warm! Heat dissipated through the thin metal roof long before reaching them. To help keep the cold out our first engineer and top turret gunner, Staff Sergeant Gerald 'Jerry' Carroll, nailed shut the door at our end of the barracks. In the seven months I was there that door was never opened again. The other door at the opposite end of the barracks bore all traffic. Nailing the door shut was dangerous. We could have been trapped inside and our bomb shelter was 20 feet beyond the operable door! (We would be bombed once and strafed probably ten times at night. A bomb missed our bomb storage area, an earthen surrounded revetment, by 50 yards.) I chose a top bunk beside the stove. Crews 12 and 13 shared space next to us. (During the six months it took to complete my thirty missions, six and a half crews from my barracks were lost; killed in action (KIA), imprisoned in German PoW camps, or interned in Sweden).[1] My bunk selection was good because I was never cold but it was bad because the table near my bunk was the focus of a never-ending poker game. Each payday the poker game would begin and last for weeks, all day and all night! It stopped only when some individual won all or most of the money. It is a wonder I ever slept through the gambling bedlam, drunken arguments and general hell raising that went on beneath me but I did! I did not participate in those games.

In the first week of our arrival at Seething, 'Lord Haw-Haw' the German radio propagandist came on the air on a barracks radio. In perfect English, he said, 'I would like to take this occasion to welcome the 448th to Europe. We'll be seeing you.' His 'welcome' statement visibly upset some of the crews, although we belly laughed. Carroll jumped onto a table and shouted, 'Boys, let's sing that guy a hymn.' Thirty voices boisterously sang in unison, 'Him, Him, Fuck him!

Men of the 448th soon discovered that there were three pubs near the base. They could choose between the 'Tumble Down Dick', the 'Cherry Tree' and the 'Mermaid', or the 'Swinging Tits', as it was called; a short bike ride from the back entrance to the base. Local boys and girls did not take long to get to know the 'Yanks' greeting them with the familiar 'Any gum, chum?' Americans quickly became familiar with the area, especially the quaint old pubs with beamed ceilings and walls bulging with age and history. The English were supposed to be reserved, but as the Americans mixed with them they found them to be warm and friendly. They were concerned about their new-found friends. They welcomed the GIs into their homes and invited them to dine with them. Everything was rationed. They were living on a few ounces of meat, butter and sugar each week. They had 'victory gardens' producing cabbages, potatoes and beans that they were willing to share with the Americans. Some of the women were willing to do their laundry. They returned their kindness with money, candy, cigarettes, liquor or whatever they could pilfer from the mess halls. Many men bartered cartons of cigarettes for items of local origin.

Wallace Patterson and five others hitchhiked to Bungay, a pleasant and charming sleepy little market town and bussed into Norwich, fifteen miles away. Norwich had been badly blitzed by the *Luftwaffe* in 1942. Patterson noted 'that the damage, even at night, was very apparent; whole blocks have been wiped out and many of the bombed areas are full of water or still unsafe due to cave-ins. The blackout is the blackest thing I have ever seen. The only way we can find the pubs and theatres, etc is by cracks of light in doors and with our flashlights.'

The city's narrow, winding streets, 900-year-old Norman cathedral with the second tallest spire in England, eleventh century Norman castle and large open-air market had survived the bombing when it had been blasted by bombs and numerous buildings were gutted by fire. Even in winter it was surprising for American GIs to see fresh meat hanging out in the open in the market place. The supply of warm English beer was rationed daily and did not last long after the pubs opened their doors each evening. GIs bought their first fish and chips wrapped in newspaper from a street vendor and were surprised to find that the chips were not like American potato chips but rather were French fries. As one who always had a keen interest in history George McCullah found the city of Norwich to be a fascinating place.

During the first two weeks we adapted to the base and went to Norwich, a trip of twelve miles, several times. We usually went by truck but sometimes rode the shuttle-bus. We mingled with English civilians who did their best to make us welcome. We laughingly drank their warm stout and tried their warm mild-and-bitters. We were used to refrigerated beer and the warm stuff was hard for us to swallow. Warm beer triggered our gag reflexes, some having to gag it down. Gradually, we learned to like it. Warm beer is an acquired taste. The English had a disquieting habit of closing their pubs early, just when we were getting on a good head of steam. They would give us a lead-time of maybe five minutes, saying, 'Time gentlemen please,' meaning they were closing the pub. They would hustle us out. It was irritating as hell but it was probably a good thing. Being young and inexperienced, we drank too much, too fast, almost competitively. Closing the pubs in the afternoon left us with nothing to do but walk the streets of Norwich, return to base, or go to a movie. I enjoyed the movie house and the sacks of small shrimps that substituted for buttered popcorn. Getting past my first winkles (small snail-like creatures) I found them delicious. Fish and chips were amply available and good, despite being served on newsprint. I didn't like the thin servings of fish paste and watercress that masqueraded as sandwiches. *Pais-'n-kres*, the waitress said to me again and again, leaving out the 't' in paste, running the words together. (She finally had to spell it!) Those sandwiches came close to qualifying as 'jam' sandwiches, where one takes two slices of bread 'then jams them together?' Good food was non-existent but we understood why. It was not unusual for a restaurant to be sold out of food altogether. When it came to ordering beef, pork or chicken, forget about it! They didn't exist. I later learned of the American food assistance program that provided food for those who befriended and fed us; those taking us into their homes in Norwich and other locations. In those instances, we stayed the night, or nights with them. I would pick up sacks of rations for those occasions from the combat crew Mess Sergeant. The Sergeant allowed generous portions of pork, beef, chickens and fresh eggs and other scarce items. Our British hosts were very appreciative, as it had been years since they'd seen some of it. This was payback for their gracious hospitality.

We stumbled about the streets of Norwich in pitch-blackness

wondering how in hell we would ever find the place we sought without killing ourselves! Despite our groping, stumbling and getting lost, we somehow found our destination. 'Turn that torch off Yank' was a familiar theme. How did they know we were Yanks? Was it that no one else was dumb enough to turn on a light? I guess so. I tried my hand at the Samson and Hercules dance emporium. I became proficient at 'The Grand Old Duke of York' and 'The Polly Glide, a silly dance that years later became popular in the States. An unscrupulous American tried to take credit for it but we who had been to England knew better. The English women forced us to dance. Had they not, we still would be seated on the side benches, forever remaining wallflowers. We had a lot of fun. My favourite music was American swing but I heard little of that in Norwich. In America young people frequented our dance halls. In England dances were attended by all ages, from the very young to the ancient.

I fancied myself an expert pool player and was something of a kid hustler before the war. Each Friday my Dad gave me a $3 allowance, which I took to a billiards parlour, usually doubling or tripling it; that done, I had enough money for a date and an evening of dancing. Though I liked pool, I preferred snooker, which is played on bigger tables with small pockets. Snooker is a game of skill and I liked the challenge of the game. Alone in Norwich, I went into a pub that had the biggest snooker table I ever saw. Three people were in the room, an old gentleman, the bartender and me. Fooling around with a cue, the elderly gentleman approached, asking if I would like a game. 'He must be 90' I thought! I said 'OK' and we commenced. He shook with palsy as he cued the ball. I have never been so badly beaten! The object ball looked like a sweet pea. One game was enough. I left the room with my tail between my legs. He made my ass want to chew tobacco! I was impressed that men of all ages belonged to some defence function or other. There was the 'King's Own' this and 'The Queen's Own' that. Old men worked when they should have been retired. Titles and functions? Everyone had them. It was confusing. A few minutes from the continent and the threat that imposed, there was a casualness about the blokes that baffled me. They were a different cut of cloth.

McCullah described London and Norwich as 'drab; no lights, but it was wartime'. The country had been blacked out since 1939. All towns and villages had air raid wardens. No matter where, people were careful to draw the black-out curtains each night. Even a crack of light was not permitted. A glimmer of light – even the striking of a match in the deep darkness – could be seen from the air. It made getting back to base difficult. The English drove 'on the wrong side of the road', the narrow roads were dark at night and GI truck drivers had a terrible time. The Liberty Run was a test of their mettle. Headlights were masked, permitting just two small slits of light, hardly enough on the narrow roads with deep ditches on each side. McCullah recalls:

> Except for its cathedral I was not the least impressed with Norwich. Except for its church, the little village of Seething also failed to impress. The base held two or three dances while I was there. Without the local girls who were good enough to come, there would have been no dances. We closely monitored them getting off the buses, trying to select a dance partner for the evening. We had a good time and believe that they did too. Officers were all over the streets of Norwich. American troops were not big on saluting because at heart we were civilians. We did not cotton to saluting or taking orders and we did not salute the British officers, though we should have, thereby eliminating half of our requirements. We grudgingly (and it showed) saluted American officers but that was it. Nevertheless, every thirty steps or so we were saluting, saluting, saluting! It was a pain to all, as most officers rendered half-hearted returns. If you failed to salute you flat gambled on a public ass chewing; a Catch 22! One day in Norwich, sidewalks relatively clear, I spied a young lady talking to a neatly uniformed British officer one hundred steps ahead. They were chatting, having a good time. On sudden impulse, I gave him my very best. Startled, he jerked to rigid attention, bringing it up, his arm vibrating in the British manner. His salute was good enough for Eisenhower, the sharpest I ever received. What the hell, they wrote the book! It made me feel good and broke my mould. From that moment, I saluted British officers.

When a sufficient number of crews were ready the 448th began preparing for its introduction to combat. William O. Ross and Crew 73 finally arrived at Seething after their enforced delay at St Mawgen and they had some crates of oranges and tangerines, which proved a very welcome treat for other members of their hut. The training started with crews making numerous orientation flights around East Anglia to get used to the surrounding countryside. 1st Lieutenant Alvin D. Skaggs, a pilot in the 715th Squadron, recalls:

> Prior to our introduction into combat, we spent many hours being

briefed on missions, taking off and forming up in combat formation and then returning to base for debriefing. We had been through all of this many times before back in the States but somehow being in a combat area made it different. With the enemy just a few short miles across the Channel, we were all aware that each time we took off we could possibly be confronted by him, so we were always alert just in case. A popular British pastime in Norfolk, where we were stationed, was to go sailing in small sailboats along the canals and small streams. This pastime prompted us to develop another sport of trying to blow over or capsize these boats while on training flights. On one occasion (George must have been at the controls), we made a couple of passes but couldn't capsize one, so we made another pass very low and directly at it. This must have been too much for the sailors because they dove in the water as we pulled up to go over the top of the mast.

We didn't think it unusual to be on duty seven days a week while in England but we did enjoy the occasional two-day pass awarded us when flying would slack up a bit. We made several trips to London about 100 miles away and we could make the trip by train in about four hours when there were no unusual delays. Things were not always as pleasant in London as the Nazis took great pleasure in dropping bombs on the inhabitants. Usually, the Nazi bombers would come only to the outskirts of London, drop their bombs on the suburbs, and high tail it for home before the AA got too heavy. Occasionally, however, they would bomb the heart of the city. Most of our crew were in London on this occasion when the Nazis mounted a large-scale attack against the centre. It was well after dark, between 9 and 10pm on a moonless night. On such nights, blacked-out London was about as 'black' as any place could be. We actually had to use flashlights to see the sidewalks under our feet – small pen-light flashlights at that! If we used our regular GI flashlights, a British 'Bobby' would tell us in very stern tones, 'Put out the torch, Yank!'

When I realized that the bombs were getting close to my hotel (the Red Cross Reindeer Club), I went out into the street to get a better look at the action. Searchlights were lighting up the skies and picking up many Nazi bombers. They would hold a plane in their beams until one of the AA crews shot it down and then pick up another one. The British planes were also in the melee and their tracer bullets could be seen streaking across the sky. I have often wondered how those Limeys could fly their fighter planes at night, avoiding each other and their ground gunners, while very systematically shooting down the intruders. Many of the bombers found their targets and dropped bombs all over downtown London. As I was viewing all this in awe and wonder, the people near me were running in various directions. Soon, a zone air raid warden happened upon me gawking up at the sky. He looked at me in exasperation and asked if I had never seen an air raid. Before I could answer 'No' he took me to the nearest air raid shelter and ushered me inside. There were so many people in the shelter, calm and collected, as if they took such refuge frequently. It was then that I realized where all those people I had seen earlier were hurrying to. In less than an hour, the raid was over and we emerged to view the damage and be about our usual business. Several buildings in the area were damaged and a couple were burning slightly, but the London Fire Department was already busy putting out the blazes. My hotel was undamaged so I went back to the lobby where the others had gathered to exchange tales of their experiences. I was rather stunned to realize that I had been through an air raid but thankful that I had suffered no injuries and very few inconveniences.

The GI food on base was not too bad but we really enjoyed the various types of food offered in the British restaurants. On one occasion, we decided to celebrate and have a feast at one of the nicer Chinese restaurants in London. Most of the crew members were there and we ordered several different Chinese dishes with all the trimmings. These were served, more or less, boarding house style so that our large table was well laden with continuous servings of Asiatic delicacies as we leisurely enjoyed the many courses offered, savouring every bite. This was one of the tastiest meals I had in England and all of us enjoyed our banquet that night.

Another newly arrived bomb group in England at this time was the 401st, which was the first Bomb Group to be activated with the all new B-17G model aircraft. The Group was based 80 miles north of London at Deenethorpe airfield in Northamptonshire, built upon part of the Brudenall Estate, which dates back several hundred years and is a famous family name with Crimean War and 'The Charge of the Light Brigade' connections. The Group's first mission was briefed on the morning of Thursday 25 November and then cancelled. At 0500 hours the next day, a mission to Bremen was briefed and flown, the nineteen Forts of the 401st being led by the CO, Colonel Harold W. 'Hal' Bowman. Though small in stature he was a fine sportsman and born leader. Bowman spent his boyhood in Waverly, Nebraska – where his father was a school teacher and school administrator – and in Texas and Kansas, before the family moved to California. He qualified for a teacher's certificate and spent the years 1921 to 1923 teaching 8th grade students at a small town in California. In July 1931 'Hal' met and married Etta Buchanan, a lovely San Diego belle, and much of his early career in the Air Corps was spent flying medium bombers and serving in the Philippines where he was assigned to a fighter group. In 1943 he checked out in a B-17 and a B-24 and he took command of the 401st, which were then in training at Spokane.[2]

Four of the B-17s failed to take off on the morning of 26 November. One Fortress ran off the perimeter track and in so doing, trapped the following aircraft. Then two more B-17s collided after suffering brake failures, the tail of one being demolished by the propellers of the other. The first combat casualty occurred when *Fancy Nancy* was hit by a B-17 from another Group, which went out of control and roared up into *Fancy Nancy*, cutting off the ball turret and taking the gunner, who had gone into the turret to effect repairs, with it. The pilot managed to land *Fancy Nancy* at Detling airfield in Kent where it was deemed beyond repair. The Group's second mission came on 1 December with a raid on Solingen, which was led by Lieutenant Colonel Harris E. Rogner, the second in command.

George Coleman, the tail gunner on Howard Hunter's crew in the 305th, was up at 3am at Chelveston on 1 December to fly his third mission. He and the rest of the crew had arrived in England on 15 October and a month later they had gone to Knaben, Norway, on their initial mission. Coleman had bought a English bicycle for $32 and had even managed to sandwich in a three-day pass to London before flying the second mission on 26 November when the target was Bremen. It was a long trip at just over six hours. Coleman recalled that the whole Group was out by the hangars when they came in. 'It sure makes you feel good' he had written in his diary 'when you come back from a raid and see the personnel waving and cheering you in.'

The plan was for the bombers to attack Leverkusen. The Hunter crew took off at 0745 hours for the rendezvous point. But some way or another they got mixed up in the wrong group and they had to fly 'Purple Heart Corner' because that was the only position open. Coleman recalled:

It was quiet over Belgium but when we hit the target things started to happen. A fighter came in at 2 o'clock and let go with a 210mm rocket that blew up right in our bomb bay, just luck that wasn't the end right there. The next minute the waist gunner was telling us on the interphone that he'd been hit. He was wounded in the right knee and was bleeding pretty bad. Fighters were coming in pretty fast and one of them shot out our rudder control cables and our pilot was having trouble keeping the plane under control. Another fighter let go with a rocket and shot out our hydraulic system. The ball turret gunner was covered in oil and could not see through his window. That was two gunners' positions out and we were getting worried. The other waist gunner was hit by flak next but it was nothing serious. I got a little hot powder down my neck on the first shot and the impact drove me against the amour plate but no injury.

We got away from the target and back over Belgium finally but were now running out of gas. I climbed up front to see what the plane looked like and see the casualties. The bomb bay was so full of holes. It looked like a sieve but we were still in the air The waist gunner was in pain, bleeding but he wouldn't show it The radio operator showed me where a piece of flak went through between his feet and tore a hole in the ammo box he was standing on. We tried to make an emergency landing at another field but planes kept cutting us off and we had to go to our own field. Gas was getting lower all the time and we finally made it to our own field. The pilot told us to prepare for a crash-landing. We were more scared at that than we were when we were being shot at. We needn't have been though, because he made a perfect landing on autopilot, which is very hard to do. Our brakes were gone and we had to swing onto the mud in order to stop. The ambulance was waiting for us to take the boys that were hurt to the hospital. There was a big write up in the paper about us and we had our pictures in too.[3]

On Sunday 5 December about 550 bombers set out for airfields in France. At about 0830 hours at Deenethorpe the 401st took off for a mission to Paris. Lieutenant Walter B. Keith was piloting *Zenodia El Elephanta* down the main runway when he realized that ice was forming on the wings. Blasted by propwash from the preceding Fortress, *Zenodia El Elephanta* slewed off the runway at about 100mph and went across the grass and down the hill before crashing on top of a barn. The tail of the aircraft had broken off with Sergeant Bob Kerr inside the turret, but he stepped out unhurt. The navigator and bombardier were trapped in the front of the B-17 and were rescued by ground personnel from the base. Eight of the crew managed to scramble clear of the wreck and they dashed around the village warning residents to run for their lives before the burning plane exploded. Twenty minutes after crashing the aircraft exploded, causing immense damage to the village, but, incredibly, nobody was killed. The sudden enormous blast rocked Nissen and Quonset huts on the base. One lieutenant in Special Services, who had left word he was not to be disturbed, as he was going to have a nap, came bounding out of his hut red-faced with anger, obviously furious at having his sleep disturbed, gesticulating wildly. 'Who banged the door?' he shouted.[4]

'BJ' Keirsted's crew at Knettishall flew their third mission, to Bordeaux, in *Winged Fury*. 'Goldie' Goldstein recalled:

Getting up early was routine business now. The target was an airfield near the city. A very long flight; longer than we were prepared for. While over the Channel and not yet on oxygen the bombardier usually came back to remove the pins from the bombs, arming them. For the second time in a row the target was cloud covered and we returned with the bomb load. When we were at a lower altitude and off oxygen the bombardier again came back to the bomb bay to insert the safety pins. This was a bit scary because if we dropped one or lost one, we might have an armed bomb aboard on landing. A few enemy fighters were encountered but not nearly enough to cause much damage. The flak, however, was plentiful and again I 'sweated it out'. Fighter support was plentiful and there were P-47s all over the sky. Returned early to dear old Knettishall. We were now credited with three missions!

On 11 December the weather cleared sufficiently for 523 bombers to hit Emden, the seventh trip to the city and one of the most costly. Flak and rocket-firing Me 110s and Me 210s accounted for the loss of seventeen heavies, including the lead ship piloted by Captain Hiram Skogmo in the 390th.

Penny's Thunderhead in the 401st flown by 1st Lieutenant E. E. Kaufman was one ship that made it back but at the cost of eight crew members. Over the target the B-17 was hit by flak and so badly damaged that by any normal standards it should never have survived. With two engines out and damage to the nose and bomb bay he headed for England. The No. 1 prop was feathered and No. 3 began to windmill and although the bomber could fly on two engines the drag from the unfeathered prop made this almost impossible. No. 3 finally caught fire and all efforts to extinguish the blaze failed. The B-17 gradually lost speed and was forced to fall out of formation. Within minutes Bf 109s and FW 190s were being called from all angles and the battle vas on. The fighters inflicted more damage on the already battered ship until Kaufman was forced to call 'Abandon ship'. The B-17 was down to 18,000 feet at this point and three men jumped out, closely followed by a further five. Being over Harlingen on the Friesian Coast, two of the second group must have realized that the wind was liable to blow them out to sea and they accordingly made a delayed drop, which nevertheless put them into the sea just off Harlingen. However, they were quickly rescued by the Germans. The other three men opened their chutes at 18,000 feet and were blown out to sea, which was deadly cold at this time of year. The Dutch lifeboat, *Twenthe*, on seeing the chutes, put to sea without German permission, but only managed to find the radio operator, Sergeant Don Carlson. The bombardier, Lieutenant R. C. Fitzgerald, had difficulties in putting on his chute so was left in the Fortress with Kaufman. Just as he was prepared to leave the plane he heard Kaufman calling on the interphone that the engine had stopped burning and had stopped windmilling. Fitzgerald stepped back from the escape hatch and almost certain death in the icy waters of the North Sea. Seeing the eight members baling out must have convinced the German fighters that the crew had abandoned the Fortress and left it on auto-pilot to crash into the sea. They peeled off and left her to her fate, as they thought, but some hours later Kaufman landed *Penny's Thunderhead* at Lindholme, Yorkshire.[5]

Next day *Stars and Stripes* reported an incident involving the 96th, when one of its B-17s bombs that were dropped on Emden never got to the ground. It came all the way back to Snetterton Heath swaying dangerously on the wing of a second Fort, whose crew pinched themselves occasionally, just checking to see if they really were alive. Twenty-eight-year-old Lieutenant Edward D. Martin, of Greensboro, North Carolina, pilot of the second Fort, sustained the stowaway bomb.

> We were directly over the target. All the ships had their bomb bay doors open, their bombs dropping down. A ship flying above and ahead of us had a bomb release malfunction and one of its bombs released late and landed on our wing just to the rear of the No. 1 engine. The ship lurched down on the wing, as though the controls were hit. I then saw this bomb, live fuse and all, out there on my wing. It had broken open and a jelly-like substance was oozing from the casing. Why it didn't go off on impact with the wing or ignite from the heat of the engine we'll never know. Someone must have been praying for us.

During the time the Fort was over the target and for part of the way back home, enemy fighters zoomed and whizzed around. A single bullet from any of them could have set fire to the bomb – an incendiary. But none hit and the ship, being handled 'very tenderly' by Martin, continued on its way. Over the North Sea, the generator on the No. 1 engine burned out. Smoke curled up and around the bomb.

'All of us were really sweating that out; for we were sure it was the bomb,' said Martin.

With the crash wagon, ambulance, fire truck and assorted ordnance and armament workers lining the runaway, Martin set down the Fort (a borrowed machine, his own *Patricia* being in the hangar for repairs from previous raid damage) 'ever so gently' and then headed for chow. Crews quickly made the bomb harmless and wheeled the Fort away.

On Monday 13 December 640 of 710 B-17s and B-24s dispatched bombed targets in Germany. The 2nd Bomb Division, which included twelve Liberators of the 445th Bomb Group at Tibenham, on their first mission, attacked the U-boat yards at Kiel, while the Fortresses hit Bremen and Hamburg. Next day the 448th was alerted for its first combat mission, but it did not go according to plan, as Lieutenant Alvin D. Skaggs, pilot of Crew 64, recalls:

This was what we had been preparing for, for so many months and we felt we were ready. Although everyone was very excited, it was well hidden. Before daylight the CQs began making their rounds waking up the alerted crews. They had very little trouble doing their job because it's doubtful if anyone got very much sleep. There was very little conversation at breakfast or on the trip to the briefing room. The officers reported to one briefing room, while the enlisted men were briefed separately. This was because each group needed different types of information and data. As we sat waiting for the briefing officers to arrive, we could feel the tension building. When the cover protecting the map marking the route of the mission was raised, it caused every man in the room to groan. This reaction was to become standard regardless of how long or short the mission was. The briefing was usually short and to the point, ending with a prayer by the Chaplain. After the briefing, the Chaplain was always available for those who wished to have 'Holy Communion' before the mission.

After the briefing, we were taken by truck to the hardstand where our planes were parked. We immediately set about pre-flighting our respective equipment – the flight engineer and pilot – the airplane, the navigator and bombardier – the equipment concerning their duties, the gunners – the turrets, guns and other equipment. When everyone was satisfied with the condition of things, we gathered beside the plane and awaited the green flare to start engines. The green flare soon lit up the tower and everyone began to take their positions on board the plane. Since the *Harmful Lil' Armful* and its crew were to lead a section of this group, we moved out early so we could take a position in front of the section we were to lead. It seemed that we had trained and waited a long time for this day and now it was here. The green Aldis lamp was finally aimed at us and the *Harmful Lil' Armful* started down the runway to our first planned test under fire. After take-off, the 448th aircraft began their climb out, following the prescribed route. Each plane attached itself to the one in front of it and continued to climb until all had reached the assigned altitude and were in a combat formation. After about two hours of flying time, the group and wing were ready. As the formations turned and started across the English Channel, the order came for the 20th Wing to return to base. It seemed that we weren't quite ready after all. We would have several more of these false starts before headquarters was ready to turn us loose on the Germans.

The 3rd Division was assigned the docks at Kiel. Larry Goldstein now had a system of doing things for this type of mission.

One of my personal hang-ups was to wear my GI shoes into the plane, change into my heated slippers and flying boots, then place the shoes tied together in a place where I could reach them easily in case of a bale-out call. Somehow I believed that in an emergency I could pick them up, tuck them into my jacket and have a comfortable pair of shoes to wear when I hit the ground. In retrospect the shoes were to be long gone once the chute jerked open.

There was heavy flak again, especially from flak barrages off the shore. We returned with a few holes in the ship. The trip was rather long and it was cold at altitude. We returned safely to the field but I could truthfully say that I 'sweated' a bit that day.

At Flixton about two miles from Bungay in the Waveney Valley the 446th Bomb Group was nearing the time when it would fly its first mission. On the trip over in November one of the Group's navigators mistook the Brest Peninsula for Land's End and the B-24 was shot down. They never reached England, although one of the gunners evaded capture and appeared at Flixton nine days after the Group's arrival. One of the Liberators was named *Ronnie* in memory of S/Sgt Ronald Gannon of Zanesville, Ohio, a waist gunner on the model crew of his squadron. On 16 September he and Olive H. Fulkes married at the chapel in Lowry Field. Ronnie walked gingerly through that service because of sore feet. They went off on a honeymoon but came back almost immediately. He went to the hospital but died of a blood infection within a week. The crew named their B-24 'Ronnie' and flew the Southern Ferry Route without him.

There was so much history on the doorstep. Settlers in Jamestown, Virginia, came from Bungay and sections of East Anglia. John Harvard and Thomas Paine were from the area. There was tranquillity even with a war going on. Yet it had seen stirring times and the history of England could be verified in it. It was a market town for the agricultural area, the staple industry of the county. Wheat and barley were the chief crops, although Americans could be forgiven for thinking that Brussels sprouts were the leading crop. The farmers were proud of their horses, black-faced sheep and large black pigs. The men of Station 125 found the towns-people friendly and hospitable even though the base personnel had a greater population than Bungay. The weather, as a rule, was dry and pleasant with the yearly average rainfall only about 24 inches. However, some thought the weather was abominable. Samuel Johnson observed in 1758: 'when two Englishmen meet their talk is of the weather.' It abated on 16 December and 535 bombers, including Liberators in the 'Bungay Buckaroos' made their 2nd Bomb Division debut, when the target was a follow-up raid on Bremen for the first of three raids that month on the German port.

At Shipdham Tech Sergeant Donald V. Chase flew his first mission in more than four months. It was also his first flight over Germany. He noticed that compared with Sicily and Italy the flak coming up was thicker, more intimidating and fired with greater accuracy. The ack-ack proved frightening and at the post mission interrogation he downed his two ounces of whisky, which was standard procedure following each mission. It hit his empty stomach like 'an exploding star'.

Larry Goldstein wrote:

This was an all-out effort to blast Bremen off the map. There were more planes in the air than I have ever seen before. We were in formation and well on our way when I looked back from my radio hatch – all I could see were bombers all over the sky: high, low, left and right. It always gave a man chills to know that so many planes were going into the flak after you. We were told that it took time for the ack-ack gunners to line up on the first planes. We were somewhat relieved and luckier to be in the lead group. The flak over the target was very heavy and there were a few ships hit. Just after the target and on our turn for home we met our first enemy fighters. Our bombardier said over the intercom 'Those guys are blinking their landing lights at us'. Immediately, 'Ace' Conklin, our co-pilot yelled, 'Those aren't lights, they're wing guns.' Then, as if by impulse, every single .50 calibre gun in the formation opened up. We felt like sitting ducks up there as fighters swept through our formations. Reluctantly we admired those enemy pilots making a pass through our formation in the face of so many guns firing at them. We often discussed how the German fighter pilots had the guts to fly through a formation of B-17s with all of our guns firing at them at the same time. It took some kind of courage. Our group was not hit but those on our right and left were. We saw six B-17s go down. It's rough to think that sixty men were involved and we would try and count the chutes as they baled out or at least those that could get out.

This was our Air Medal mission. If you completed five missions the Air Medal was awarded. These first five were tough with heavy flak and rough targets. It was hard to believe that we had to do twenty more to go home.

On 20 December during the third raid on Bremen in a week bundles of chaff were dropped to confuse enemy radar.[6] More than 470 bombers hit the port area but twenty-seven heavies were shot down and some of the returning bombers had dead and wounded aboard. Hubert F. Radford, bombardier in Frank J. Rezek's crew in the 409th Squadron, 93rd Group, recalls:

We had already made one mission to Bremen just four days earlier so we knew we were in for a rough time as fighters had been plentiful and they were all German. We did have Spitfires to escort us over the Channel but their range was not about to reach into Germany. This was a couple of months before our P-51s, P-47s and P-38s were available to make our flights easier. There would be flak so thick you could almost walk on it. Flak smoke was not dangerous, but those red centres of the burst were really dangerous and deadly.

We were flying an old and famous B-24, *Teggie Ann*. We flew this plane on five missions. The day started without problems. We took off and were to hit Bremen at 26,500 feet. This meant that the temperature over the target would be around –50 degrees to –55 degrees. Just before we reached the target, we were hit very badly by flak that sounded like rocks hitting a tin roof. I checked all gun positions, as was our crew procedure, and could not contact our new replacement tail gunner, Fred Wrablik, a young man who had not reached his eighteenth birthday. Our waist gunners reported that he was slumped over in his turret and had probably been hit. I took a 'walk around' oxygen bottle and went to the tail position taking our radio man, Harry Schuil, who was not manning a gun, with me. We saw that Wrablik's oxygen mask was not working and that he was unconscious so we pulled him out and dragged him to the flight deck. We plugged his oxygen in but he was not breathing so we prised open his mouth and forced oxygen down his throat and he started moving and breathing. Rezek noticed that our oxygen supply was rapidly failing and he alerted us. He quickly left the formation and dove for the clouds coming to a flight level of 11,000 feet.

We remained in the clouds on instruments to protect ourselves from fighters. The clouds ran out just before we got to the North Sea. Our navigator, John Heisl, pointed out to me that we were still over Germany and I spotted a small town just ahead, picked the town up and opened the bomb bay doors and dropped my bombs at 100 feet intervals. We then flew back to Norwich over the North Sea at 50 to 75 feet altitude to evade the fighters. I know we were a lucky bunch because we made it OK. Wrablik was still out and covered with frostbite but still breathing. We turned him over to the medics upon landing, never expecting to see him again.

Wrablik remembered trying to get his guns unfrozen but that his hands were so cold he could not use them. He tried to call in but his microphone was out also. He remembered getting sleepy and almost dozing off, which happened due to his oxygen line being shot into. He remembers at the hospital that he had been put into a large tub of ice water and had his clothing cut off him. He also remembers at one occasion on the flight deck that Bob Johnson the co-pilot looked at him and shook his head in doubt.[7]

One of the B-17s that failed to return was *Jersey Bounce Jr* in the 'Hell's Angels', which was damaged by flak and was ditched east of Cromer. A 20mm shell exploded in the radio room while twenty-year-old Tech Sergeant Forrest L. 'Woody' Vosler, the radio operator, was firing his .50 calibre machine gun at the enemy. He was hit by splinters that lodged in his face and chest and he was partly blinded by blood streaming down the retina inside his eyes. He believed he was going to die and the fear became so intense that he went completely berserk. And then he became calm. He was ready to die but he remained at his post and clung to life. Vosler even managed to repair his radio by touch. Then he lapsed into unconsciousness and when he came round he sent an SOS to Air-Sea Rescue. His duty done, Vosler asked the crew to lower him out of the aircraft without a parachute to help lighten the aircraft but they refused. After the ditching Vosler scrambled out onto a wing unaided and prevented another wounded crewman from drowning. The crew were finally rescued by a passing Norwegian coaster and put ashore at Great Yarmouth. Vosler, who for a year had worked as a drill press operator in Livonia, New York, before enlisting in 1942, was awarded the Medal of Honor for his actions. He received the award the following August when President Roosevelt pinned the medal on his chest in a ceremony at the White House. Vosler was discharged from the service after ten months in hospitals.

Donald V. Chase felt helpless as bandits swept through his formation. The other sergeants manned gun positions but he had only a Very pistol for firing signal flares. While under attack he stood behind the armour plate located on the back of the co-pilot's seat. Hunkering as low as possible but still able to observe enemy aircraft anywhere from 9 through 3 o'clock, he watched the red 'wink-wink-wink' of German 20mm cannon fire and heard their responding .50s. On a later raid the top turret gunner on the B-24 Chase was flying got off several bursts and the empty casings clinked against one another as they fell onto the cabin deck. Once again Chase crouched behind the armour plate that protected the co-pilot's back, only his helmet and eyes above the armour as he watched the action.

Oh, how I wished I could shoot back. Please, don't let them strip my bed. When a crew went down, footlockers were pried open and personal belongings were collected, minus any objectionable material or firearms and shipped to their next of kin. Their beds were stripped and the thin mattresses folded. Soon newly assigned young men would arrive and the beds would be made again. Finally, I couldn't resist anymore. I just had to do something positive. As an enemy aircraft came barrelling through our formation I pulled the trigger of my Very pistol and fired a signal flare at him. Useless? Foolish? Certainly but I did get to fire one futile 'shot' at the enemy.

There were no 'easy' missions but some were much less difficult than others, especially when no enemy action occurred. Regardless of enemy activity many lives and ships were lost. Accidents plagued all operational Groups. Some crewmen were blown or fell out of aircraft. A couple of days prior to my thirteenth mission, a radio operator, seeking to obtain forgotten orders, left his aircraft and walked into a whirling propeller, killing him instantly. Airmen died from oxygen starvation when icing conditions froze shut their masks' intake valves. Mid-air collisions claimed many lives and ships. When several hundred aircraft climb through layered clouds, sometimes up to 20,000 feet, a slight tracking error occasionally brought two ships together on a collision course. A few ships were knocked out of the sky when bombs from higher flying aircraft ripped through the planes of a lower formation. Errant B-24 gunfire too, added to our own toll. Several B-24s, their IFF code (Identification Friend or Foe) inoperative, were shot down by British AA. There were no easy missions.

At bombing altitude temperatures of 50–55 below were not uncommon. An aircraft's enclosed forward cabin, while not heated, did protect us from wind. But aft, especially at the waist gun positions, the 170mph-plus winds, coupled with arctic-like mercury readings, caused much suffering to crewmen. Minor to severe cases of frostbite occurred. The advent of electrically heated, snug-fitting bunny suits minimized the problem. Sometimes, however, the suits shorted out (mine did once) and it was essential to don fleece-lined jackets and pants hurriedly. Incidents occurred where a wounded crewman, unattended for just a few minutes while his fellow crewmen fought off enemy aircraft, died from exposure; others, still alive and in need of morphine, suffered extreme pain because syringe needles broke when attempting to penetrate hard, deep-frozen skin. Conversely, frigid temperatures have saved some lives. Reportedly, an artery-severed, blood-spurting limb of a crewman had been freeze-cauterized and his life saved by baring his injury to icy blasts.

For every mission flown to its conclusion there was, or so it seemed, a scrubbed or cancelled mission due to severe icing conditions, very high and dense cloud layers, hurricane-force winds aloft, or a change of plans at Bomber Command. Naturally, a scrub or early call-back did not count toward an airman's mission tally but it did raise his anxiety level.

Soon all of the 44th's well known ships were gone and scores of others fell to enemy action. We changed operational ships often, not knowing for sure from one mission to the next which ship we would fly. When our crew stood down, another crew might fly our ship either on a mission or for a training flight. The personal touch, the allegiance toward any one individual B-24 diminished. When Lieutenant Hill and his crew flew their twenty-fifth mission their combat tour was over. Prior to landing, Hill buzzed a base perimeter strip with full power at an altitude too low to estimate. He then climbed at a steep angle, rocked the wings and put the plane through a modified chandelle, the resultant G-force of which made my body feel as if it were filled with cement instead of thin, scared blood. Of course I felt joyous that my second crew had completed their tour successfully; previously, few had. But I still had eight missions to fly before ending my tour. I kept checking with Squadron Operations, waiting for a chance to join an experienced crew. Then Squadron Operations passed along the news that each crewman must fly thirty missions, not twenty-five, before his tour of combat was over. This meant that instead of four I now had nine missions to go. It was disturbing news. I didn't think I had enough luck to take me through nine. Operations called me in and said I'd only be required to fly a total of twenty-eight, based on the number of missions I'd already flown. Okay, fine but that still meant three extra missions. On one of these missions, as I straddled the catwalk during the bomb run and pressed the bomb bay anti-creep lever, a chunk of shrapnel ripped through my bunny suit, nearly making an instant soprano of me as it shorted out my suit. It was a cold flight home. The two-ounce shot of 86-proof was especially welcomed at the end of that difficult day.

On another the majority of AA shells burst just below us. I took off my flak jacket, sat on it and promised I'd go to chapel the following Sunday, if He'd let me. Middle Ages Crusaders' armour suits, updated with full-length zippers for quick removal, I thought, half seriously, that's what we needed. Instead, we were issued flak vests not unlike the shape of a baseball umpire's protector except it covered our backs as well. These vests, together with our GI helmets, saved many lives and helped to minimize some otherwise serious shrapnel wounds.

After another eight-hour mission there were a few flak holes and the 'Little Friends' looked so good, shuttling back and forth, like protective Border Collies shepherding their flock. There were so many new faces, new crews. It was difficult to find an experienced crew in need of a radio operator. I felt like a wandering Bedouin searching for an oasis. I considered leaving a conditional 'goodbye' letter in my footlocker, thanking my parents for twenty-three good years but couldn't summon the courage to tempt fate.

Finally, after twenty-eight missions of varying intensity and the loss of many friends, I was through with combat. And I wished that nobody, anywhere, ever had to go to war again.

On 20 December Howard Hunter's crew at Chelveston found themselves going to war again for what was only their fifth mission, having flown a fourth to Bremen on the 13th which this time, according to George Coleman, the tail gunner, was 'nothing very exciting'. On the 20th it was Bremen again.

We were awakened at the usual time. We had a good breakfast of ham and eggs and then went for briefing. Bremen was getting to become a habit. Everything went along fine until we got to the target and then things started to happen. There was an explosion and the whole plane shook like a leaf in a storm. The tail started whip cracking and I thought for sure that it was coming right off. A burst of flak took our No. 2 engine clean off the plane and part of the nose with it. We started losing altitude fast and the fighters were coming in for the kill. Then our No. 2 engine was put out of commission and the bombardier was showered with flying glass. Then I heard the order to bale out. I scrambled out of my flak suit and crawled up to the waist. The two waist gunners were struggling with the door. It was stuck and wouldn't come off. We finally got it open though. Then some way or another one of the waist gunner's chutes opened. There was silk all over the plane. We picked it up and folded it up as best we could, tucked it up under his arm and kicked him out. The other waist gunner jumped and I was right behind him. I landed in a farmer's yard and he came running out and picked up my chute right away and hid it. I thought he might be going to help me but he just wanted my chute. A few minutes later a car drove up with a German officer in it and he took me to the Mayor's house. We met the navigator on the way and he was taken in too. We were interrogated there and then we were marched to a little abandoned school where we waited. They picked up one waist gunner and took him there too. From there we were taken to a German Air Force base for the night. Next morning we were given some cheese to eat. The guard brought it in along with what looked like a piece of wood. We ate the cheese and were trying to figure out what the wood was for when we discovered it was black bread. It didn't take us long to eat it, because we hadn't had anything to eat since we left England the morning before. Next day we found out that the bombardier was dead.

At Seething Bill McCullah was in base operations when *Ye Old Pub*, a heavily battle damaged B-17 in the 379th piloted by Lieutenant Charles Brown, landed on the long runway. It was shooting red flares, a distress signal. Brown stopped near base operations where an ambulance waited. His curiosity raised, McCullah walked to the plane.

There was a big hole in the side of the tail gunner's compartment, made by a German fighter's cannon, which cleanly decapitated the tail-gunner! The single hit told me it was a fluke but that round had the gunner's name on it. Ambulance personnel hauled the body away on a stretcher. It ruined my day.

Charles Brown recalls:

After brief visits with intelligence personnel and the unit commander [Colonel James Thompson] I went back to the aircraft. It seemed as though every camera in England was focused on what appeared to be an unflyable aircraft. As a badly crippled bomber, operating with a maximum of three functional defensive guns, we had survived attacks by between thirteen and fifteen German fighters, as well as a harrowing return flight to England across the deadly North Sea. I realized that survival of the flak damage, our survival of the fighter attacks, our return flight, the timely assistance of our 'Little Friends', the P-47 pilots and my own decisions enabling the successful completion of our mission had been guided by a higher power.[8]

The 8th was stood down on 21 December. Bill McCullah and the rest of 2nd Lieutenant Paul Helander's 'Crew 11' in the 448th at Seething were in their sacks by 2200 hours but they had difficulty getting to sleep. It was doubtful if any crew members could sleep for on the morrow the Group would get its first taste of combat since arriving in Norfolk. Ground armament crews loaded the bombs and guns during the night. McCullah said that they 'could hear the beat of the music as they stood on the edge of the big dance floor'. Tomorrow they would dance! They would get down the line with Maggie Klein! Crew 11 had pre-flighted their B-24; dry-running the bomb racks for proper operation and at the base armoury they had cleaned, oiled and set headspace on their guns (backed-off two clicks as instructed). Teletapes that came in during the night instructed 439 B-17s and B-24s to bomb marshalling yards at Osnabrück and

Münster. Osnabrück was a manufacturing centre and an important railway junction between Bremen and the Ruhr and this first assignment for the 448th was a tough one. Wallace Patterson noted that they were awakened at five. At 0400 hours Helander's crew were rolled out of their sacks by the charge of quarters (CQ). McCullah recalls:

We quickly dressed. We donned T-shirts, boxer shorts and one-piece cotton underwear (long johns) that covered our bodies from necks to ankles. Over that went a single-piece summer flying suit, topped by a heavy woollen sweater that covered our upper torsos. A huge bath towel was wrapped around our necks and shoulders. This was covered by zippered, sheepskin-hued trousers held by shoulder calluses. Last, we put on our sheepskin-lined jackets. On our feet were silk stockings (to trap the warmth) covered by three pairs of thick woollen stockings. Over this were our sheepskin lined boots. My A-3 bag contained my chest-pack parachute harness, with detachable parachute pack, a pair of walking brogans, an extra bath towel for warmth, leather helmet and glass goggles. Enclosed in my leather helmet was my interphone headset (earpiece). Also in the bag were my throat mike, oxygen mask and loaded Colt .45 semi-automatic pistol, my Mae West and flak jacket (waist gunners and other crew members carried backpack parachutes. The pilots wore seat packs.)

Bill McCullah had been inducted into the service on 23 January 1943 and now, eleven months later, short of one day, he would fly his first mission. He thought that it was impossible! What a trip it had been. It had been a cramming, jamming, frustrating year; the worst of his life! But he did not know the half of it. (The first six months of 1944 – his hell year on earth – would turn out even worse.) Then it had happened. They were placed on alert. The Group's 'time-in-the-barrel' had arrived. A couple of days prior 'Crew 11' had been designated Lead Crew. They took this news as a mixed bag. It meant that they would fly every fourth mission only. It meant also that McCullah would be in the Emerson electric nose turret and not the ball, which was 'a death trap'. He also considered another downside; that it would take 'an exceedingly long time' to complete twenty-five missions.

That was a bummer. Our selection as a lead crew was almost certainly based on Helander's ability. He was an outstanding pilot, with fantastic reflexes, unanimously acclaimed the best instrument flyer in the Group.[9]

Getting into the back of a waiting 6 × 6 truck, we were delivered to the combat mess. We had the works: bacon, orange juice, fresh eggs, milk, toast, fruit and coffee. Pancakes and SOS (shit-on-a-shingle, creamed beef on toast) were available. Finishing breakfast, trucks delivered us to the briefing room at base operations. We had a good mess sergeant – good food – always having fresh eggs. Some groups did not.

Crew 11 entered the briefing room. We took seats near the front. The room rapidly filled. Three operations officers stood on an elevated stage at the front of the room. Two white sheets covered a large map of Europe on the wall behind them.

'*Ten-hut-ttt!*' someone bawled, as a Lieutenant Colonel entered the back of the room, flying crews quickly coming to attention. 'Seats, gentlemen' the Commanding Officer said, stepping onto the wooden platform. Checking his watch, he began, 'Synchronize watches on the hack.' Establishing the exact time of day, starting from the count of ten, he counted the seconds backwards, 'Five, four, three, two, one, hack Flying officers and radio-operators pushed watch fobs in on the 'hack'. The Colonel indicated the target with a wooden pointer. 'The target for today is the Osnabrück marshalling yard,' he continued, as two operations officers pulled aside two white sheets that revealed a jagged line of red ribbon leading to the target. Coming in from the North Sea, we would enter the continent via Holland. A green ribbon showed our return route. 'You're carrying 2,600 gallons of fuel and twelve 500lb high-explosive bombs.' This was followed by a shorthand delivery of mission particulars. The briefing procedure was clean, precise and to the point. An operations officer continued the briefing, indicating on the map with a wooden pointer where we would encounter light flak and where we could expect heavy flak. 'Your approach to target will be from the south-east. Expect fighters over the target and anyplace between. You'll be picked up by P-38s at the Dutch coast.' He pointed to where they would take us and where they would leave us. 'They'll pick you up again on your way home' he added. The weather officer came on next, giving a detailed briefing of weather over England as well as the continent. The 22nd of December was a bad day to fly. There was turbulence and heavy overcast over England.

The general briefing concluded with, 'For those wishing to consult with a chaplain, Protestants will assemble over there'. He pointed. Then he said, 'Catholics over there and those of the Jewish faith over there', indicating direction and location. Various chaplains present led small groups through prayer. As I observed little enclaves kneeling, praying, heads bowed, hands clasped, priests making 'signs of the cross,' it gave me a feeling of uneasiness. It was a sobering sight (I went to Sunday school every week when growing up but I hadn't been inside a church in years.) The prayers made me realize the seriousness of our undertaking.

Lead pilots and navigators attended separate, specialized briefings, where precise mission aspects were covered. (We would fly No. 2 lead in the first section.) Co-pilot 2nd Lieutenant Henry M. Snyder and I attended the bombardiers' briefing. Since I would be in the nose turret, I would help to identify visual checkpoints in the target area. Should the No. 1 lead be shot down Snyder would be the back-up first section bombardier. He would sight the target through the Norden bombsight if all went well over the target, cueing off the lead aircraft as its bombs were dropped. I would drop the bombs. (Of sixteen lead missions flown, I would drop our bomb load eight times). The remainder of Crew 11 either walked or caught the shuttle to our hardstand. Once all of the crew arrived, A-3 bags were loaded and a second aircraft 'walk-around' inspection was performed. Our bags also contained fleece-lined leather gloves and steel helmets. In the event of bale out, a pair of brogans was essential, as the chute opening-shock would pull loose fitting sheepskin boots from our feet. Carrying our Army .45 semi-automatics was optional. (They were often left in barracks. If you carried one and if you did bale out, you had better be prepared to use it! A gun in hand in enemy territory could get you killed. You might have to use it against civilians.) Crew gunners climbed aboard and checked ammunition alignment in ammunition belts and chutes. Cartridge ends had to be perfectly aligned, as long or short rounds would cause a firing stoppage. We carried from two to 300 rounds per gun, sometimes carrying an extra box of ammunition, just in case. This sequence of events was not mandatory; it was the way my crew did it.

Once the complete crew had assembled, just prior to boarding aircraft, Helander set a precedent that continued for the remainder of our tour. He gathered us under the right wing and said a prayer! I wished he had not because prayer stripped away my protective shell. His prayer forced me to look down the gun barrel of reality; my mortality. I did not want to do that. 'Don't do this to me! Let me bask in my ignorance' I thought. I stole a glance at Carroll, the engineer. Nothing was there to give himself away. One side of my conscience experienced relief; a weight was lifted. But my other side was disturbed. I wanted Helander to leave me the hell alone! Don't get me wrong. I prayed, many times. Helander then said a thing that I hadn't thought about. 'I want each of you to know that if we ever have to bale out, I will be last to leave the plane. I won't leave until the last man is out.'

It was common knowledge that a renowned US football hero had baled out of his B-26, leaving his crew to perish. That could have prompted Helander's statement. But Helander said it as a simple statement of fact. I believed him! It was a comforting thought and especially when I had to be in the ball. I had a strong belief that the good do die young! My barracks experience bore out what otherwise would be ignorant, redneck superstition. Guys, who had their heads stuck in a Bible, the fanatically religious and scared, were 'Short-timers!' They didn't last. Did they have a premonition? Was it because they were 'ready' and us hell-raisers were not? It happened frequently enough to ensure me that there was a God! It seemed that drinkers, debauchers and whorers and those in between were the ones who made it. (He gave debauchers a second chance.) I could almost make side-bets on who would make it and who wouldn't.

At 'board-aircraft' time we climbed into *Boomerang*, our 'new' B-24 and put on our chutes and Mae Wests. (I donned my harness.) Assuming a crouched position, I tugged at my adjustment straps to make the harness as tight as possible. My chute-pack (my constant companion) was carried by its cloth handle. We never knew when we might have to leave the plane. A few minutes later we started engines. Helander faced *Boomerang* into the wind, running each engine to full power, checking magnetos and instruments. Waist and tail gunners would be in the rear of the plane on take-off. With the remainder of the crew I was on the flight-deck bench behind the divider that separated us from the pilots' compartment. At the radio table sat Technical Sergeant Ocolotlan Ulysses Richmond. Carroll stood in the doorway behind and between the pilots. He would monitor critical instruments during take-off. Finishing engine run-up, we taxied. We approached the long runway from the left side. As the No. 2 lead plane we were at the head of our line. Twelve planes taxied behind us. The 448th was putting-up twenty-six bombers, two sections. We would be in the first section.

Al Northrup's crew had been detailed to fly in one of the three of the aborting elements, which would fill in the place of any ship that aborted before leaving the English coast. From the skin out Wallace Patterson wore long winter woollies, his uniform, electrically heated suit, shoes and gloves, flying suit, Mae West, parachute harness, flying boots, over-gloves, helmet with oxygen mask and goggles. He carried his chute and fur pants and his kit. He inspected the twelve 500-pounders, gun and interphone. Patterson noted that it was 'a swell ship'. The only thing wrong was that one tail gun was out of commission. They would take off last.

Bill McCullah continues:

Helander swung the B-24 in a tight semi-circle, stopping at the extreme left side of the runway. We would be the second plane off. The No. 1 lead was adjacent to us, on the right side of the runway. Twelve airplanes were behind him, awaiting entry to the right side of the runway. Left, 100 feet ahead sitting on the grass was a green starter van. The starter, wearing headphones, holding a furled green flag, stood beside the van. There were red and green lights at the back of the van. The red light was illuminated. I wondered if people in the little village of Seething heard us that morning. They probably did. The noise from our engines was deafening. The Commanding Officer with ranking officers stood on the second-storey platform of the control tower, watching. Spectators, ground crews and the curious lined the area in front of the tower. Ground maintenance crews were already sweating our take-off roll. (They would be in the same position when we returned.) The familiar cockpit choreography began:

'Brakes,' Helander said.

'Brakes on and locked,' 2nd Lieutenant John J. Schneider, the co-pilot replied.

'Take-off flaps.'

'Flaps 25 degrees.'

'Mixture is rich; applying full power' Helander said as he milked the four throttles on the centre pedestal fully forward. (With the mixture rich, engines were gulping 100-octane gasoline.)

The light on the van went 'green'. The starter vigorously waved his green flag to the plane on our right; giving him the 'GO!' The No. 1 lead was moving. Eye-balling Helander, the starter pointed to the red light on the van. Engine rpms mounted as the B-24 strained at her brakes. Propellers became a blur of motion. The Liberator quivered and vibrated and then began to shake and then bounce. Her Pratt & Whitney engines strove to pull themselves from their roots.

Her whining engines were deafening. The hair on the back of my neck stood as I felt goose-bumps of fear and exhilaration that occurred on take-off. With engines running full blower the B-24 was a living thing! The total sensation was 'P-O-W-E-R!' (Spelt in BOXCAR letters!)

The light turned green on the van. Waving his green flag, the starter pointed to Helander.

'Brakes off,' Helander said. He was cool and contained.

'Brakes off,' replied Schneider.

We lurched left and right – skittering – as her tremendous power took hold. First, tapping the brakes (then with increasing speed) foot rudder-action kept her left and parallel to the centreline.

'Fifty-60-70-80-90-100,' chanted Schneider, with increasing ground speed. We were accelerating at an accelerating rate. The nose-wheel began to lift but Helander pushed her back down. With the end of the runway coming up, only then did Helander allow her to fly. (We were off the deck and moving fast.)

'Airspeed, airspeed, airspeed,' Helander preached. Without airspeed, you have nothing! Helander did not wobble planes off runways (as many were wont to do); Paul Helander flew planes off runways! They left them smoothly, efficiently and fast. When Helander took a plane off, it wanted to fly! (As an emergency measure in the States, Helander insisted that each of the crew have some flying time. All were given wheel and rudder training. I acquired six hours' 'stick-time'. I followed railroad tracks, performed banks, centred the ball, kept the nose level with the horizon and kept the nose high in banks.

'Gear up,' said Helander to Schneider.

'Gear coming up…Gear up and locked,' said Schneider.

'Climb flaps.'

'Flaps 15-degrees,' replied Schneider, making the adjustment.

'Climb power,' said Helander, fiddling with throttles and fuel mixture controls, reducing power, adjusting prop pitch and checking instruments etc. Only then did the loud whining of our engines abate as we seemingly shifted into a lower, quieter gear. Gunners went to their assigned positions. I lead wired (safety wired) my chute-pack to the skin of the plane and put on my steel helmet and flak vest (fastened only on one side) and climbed into the nose turret. I lead wired my chute to the fuselage in the navigator's compartment, a known location, because I did not want to undergo a time-consuming

Easter egg hunt for my chute if my plane went out of control. I could wear a chute inside all of the turrets but I did not. I could not properly position my head behind my sight. If I could not correctly aim my guns, why was I aboard? Besides, I wanted to be an 'ace'.

We were climbing out, headed for the Buncher. The weather was a bitch! Flying over socked-in, cloud-covered England was a deadly sporting event. It was an exercise of near misses and head-on collisions, a real asshole grabber! Though it was impossible to fly all planes on any given day, the fact remains that heavy bombers became airborne at about the same time. If we put up a third or one-fourth of the total force, we are talking about a crowd, a jumble of airplanes; a situation where hundreds of singly flying aircraft were attempting to assemble over radio beacons at fixed, predetermined altitudes. Planned or otherwise, some bomber flight patterns overlapped! We were flying singly and blind in thick cloud cover. We couldn't see them. They couldn't see us! England is small and the area in which we flew was constricted.

'Hard right! Hard right!' someone would shout over intercom, as we nearly collided with another plane, followed by a straight-up vertical bank! About to be rammed from above we were subjected to frantic dives. When threatened from below a precipitous climb would slam us to our knees. This happened again and again, as we gained visibility only to lose it a couple of seconds later. Sudden moves in a blind direction left a grab bag of disastrous possibilities. We never knew for certain who was beside, beneath or directly above us. 'God was checking our hole-cards,' we said. Without warning a group would slice through another group, similar to shuffling a giant deck of cards! This happened many times. It was enough to make one a nervous wreck. Such circumstances created havoc and were the cause of many mid-air collisions. Flying into or letting down through heavy cloud cover was a dreaded occurrence, though we did it almost every time we flew. I'm surprised we did not lose half of our planes to weather![10]

Verbal warnings struck terror into one's heart! On the B-24, the most terrorizing utterance occurred during take-off with the words, 'Abort! Abort!' Now that would chill you! More terrorizing still was when the pilot came back with 'Gotta go! Gotta go!' When that happened, it was too late; we were committed. (One day while standing in the aft section, letting-down singly through low, dense clouds near the base, Helander flipped the plane into a hard left bank and held her there! I was flung halfway through the open waist window as a tremendous 'G' force slammed me, then gripped me, pulling me from the plane! With waist gunners Norbert 'Mike' Duginske and Benjamin 'Benny' Means' watching helplessly I scrambled and fought for my life! (I was wearing my harness but my chute-pack lay on the floor of the plane). Only quick reflexes and strength kept me from going out the window! From that moment, unless inside a turret, my chute pack was attached to my harness. We learned from those experiences. There were some hard, commonsense lessons.

The nose turret was a clear, Plexiglas bubble that afforded outstanding visibility. I wore my metal helmet and draped my heavy, unwieldy, cloth covered flak vest across my left shoulder, leaving the right side unfastened. I hated this piece of gear. With both sides of the flak vest fastened, it was a difficult, time-consuming, reluctant bastard to unfasten. When trying to clear a plane, time was your enemy, so I kept my split-turret door half-open, allowing for quick exit. Though frigid outside air came through the half-opened door that was small cost should I have to jump. Seated in the nose turret, I enjoyed a panoramic view of everything forward of the plane, a broader view than the pilots did. I could look up and back over 90° and could look down minus 45°. My horizontal view exceeded 100° on either side. When I elevated my guns my seat sank. When I lowered them my seat rose. Seat movement kept my head squarely behind my gunsight. There was a 2 feet by 3 feet, 4-inch thick slab of plate-glass in front of me that served as armour plate. The glass moved up and down with the elevation of my seat. The Emerson Electric was a Rolls-Royce of turrets. The bomb toggle switch located beneath my seat was easily reachable. I had the best seat in the house! As concerns smoothness of operation, the Emerson Electric nose turret was by far the best turret on the B-24. The Sperry ball would be second and the Martin upper turret third. The Consolidated Vultee tail turret, hydraulically driven, afforded the most room but its movement was jerky.

Airplanes were all over the sky. Group planes appeared to mill about when, in fact, pilots fought to attain a predetermined position in the formation. (On later missions, with assembly time running-out, pilots often filled in anywhere they could, even tacking on with other groups.) We busted in and out of bad weather, flying through angry, dark clouds with high winds buffeting us. We flew mostly blind as we climbed toward our rendezvous point over the beacon. Finally arriving, Helander jockeyed the B-24 into position. We were exactly where we should be, in the first section, No. 2 plane of the lead element. We were behind and to the left of the No. 1 lead that flew 40 feet ahead, a plane's width to the right of us. When we flew lead in the first element, identifying group stabilizer markings was easy. When we flew in the rear of a formation, finding our position by tail numbers was difficult, time consuming and dangerous.

On this and subsequent missions the 448th was divided into two parts, the first and second sections. A section was composed of several mini-formations called elements. Ideally, distance between sections was 100 to 200 yards but actual distance often varied; sometimes too dangerous extremes. The latter condition was not by design. When a section was out of position, it was usually far to the rear. Sections were 'stacked-down to the left'. From a plane view, a section formed an inverted 'V' formation, the lead element being the apex. This stacking arrangement was used because no two elements flew at the same altitude, a flak consideration. An element consisted of four planes. Three planes in each element flew at the same altitude. The fourth plane flew behind the No. 1 element lead but beneath and behind the other three. The fourth plane was called the 'bucket', or the 'slot'. Because it was a hard plane to fly, the B-24 was not a good formation airplane. The tighter a section formation the better. Tight formations concentrated defensive fire against attacking fighters, affording a tight bomb pattern on the target. Catch 22: the tighter the formation, the easier target you presented to flak gunners and fighters. It was clearly a 'damned if you do, damned if you don't' situation.

Four bombardiers in the lead element of the first section and four bombardiers in the lead element of the second section were the only bombardiers that aimed the bombs. Bombardiers in all remaining aircraft rode in nose turrets and performed the function of nose gunner and bomb togglier. These latter personnel cued off the element lead plane, dropping their bombs when it dropped. Bombardiers were commissioned officers but the vast majority never once aimed the bombs, flying their missions in the nose turret. The downside was that they had only the barest gunnery training. They lacked hands-on experience (equipment and theory) while enlisted gunners had extensive training. Bombardiers in nose turrets did not give one a heady sense of security during fighter attacks.

The No. 1 section lead was assigned the highest bomb drop priority, sequentially followed by Nos 2, 3 and 4 leads. If the No. 1 lead was shot-down the No. 2 lead took over the primary bomb aiming function etc. The same thing happened in the second section. It was a redundancy deal, three back-up bombardiers in both the first and second sections. During our bomb-runs it was Snyder who actually flew the plane via the Norden bombsight. On bomb runs Helander relinquished aircraft control to Snyder. Hunched over the sight, turning dials, Snyder flew a straight course at the target. It was during bomb runs that crews were most vulnerable.

Despite the hoop-la about precision bombing lead bombardiers deliberately dropped their bombs short of the target. Fractional delays caused by human reaction time (cueing their release from the lead aircraft drop) resulted in walking the bombs through the target. Many bombs fell short of or long of the target. Bombs in the middle of the string are the ones that did the damage. Was this saturation bombing or what? During bomb-runs, nothing deterred the course of our planes! Nothing! We hewed to a suicidal straight line run at the target and this is where the flak gunners had a field day! We were locked-in, straight and level all of the way and neither hell nor high water broke us from our path. We lived or died with that commitment. No matter how thick the flak or how bad the fighter attacks, evasive action was totally out of the question. We maintained straight and level flight until our bombs were dropped. Bomb runs lasted an interminable amount of time, three through ten minutes etc. A lifetime! I sometimes thought the bomb-run would never end! Don't you kno+w German flak gunners loved it? We were targets in their 'shooting gallery'!

We were over the Buncher and with scheduled departure time running out the first section formed and in position, section lead pointed his plane in a north-easterly direction toward the Continent. (Thirteen of the original twenty-six bombers put up by the Group aborted the mission and returned to base! Due to extremely bad weather and pilot inexperience, second section pilots could not locate the rendezvous point! The Osnabrück mission was flown by the first section only – thirteen aircraft. That was a bummer).

Al Northrup's crew cleared out of the overcast at about 9,500 feet.
Wallace Patterson wrote:

There was a white sea of clouds under us and the air was filled with ships. The 93rd was well formed and several groups of B-17s passed us by. We looked in vain for any formation. Our ships were mixed up with all sorts of other groups. We did see a few of them together and when we tried to tack on they shook us off. We had a bad scare when we hit a current of air in a thunderhead and lost 2,000 feet in a matter of seconds. Everything movable in the ship, including heavy ammunition cases and crew, floated around within the ship during the descent. Finally we found ourselves 68 miles out over the North Sea and all alone. We had been unable to find anyone to fly with; so we came home and found the other two abortive ships over the field. In all, eleven other ships had to abort, one carrying the Colonel, fifteen minutes from the target.

McCullah continues:

At scheduled departure time we flew a north-easterly heading over the North Sea toward our entry near the Zuider Zee. Once over water we test fired our guns but bearing surfaces were frozen nearly solid. Too much oil had been applied and there was insufficient headspace.[11] The temperature was 40 below. A straining, grunting effort was required to pull charging handles fully rearward and when released, driving-springs just barely chambered the rounds. Normal release produced a slanting effect but actions were still and the slant was gone. My right gun would not fire at all! *Pop-pop-pop-pop* reluctantly went my left gun, skewing my turret sideward with each pop. The usual ear-splitting sounds of exploding rounds were swept away by the slipstream. It was a hell of a fix to be in. The base armament officer's instructions were specific and we followed them to the letter. My crew made a balls-busting effort but to no avail. It was not just my guns that misfired; it was all guns. We were crippled and could not effectively defend! We were scared and pissed. As I grew older, I learned that incompetence abounds at all levels. 'Pull back plates and remove excess oil. Back barrels one click,' I suggested but we hadn't enough time. Raising both gun covers with screwdriver and half-frozen hands I backed off both barrels one additional click. Working space inside a turret is minimal. I did it the hard way; gun mechanisms inside receivers. Actions still stiff, all guns fired, though slowly. We were nearing the Dutch coast!

Our bombers screwed their way through moisture-laden air, throwing vapour trails remaining visible for 200 miles. The condensed vapours from churning propellers clearly marked our trail. Hundreds of bomber tracks criss-crossed the sky providing perfect screens for German fighters to fly up our rail-pipes. The vapour streams produced an ethereal effect; that of being caught in a time and space warp. Everything was white and dream-like. We were detached from those so far, far away on the ground. We flew the Osnabrück mission (and others) at altitudes ranging from 20,000 to 26,000 feet, 3½ to 5 miles. Here, the Flying Forts one-upped us, flying at higher altitudes. When we exceeded 10,000 feet, we had to suck-hose, going on 100 per cent oxygen. Our oxygen masks had been tuned and tested, allowing 5 per cent maximum leakage. When we exceeded 10,000 feet it was getting cold and the higher we flew the colder it got. Temperatures ranged plus or minus 40 below zero. Every half-hour we would unfasten one side of our rubber oxygen masks, crushing them in our hands, breaking and shaking-out ice accumulation. We broke ice from our eyelashes. We kept a wary eye on our oxygen flow blinkers. To lose oxygen was to pass out and die. And cold, so goddam cold! It was a crackling, flesh-sucking-to-metal cold. Despite our exaggerated dress, still we were cold. We were an overdressed, pregnant looking bunch, when in fact, we were lean-and-mean, all dressed up in our flying machine!

There was the Dutch coast! In a few minutes we would make landfall. From our altitude it looked no different from England; everything green but blurred. Remembering why I was here, I scanned the sky for fighters. All was clear. We were overtaking a B-17 group flying in the distance to our left. Another B-24 group flew a mile ahead. Other than them and the suspended contrails from other planes there was no forward activity. Other groups flew behind us. In the B-24 group flying ahead of us there was flak! It was our first. I was fascinated as I sat theatre-front, watching. A coastal battery was shelling them. The 448th lead banked gently to the right. Helander followed. We were beginning evasive action. It was a good fly but hardly worth the effort. When we were adjacent to where the previous group had been *Whoo-oom-Whump* went the sound and a greasy black, vertically elongated blob of smoke hung, then expanded off our left front. *Crr-aaa-kk* came another 40 feet ahead and I saw the fire from the centre of the burst. We flew through the smoke. I smelled the acrid, burning, biting odour through my oxygen mask. There were more bursts ahead and behind us. Then we were through it. 'It wasn't bad,' we said. 'I wasn't scared, were you?' we asked. 'Yaw, were you?' And do you know what? I don't think we were. We were invincible weren't we? 'Damn straight! We're not afraid of that Mickey Mouse crap!' We flew on.

'Sombrero, High Hat here. We're leaving you, Big Brother. Good luck', said the fighter leader (on Command Channel) to group lead. They were going home to refuel. 'We'll pick you up on your way back, Sombrero. High Hat out Tally-Ho!' he said, hanging-up the phone. I did not see our fighters though they had been with us all along. When our fighters were present, it was usually from a look-down position, enabling them to hide in the sun. With this conversation (real except for call signs), our P-38 escort turned back, severing our umbilical cord. We were cut-loose, released to do our own-thing.

Again we picked up flak, heavier and more concentrated. Several close bursts lifted the B-24, bouncing her. The sides undulated, flexed and breathed with the concussion from exploding shells. Concussion meant too goddam close! We were inside a steel drum and someone was banging it! Someone threw a handful of rocks against the plane and the staccato clatter reverberated like hail against a Nissen hut. We knew we had been hit but didn't know how badly! A burst to our left front banged the B-24 with shrapnel A cursory search by Lieutenants Alfred Cannon, navigator, and Snyder revealed no holes. The clean, snapping bullwhip sound of exploding shells was as frightening as hell! Mostly the explosions were oblong, vertical forms and oily black but they could be balls, snow white and varying shades of grey. Their smoke quickly dissipated but at times it hung, ominously maintaining shape and position. Different calibre guns caused sound variations like big bass drum, lingering and drawn out sounds and deafening 'KRAAKKKKs', some with a snap on the end. The amount of moisture, the direction of winds aloft and temperature had a bearing on sounds, as did the speed of our plane. Achieving a state of detachment was easy. I would shift mental gears (a trick learned as a kid) and guess what? I was detached. A part of me stood to the side, watching. I was sitting in a front row seat of the Princess Theatre (the north side greasy seat), Springfield, Missouri, watching a bad movie. What was going on around me was not real.

Suddenly there were tiny specks on the horizon! I intently watched as the specks got bigger. 'God, look at that! German fighters; 11 o'clock level. The sky's filled with them!' I said over intercom. The *Luftwaffe* were way out front, getting bigger and closer by the minute. We estimated their number to exceed 200 planes. It was the biggest number of enemy fighters we would ever see in one bunch. Theirs was not a formal formation – no fixed distance between planes in azimuth or elevation. They flew as a swarm, loose and sloppy, meandering side-to-side, up and down. The haphazard formation rattled my preconception of the precise German mind. The frightening thing was, they were coming straight at us! We fired our guns to warm and loosen working parts. Knowing that the large number of fighters would generate excitement I switched to command channel. Our lead pilot was talking.

'Tighten it up boys; tighten up!'

'With that Helander stuck our right wing tip near the lead plane's vertical stabilizer. We had a tight formation and when it seemed certain that the fighters would come through our formation, they veered right, hitting the Fortress group to our left. What changed their minds? They probably bypassed our little thirteen-plane formation for bigger prey; the B-17 formation was a full group. We did not fire a shot in their defence, as we could have shot down more of the Fortresses. The fighters sliced through the formation, head-on, firing all the while and knocked down half of the Fortresses in one pass! Some of the attacking fighters went down from bomber counter-fire! The attack was over in seconds. The rate of closure was 600mph. It was mind-boggling, a scene of bedlam, a bad dream! Fortresses blew up, broke up and disintegrated. Wings, tail sections and engines and parachutes filled the sky. Planes trailed sheets of flame 100 yards behind. Many of the crews were doomed, trapped, dead and dying. Some planes spun out of control as they plunged. Some airmen in the spinning planes had to be pinned by the centrifugal force. I only saw the B-17s go down but that was enough. The onslaught happened at maybe 1,000 yards. Some of the damaged Fortresses turned back, becoming sitting ducks, as they attempted to fly home alone. The remaining Forts, now widely dispersed, continued toward Osnabrück. That was probably where, in the rear of the formation, that we lost 2nd Lieutenant David E. Manning and crew to fighters and where 2nd Lieutenant Ed Hughey Jr fell behind the formation only to be shot-down by fighters. Hughey lost eight of his ten-man crew. Only the assistant engineer and top turret gunner got out alive.[12]

I was spent and physically and emotionally exhausted! As bad as it was, it did not stick. A week later, it was gone, wiped it from my mind! You must forget, or you will surely lose your mind. Each of us was the centre of his universe. The way I saw it, 'it happened to them' and not us. Crew 11 was exceptionally quiet as we flew on. I believe that our crew was reflecting on the horror we had just seen. We were scared shitless at the time but by the time the next mission rolled around that memory was reduced to an intellectual exercise.

Osnabrück lay before us and we were finally on the interminably long bomb run. Snyder, hunched over his bombsight, flew our B-24 toward the target. Our front and rear bomb-bay doors opened; bomb fuse safety wires long since pulled over the North Sea. We flew straight and level; no evasive action whatever.

With groups flying at mixed altitudes, there was a jumble of American bombers over the target. Groups crisscrossed the target from several angles and altitudes. Heavy flak exploded around us, barrage stuff. Watching the lead plane flying 40 feet ahead and to the right of us, I awaited my cue to drop our bombs. His bombs fell. I hit the toggle switch saying, 'Bombs away! The B-24 surged upward with the sudden weight release. Helander was back on the yoke, again flying our plane.

Disaster struck! The formation above us dropped their bombs through our group! One of their bombs struck a B-24 flying behind us! It broke-up the plane, taking out Lieutenant Joe Smith and crew! His plane plummeted to earth, killing all aboard. It was a gigantic 'fuck-up'! Other words would not adequately describe it. We talked dirty to express true feelings. Yes, we should be ashamed but we were realists caught-up in a war! We wanted to take names and kick ass! And it was a miserable, goddam shame when Americans killed our own people! That we completely missed the target was a kick in the ass! That was the capper to a horrendous day.

Osnabrück was mission number twenty-three for Luther S. Bird and the crew of *El Toro* in the 'Travelling Circus'.

Sergeant Harvey B. Lyons and the belly gun did not make the mission in order to remove weight, as it was anticipated that we would have to go to a higher than usual altitude. The group was approaching the target at 27,500 feet, barely above cloud cover and making dense vapour trails, when we were hit by a rocket and 20mm bullets from a fighter. Numbers two and three engines were on fire. A big hole was blown in the right side of the flight deck behind the radio. Fire was sucked in through the big hole and the flames extended back into the bomb bay. The heat caused condensate to form on all glass surfaces, windows and instruments. Thus, a flying blind situation was instantly created. Because of the altitude, we were operating at about 90–95 per cent of available power. Flight characteristics indicated all power from number three engine was lost instantly. *El Toro* went into a spin to the right, then levelled out and exploded. We had at least half a load of gasoline and twelve 500lb bombs on board. Radio man Francis A. Sullivan jumped into the flight deck well and the bomb bay doors would not open. Sullivan was last seen going into the crawl tunnel towards the nose wheel. In the rear, waist gunners George H. Kelly and Herschel W. Dodd made successful jumps out the waist windows and parachuted down. Tail gunner Robert O. Sparks was hit in the buttock by fragments of a 20mm shell. He was out of the turret when the plane lurched; throwing Sparks chin first into the bottom tunnel door. A glass pane was broken and Sparks' chin and jaw were wedged into the opening in a manner that kept him stuck. James W. Reid and Jack H. Roach, navigator and bombardier respectively, were not seen or heard from during the period of being hit until the plane exploded. Rocky Hill and Charles B. Molina, the engineer-top turret gunner, managed to get onto the flight deck. The centrifugal force was so great one could not raise the arm high enough to grab and open the top escape hatch. I failed to pull myself from the pilot's seat, so I turned back to the flight controls and placed them in the neutral position. This is when the ship exploded. Other than the fact that Reid, Roach and Sullivan were killed in action their exact fate is not known. Hill, Molina, Sparks and I were still in the ship when it exploded. All four of us came to in a free fall, pulled the ripcord and were on the ground in three to four minutes. On the way down I saw thousands of pieces of *El Toro*, the size of leaves, floating down. The largest parts were an outer piece of one wing and an inflated dingy.

The survivors of the crew were captured by farmers and taken to a rural community centre. A lady attended to Sparks' wounds. Later, soldiers came in a truck and took us to the airdrome at Quakenbrück. Sparks was taken to a hospital, and the remainder were placed in prison cells. During the next two days we were transported by train to an interrogation camp in Frankfurt. We were placed in solitary confinement on Christmas Eve and taken out New Year's Eve. On 1 January we were aboard trains being transported to prisoner-of-war camps.[13]

Bill McCullah concludes:

Out of the target area, we picked up light flak a couple of times on our way home. Our P-38s rendezvoused with us but it was too late. Fighter damage already suffered by the Group was a done deal. (You could stick a fork in it and turn it over; it was done on that side.) Over the Channel we removed ammunition belts from our guns. We later learned (the hard way) that that was a mistake. I sometimes wondered if we had any brains at all.

Back at our hardstand at Seething, we performed an aircraft walk-around. We picked up four flak holes that we could stick our fists through, with approximately thirty holes of lesser size. (Ours was not one of the five severely damaged planes.) Our ground maintenance crew patched holes during the night. Our maintenance crew, happy that we were home, grilled us for details of the flight. They vicariously fought the war through our tales.

Arriving at debriefing we were poured a shot of whiskey. When finished, they offered us another because Osnabrück was a 'two-shot' mission. Less difficult missions were 'one-shot' missions. 'Milk runs' (easy targets) were 'no-shot' missions. Disbursement discipline would allow no more whiskey than called for. My single-shot made me ill. I had trouble keeping it down. Debriefing officers quizzed us on the mission, asking questions from a standard form. They wanted details of everything seen, which they entered in a log. Was the target visible? Did your bombs hit the target? Enemy fighters? Number and make? How many planes did you see go down? How many chutes? Did you inflict any damage to fighters? And on and on. When satisfied they released us.

That was 'Crew 11's first step, our first mission. One down, twenty-four remaining and then back to the 'ZOI'; the 'Big PX', the 'World', 'Home'! Our mission was a milestone. It was good to be back at Seething. We were exhausted! We did not know whether we were coming or going. Later, only hours from nearly getting ourselves killed, we would be laughing; joking, drinking and yakking it up in a pub. Still, I would not have changed places with our guys in foxholes. Their danger was continuous, having no respite from mud, ice, snow, heat and cold, rain, or the dangers they faced every day. We in bombers traded a few hours of abject terror for the amenities of civilization. Our hell was condensed, occurring in spurts. We went through it on our way to and from targets, alternately terrorized by German flak gunners and fighter pilots who tried their goddamndest to kill us! Back home at Seething, safely on the ground, we were ebullient and we lived it up. We had hot meals, hot showers and slept in warm bunks beside a fire. We attended movies, drank, danced and caroused hundreds of miles from the action. That's the total unreality of our on again, off again, war existence. It was a jerk-around way of living. Due to my ability to hide from reality and later, the company of my English girlfriend who helped me forget, relatively speaking, I floated through World War II. The pressure of personal fear dissipated somewhat and for the most part, disappeared. My English girlfriend, Sybil, was a beautiful, vivacious girl. We enjoyed each other's company and were very much in love. We never once discussed marriage. Knowing that I could not properly support her, I returned to the States without her. I actually did her a favour but she was very bitter. I was untrained but ambitious and wanted a college degree. Being with a woman was not new to me. At sixteen, I was seduced by a twenty-four-year-old divorcee neighbour and carried on a secret affair with her. A second, younger woman became part of my little harem. Because sex was available, I was free to pursue serious efforts as a student. I was discreet. I did not want my mother to ever find out what I was doing. Thousands of miles from home, my forced abstinence would be a problem but a minor one. Sybil was nothing short of a godsend! She relieved my tension and anxiety. I would never tell! We had gotten our wish. Though our first mission was a miserable bust, we were veterans, flying with the Mighty Eighth Air Force! No matter which way you cut it, 'we were running with the big dogs'!

We wanted something to eat; a hot shower and a long sleep in a warm bed. We took someone's jeep from the front of base operations and drove it to the barracks. We showered and changed clothes. Upon our exit from barracks, the jeep was still there. (Later, when we returned from any mission, we would steal a jeep! This happened so frequently that it seemed Crew 11 had its own jeep. Back from a mission, physically and emotionally spent, we would climb into one of the jeeps parked in front of base operations. Five or six were always available. Risk-takers to the core, we were careful not to take the same jeep two-times running. Arriving at our destination, we would abandon them, leaving them where they sat. Someone would return them or the owner, pissed to the gills, cussing like a maniac would scour the base searching for his jeep! Four squadrons are a big search area and owner frustration ran rampant.) We drove it to the combat mess where a hot meal awaited. We drove back to the barracks, parked the jeep and then fell into our bunks. It had been a heavy day.

The 448th put up twenty-six planes for the mission but only eleven made it to the target. Thirteen planes could not find the RV and turned back. Two of these did not make it to the target and we lost another over the target – twenty-eight airmen killed – 22½ per cent of our people and 23 per cent of our planes! This was our first mission! Hell's fire. We had twenty-four to go! When back on the ground, we learned that five of our planes had been severely damaged. Counting the three planes that were lost, eight of thirteen planes had been severely damaged; 61½ per cent was a bad showing. Aerial reconnaissance photos taken two days later showed that no damage was inflicted on the target! The Osnabrück mission accomplished absolutely nothing! It was a 448th disaster! We were bitter. It was a helluva way to begin a war!

Notes

1. There was no Crew 13 in the 448th BG, presumably because it was an unlucky number. 2nd Lt Donald C. G. Schumann and Crew 12 were one of two crews lost on 11 January 1944 when *Prodigal Son* was shot down by fighters over Holland. Schumann and four of his crew survived and five were KIA. The other B-24 the Group lost was *Thirty Day Furlough*. All ten men in Lt James Urban's crew were killed. See *The 448th Bomb Group (H): Liberators over Germany in WWII* by Jeffrey E. Brett (Schiffer 2002).

2. *401st BG; 'The Best Damn Outfit in the USAAF* (Turner Publishing 2000).

3. A malfunction in the Pathfinder equipment prevented the attack and instead, just over 280 heavies bombed industrial targets at Solingen.

4. Adapted from *Airfield Focus 37: Deenethorpe* by John N. Smith (GMS 1999).

5. *Penny's Thunderhead* crash-landed at RAF Woodbridge on 30 January 1944 and was salvaged.

6. Strips of tin foil cut to the exact length of the German radar signal.

7. *2nd Air Division Journal*, spring 1990.

8. See *Raiders of the Reich* by Martin W. Bowman and Theo Boiten (Airlife, 1996).

9. *We Flew The Big Ones! Crew Eleven; Memoirs of a B-24 gunner and crew 1943–1944* by Bill J. McCullah (unpublished).

10. The 1st AD (B-17s) was in front; the 448th BG flew in back with the 20th Combat Wing. Clouds interfered with the assembly so the 20th Combat Wing actually left the coast in two sections – the 448th and 93rd Groups in one and the 446th Group in the other.

11. 'Headspace was the distance between the bolt and the breech-end of the barrel. When back at Seething, I told the base armament officer to set headspace at three clicks not two. And after cleaning and oiling gun parts, to wipe all oil prior to assembly. It worked! We never had gun trouble again.'

12. Lt Edward Hughey's Crew #41 and Lt David Manning's Crew #52 in the 714th BS had the unenviable distinction of being the 448th's first combat losses. All eleven men in Manning's crew were KIA. Lt Foster's Crew #61 took a rocket hit just inside the No. 3 engine sending fragments through the radio operator's compartment, striking T/Sgt Arthur E. Angelo in the left chest and wounding him seriously. Most of the returning planes had sustained battle damage – some very minor and some very extensive. See *The 448th Bomb Group (H): Liberators over Germany in WWII* by Jeffrey E. Brett (Schiffer 2002).

13. '*Martin's Red Caps*' by Luther S. Bird writing in the *2nd AD Journal*.

Index